Laboratory Dogs Rescued

"Dogs in Our World" Series

*Dog of the Decade: Breed Trends and What They Mean in America* (Deborah Thompson, 2022)

*Laboratory Dogs Rescued: From Test Subjects to Beloved Companions* (Ellie Hansen, 2022)

*Beware of Dog: How Media Portrays the Aggressive Canine* (Melissa Crawley, 2021)

*I'm Not Single, I Have a Dog: Dating Tales from the Bark Side* (Susan Hartzler, 2021)

*Dogs in Health Care: Pioneering Animal-Human Partnerships* (Jill Lenk Schilp, 2019)

*General Custer, Libbie Custer and Their Dogs: A Passion for Hounds, from the Civil War to Little Bighorn* (Brian Patrick Duggan, 2019)

*Dog's Best Friend: Will Judy, Founder of National Dog Week and Dog World Publisher* (Lisa Begin-Kruysman, 2014)

*Man Writes Dog: Canine Themes in Literature, Law and Folklore* (William Farina, 2014)

*Saluki: The Desert Hound and the English Travelers Who Brought It to the West* (Brian Patrick Duggan, 2009)

# Laboratory Dogs Rescued

## *From Test Subjects to Beloved Companions*

ELLIE HANSEN

*Foreword by* Kathrin Herrmann

**DOGS IN OUR WORLD**

*Series Editor* Brian Patrick Duggan

McFarland & Company, Inc., Publishers
*Jefferson, North Carolina*

Library of Congress Cataloguing-in-Publication Data

Names: Hansen, Ellie, 1974– author.
Title: Laboratory dogs rescued : from test subjects to beloved companions / Ellie Hansen ; foreword by Kathrin Herrmann.
Description: Jefferson, North Carolina : McFarland & Company, Inc., Publishers, 2022. | Series: Dogs in our world | Includes bibliographical references and index.
Identifiers: LCCN 2021051191 | ISBN 9781476685014 (paperback : acid free paper) ♾
ISBN 9781476644929 (ebook)
Subjects: LCSH: Dogs as laboratory animals. | Dog rescue. | Animal experimentation—Moral and ethical aspects. | BISAC: PETS / Dogs / General
Classification: LCC SF407.D6 H36 2022 | DDC 636.7/0885—dc23/eng/20211028
LC record available at https://lccn.loc.gov/2021051191

British Library cataloguing data are available

**ISBN (print) 978-1-4766-8501-4**
**ISBN (ebook) 978-1-4766-4492-9**



On the cover: Beagles Mini and Maria (photograph courtesy of Mary Pryor)

Printed in the United States of America

*McFarland & Company, Inc., Publishers*
*Box 611, Jefferson, North Carolina 28640*
*www.mcfarlandpub.com*

# Table of Contents

**Part 2: To the Rescue**



**Part 3: Saved—Stories of Rescue, Rehabilitation, and Second Chances**

# Acknowledgments

If this book has taught this author anything, it's that we are stronger together, working side by side—with friends, family, colleagues, and other people (sometimes strangers who become friends along the way) who share in our visions and want to help make this world a better place for people and animals.

Thank you, Elizabeth Varnai (my amazing mother), for being my advisor, confidante, and most fervent supporter. I am forever grateful for the exceptional editing, sleuthing, daily phone calls, early morning epiphanies, and our mutual sense of adventure, which all went on behind the scene.

Thank you, Jeremy Hansen, for taking on extra shifts at work for me, for sharing me and our entire kitchen table with this book, and for the being the best partner and husband I could ask for. My heart is full knowing that you always support me in my rescue work, including adopting our own rescued laboratory beagles. These are gestures of true love.

I am also thankful for the opportunity to work with McFarland & Company, Inc., Publishers, who recognize the importance of this topic and chose to publish this book as part of their "Dogs in Our World" series. A special thanks to Brian Duggan for working with me for months to put together a robust book proposal and for his continued assistance when I needed it.

Many other inspirational people have added their voices to this book. They are individuals and families who have adopted former research dogs and worked with me through written interviews and conference calls, including Dave and Greta Rubello, Ryan and Sarah Webster, Kris Wood, Diane and Bruce Vanderpool, Sasha I., Shannon Malone, Brigitte Pascual, Lillian and Niels Larson, Nicki S. and Wayne T., Gail Thomssen, Erica Ridgeway, Lisa F., Paula and Jeff Bowie, Mary Beth Stoddard, Jodie Lee, Nancy House, Sarah Kite, Kelly Selcer, Sheila H., Samanta Stefano, Vania P., Lily Blavin, and Mary Pryor. Thank you for generously sharing your stories.

It's been a true privilege to work with leaders in the fields of biomedical science and higher education, who enthusiastically offered their assistance and shared their voices for this book. They include Dr. Kathrin Herrmann, Dr. Jarrod Baily, Dr. Lindsay Marshall, Dr. Katy Taylor, Dr. Stacy Lopresti-Goodman, and Dr. David DeGrazia. These amazing people have dedicated their lives to bringing about change for animals in research and I feel honored to have worked with them.

To Shannon Keith at Beagle Freedom Project and John Ramer at Kindness Ranch Animal Sanctuary, many thanks for rallying support among adopters to share stories for this book and for our candid conversations about laboratory dog rescue. My soul overflows with gratitude for all the dogs that have been saved and re-homed because of them.

I am also grateful for the chance to work with leaders in animal advocacy, including Justin Goodman at White Coat Waste Project and Katie Conlee at the Humane Society of the United States (HSUS). Thank you for bringing the plight of research dogs into the spotlight and challenging the status quo. Also, a special thanks to HSUS and Cruelty Free International for supporting this book and providing photos and other important data on dogs in research. Mary Hilley and Sarah Kite were invaluable in many fact-finding missions.

Also, a special thank you to the Show Your Soft Side Campaign and to photographer Leo Howard Lubow for letting me use the awesome photo of Lucia and Torrey Smith that appears in this book. Your support of this cause means so much.

Finally, several dogs are responsible for my interest in writing this book. My first beagle Max gave me my love for this independent, silly, and adventurous breed of dog. In June 2020, as I began writing this book, Max passed away at the age of 14. Besides his zest for living and following his nose, Max showed me the true spirit of beagles and how they don't belong in laboratory cages. My eyes are wide open, Max, as is my heart. In 2015 I adopted two former research beagles named Marty and Eddie. They have both taught me so much about the intelligence and emotion of dogs coming out of research laboratories and their resilience and ability to heal from the trauma they experienced. My education into the world of rehabilitating laboratory dogs came directly from them. Thank you, my brave and wonderful boys, for trusting me.

# Foreword by Kathrin Herrmann

My first nonhuman friend was a Newfoundland dog called Gina. She moved into our house as a family member when I was six years old, and I fell in love with her immediately. In the next fourteen years, we went on countless adventures together and were inseparable. We can feel love for many other nonhuman species, of course, but there is something special about our relationship with dogs; there seems to be a mutual understanding between us and them. They can read our minds, and we can comprehend what they feel.

A recently published cross-cultural study[1] on human-dog evolution added evidence to the evolutionary theory that humans and dogs chose each other rather than humans forcing this relationship onto wolf puppies. The study concluded that the relationship between humans and dogs has overall been a mutually useful and successful one for both species. The researchers also found that when women cared for dogs the likelihood of the dogs' being treated like people and family members was higher. Thus, women have profoundly influenced the coevolution of humans and dogs.

As you will learn in this book, our close relationship with dogs has been more harmful than useful for them when it comes to science. This special place that dogs have in the hearts and lives of many humans has not spared them from being used as test tools. For almost a decade, I worked as a federal regulator in Germany, inspecting laboratory animal husbandries and breeding facilities, as well as scrutinizing animal experiments involving a number of species, including dogs.

The most-used dog breed in laboratories is the beagle. They are such easy going, kind and trustful little beings. I remember assessing a research facility where they tested chemotherapeutic drugs in beagles. These dogs were so sick and surely had had some traumatic experiences with humans, but they were still so happy to see me, wagging their tails, seeking my attention. I was only allowed to pet them with gloves to prevent the drugs from being secreted through their skin from getting on my skin. It was heartbreaking to see their suffering, to know that their untimely deaths were imminent and still not be able to help them. I felt sad for not only the dogs I saw, but also for all the so-called "laboratory" animals, large and small.

As a veterinarian, I am trained to recognize pain and suffering in the various animal species and to assess the severity, so I could clearly see what the animals were going through. While working for the government, assessing animal research proposals and inspecting animal laboratories, I became increasingly aware not only of the pain and suffering inflicted upon dogs, monkeys, rats, mice, rabbits, fishes and many other species, but also of the flaws of animal-based research. The translatability of findings from animals to the human setting is poor, to say the least. That is what most animal experimenters don't want to acknowledge, as it takes away their scientific justification for using animals for their research.

So, what about animal welfare laws and their potential to safeguard animals? According to European Union legislation, one should first try to replace animals wherever possible; then if they are still deemed indispensable, reduce their number as much as possible, and last but not least, refine procedures with the animals to cause the least possible pain, anxiety and suffering. These principles of replace, reduce and refine are known as the 3Rs. However, I frequently observed that the 3Rs principles were not followed in practice. In my position as assessor of animal research proposals, I tried my utmost to prove that these experiments were not indispensable. Rarely did I succeed.

The animal researchers frequently were more influential in getting their way, despite this animal-based research failing to provide answers. Since retrospective assessments of animal research studies are generally not mandatory, the extent of flawed and unsuccessful animal studies goes mostly unseen. However, animal experiments that have been systematically assessed in regard to their ability to predict human responses have revealed that we (human animals) are just not like other animals. Surely, there have been animal tests in the past from which we have learned, but this limited historical success is not a reason to continue using animals, especially when looking at the complex, multifactorial and often chronic human diseases we try to find cures for today. Dogs, as well as other non-human animals, are just not good models for humans.

You may wonder, why are so many dogs, as well as other species, still being used in laboratories today? Even when the evidence points towards the failure of these animal models to mimic human disease or drug response, and therefore strongly supports abolishing animal testing? It is because animal use in research and testing is a huge industry with a powerful lobby.

As an example, have a look at a recent "Love Animals? Support Animal Research" campaign[2] by the Foundation for Biomedical Research that was endorsed by Temple Grandin, who some see as an animal welfare expert. The whole campaign is aimed at dog lovers (and other companion animal lovers), telling them that research using animals is vital to helping their beloved pets. The campaign also highlights some medical conditions that we share with our companion animals. However, it fails to mention that the differences in the underlying biology mean that these maladies are not identical.

The campaign goes on to say how wonderfully enriched the living conditions of laboratory animals are, and how caring everyone is toward these animals. All this is just an attempt to whitewash the sad, barren, lonely reality of life in a laboratory. If they really cared about these animals, they would dedicate their hours to getting these animals out of the labs and would invest their time and resources in developing animal-free, human biology–based methods. Instead, they use their money and influence to run campaigns like the one described, misinforming and misleading the public. And, combined with the lack of transparency around animal experimentation, it is hard for the public to know what is really going on.

As a veterinarian, a scientist, and a dog lover, I am grateful to Ellie Hansen for writing this book as it sheds light on the opaque, secretive animal-use industry. We need to discuss as a society what we consider acceptable, since research activities reflect our values. One hopes the knowledge gained from this book will inspire the reader to make a difference for laboratory animals by advocating for them. Animals languishing in labs today need your voice, and all our voices combined, to question the "necessity" of these practices and bring them to an end. Our beloved companion dogs, those best friends who give us their love, empathy, and compassion every single day, would expect nothing less of us.

*Kathrin Herrmann, Ph.D., works at the Center for Alternatives to Animal Testing (CAAT) at Johns Hopkins Bloomberg School of Public Health in Baltimore, Maryland. She is also the Animal Protection Commissioner of Berlin in Germany. Dr. Herrmann is regarded globally as a veterinary expert in animal welfare science, ethics and law.*

# Preface

> The fidelity of a dog is a precious gift demanding no less binding moral responsibilities than the friendship of a human being.
>
> —Konrad Lorenz, Austrian zoologist, founder of modern ethology (study of animal behavior), and 1973 Nobel Prize winner for Physiology and Medicine

In the days before I started writing this book, I was reading Pema Chodron's book *Welcoming the Unwelcome*. Chodron introduces a Mahayana Buddhist practice known as *bodhichitta*. In Sanskrit, *bodhi* means "awake" and *chitta* means "heart" or "mind." The aim of *bodhichitta* is to fully awaken our heart and mind, not just for our own greater well-being, but also to bring benefit, solace and wisdom to other living beings.

In the first chapter, titled "Begin with a Broken Heart," Chodron tells a poignant story from one of her spiritual teachers:

> Trunga Rinpoche, who had a huge capacity for being in the presence of suffering without turning away, would often bring to mind a time in Tibet when he was about eight years old. He was on the roof of a monastery and saw a group of young boys stoning a puppy to death. Though they were quite far away, he could see the terrified eyes of the dog and hear the boys' laughter. They were doing it just for fun. Rinpoche wished he could do something to save the puppy, but he was helpless. For the rest of his life, all he had to do was recall that time, and a strong desire to alleviate suffering would arise in his heart. The memory of the dog gave his desire to wake up a sense of urgency. This is what propelled him, day after day, to make the best use of his life.[1]

This book is the product of my *bodhichitta*. Like Trunga Rinpoche, I also saw a tragic event that I felt helpless to do anything about.

I was at my computer scrolling through Facebook on a peaceful morning when I came across a graphic undercover video of a beagle being used for animal testing in a research laboratory. The beagle was euthanized and thrown onto a cart like a sack of potatoes. In that moment my heart broke into a million pieces. That moment awakened my heart in a way I had never felt before. Since then, not a day has gone by when I don't use that image to raise my *bodhichitta* to help dogs in research.

Many people don't know that dogs are still used for scientific research. Mostly beagles. Mostly to test human drugs and chemicals. Human drugs are often tested on dogs in doses hundreds of times stronger than is ever given humans—making the suffering the dogs endure in these tests a real ethical concern. Not surprisingly, few dogs survive. While our heads are full of numbers and facts these days, there is an important number to remember: 55,000. There are 55,000 dogs in research laboratories today in the United States.[2] It's hard to imagine.

While much of this book is about saving dogs from research laboratories, it is also about the importance of finding more humane, and possibly more effective, alternatives to testing products. This will not happen overnight. It will take tremendous effort and patience from all of us—animal rights advocates, scientists, politicians, doctors, teachers, corporations, and consumers. One step at a time, we can all awaken our collective voice. At times we may feel like we are fighting separate causes. A cure for cancer. Child trafficking. Poverty. Animal abuse. However, these causes are all connected by one thing: coming to the aid of those who are suffering. Most of us are propelled on some level to want to help others in need. Once we realize we are not "separate" we can begin to work together to help fight against the world's many problems and injustices.

As you read this book, please take this thought to heart: Every one of us has the capacity to use our voice for the voiceless. Dogs in research laboratories need your voice, too. My hope is that you take away from this book a growing sense of understanding and courage. I also hope that you will join me in envisioning that day when all laboratory research dogs are saved. Until then, we can keep our commitment going strong ... even if it means beginning with a broken heart.

# Meet the Experts

## *Dr. Kathrin Herrmann*

Kathrin Herrmann, DVM, DipECAWBM (AWSEL), Ph.D., is a veterinary expert in animal welfare science, ethics, and law. Since 2017, she has worked at the Center for Alternatives to Animal Testing (CAAT) at Johns Hopkins University in Baltimore, where she directs the "Beyond Classical Refinement" Program.

Her work addresses the reproducibility and translatability crises that science is facing. Taking into consideration insurmountable interspecies differences, solely refining animal studies will not be sufficient to advance human healthcare. Consequently, Herrmann's program is critically appraising current animal use practices in science.

With teaching the next generation of scientists being a main focus, Herrmann is involved in several international initiatives to improve and extend animal-free, human-relevant science education. Together with the Physicians Committee for Responsible Medicine (PCRM) Herrmann co-organized and co-hosted the first U.S. Summer School on Innovative Science Without Animals in June 2020, which will take place every two years in alternation with the European Summer School, organized by the European Commission Joint Research Centre.

Herrmann initiated and co-edited the open access book *Animal Experimentation: Working Towards a Paradigm Change* (Brill Human Animal Studies Series, 2019), which features 51 authors who critically review current animal use in science, present new and innovative non-animal approaches to address urgent scientific questions, and offer a roadmap towards an animal-free world of science.

Other passions of Herrmann are to raise awareness of the important role veterinarians should play in animal protection and animal law and to a cruelty-free, vegan, sustainable lifestyle. At the end of 2020, Herrmann took an additional position. She is now the Animal Protection

**Dr. Kathrin Herrmann**

Commissioner of Berlin, Germany, a role in which she advises the government of Berlin in various animal welfare and protection issues.

Connect with Herrmann on Twitter or *LinkedIn*.

## *Dr. Jarrod Bailey*

Jarrod Bailey, PhD, is the Director of Science at *Animal Free Research UK*. He received his degree and Ph.D. in genetics from

**Dr. Jarrod Bailey**

Newcastle University, England, then spent seven years investigating the possible genetic causes of premature birth in humans, using human tissues.

For the past 16 years, Bailey has worked for a number of organizations in the U.S. and the U.K., evaluating the scientific validity and human relevance of animal experiments in many areas of biomedical research and drug/product testing, and promoting the use of human-specific research methods in their place. He has published many peer reviewed papers and book chapters, on topics as diverse as HIV/AIDS, neuroscience, drug testing, genetic modification of animals, and the use (and replacement) of dogs and nonhuman primates in science.

He has authored scientific petitions and submissions of evidence to many U.S. and European inquiries into animal research/the use of alternatives, and spoken about his work with the FDA, and with many members of the U.S. Congress and the U.K., Italian and other European parliaments. He was invited to present his work to the U.S. Institute of Medicine as part of their 2011 inquiry into chimpanzee research, which led to a *de facto* end to invasive chimpanzee experimentation in the United States.

Bailey has taken part in countless debates and interviews on the scientific case for a shift toward human-focused methods in biomedical research, and his expertise and knowledge have been sought many times for television and radio programs, documentaries, and for newspaper and magazine articles.

He is a Fellow of the Oxford Centre for Animal Ethics.

## *Dr. Lindsay Marshall*

Lindsay Marshall, Ph.D., is Biomedical Science Advisor at the Humane Society of the United States and Humane Society International (HSUS/HSI). She is a Fellow of the Royal Society of Biology in the U.K. and a Senior Fellow of the Higher Education Academy.

Prior to her current position, Marshall spent around 12 years at Aston University in the U.K.—as Senior Lecturer in Immunology, she incorporated a strong element of animal replacement in all of her teaching. This included research driven lectures that scrutinized and criticized animal models and considered how these might be improved with more human-relevant approaches, and practical classes which moved away from the traditional use of animals in teaching and instead focused on human-based studies, using the students themselves or other human-based investigations—examining human blood under the microscope or measuring the response of cultured human cells.

She introduced a level 5 module on "Bioethics" to specifically address the issues with failing animal research and enable better understanding of the scientific and ethical disadvantages of using animals and also to raise awareness of the non-animal methodologies that are available, are continually developing and offer better science. This was so well received by students that it was converted to a level 6 module to allow more students access to the material. This humane approach to science was very well-received

**Dr. Lindsay Marshall**

by the students, and she was winner of the student-led "Astonishing Academic" award for three consecutive years before she left.

Her research program during her time in academia was dedicated to the theme of human respiratory defenses, where she ultimately developed multi-cellular human cell–based models of human airways. Her models of healthy human airways were used to examine the potentially toxic effects of e-cigarette vapor on human lungs, and she also created models of cystic fibrosis airways, which were used to evaluate possible treatments for infections in people with cystic fibrosis. These, and similar, human-based approaches are vital if we are to understand the effects of inhaled toxicants (such as e-cigarette vapors) or diseases (such as cystic fibrosis), since animals do not share the same breathing patterns and lung cell composition as humans, and animals are not naturally affected by conditions like cystic fibrosis.

Marshall left academia in 2016, believing that her goal to bring about total replacement of animals in research could be better achieved through working with academics from outside their institutions.

She is now the European Advisor for the *BioMed21 Collaboration*, an initiative that brings together scientists from across Europe, Asia and the Americas with a shared vision of a new, human-focused paradigm for health research. As part of this position, her key activities are to liaise with academics to develop critical reviews of animal disease models, and support HSI-HSUS public policy efforts through the preparation of targeted briefing materials for politicians and other non-expert stakeholders.

In 2018, she was joint lead of a European initiative to review the use of non-animal models used in respiratory tract disease research—this was a collaboration between the chemical consultancy EcoMole, Professor Ian Adcock of Imperial College London and the European Union Reference Laboratory for Alternatives to Animal Testing (EURL ECVAM). The ultimate aim of this research is to develop a freely-available database of non-animal methods which scientists could access in order to help them make decisions regarding the use of these innovative human relevant techniques in their research. Other projects are creating databases for common human diseases like neurodegenerative conditions (such as Parkinson's or Alzheimer's disease), breast cancer, autoimmune diseases and cardiovascular diseases.

Along with several academic colleagues, she is currently working on a project to produce an animal-free curriculum—creating educational materials that will allow scientists, students, lawmakers, funders and other interested parties, to design and execute their research projects without using animals.

At the moment, there are no existing courses that help and encourage people to carry out animal-free research; although many college and university courses may include elements of experimental design, and many undergraduate life science students are required to take a project that could necessitate the generation and testing of a hypothesis, there do not appear to be stand-alone modules that consider how to carry out effective research in this era of technological revolution.

This may be contributing to the institutional inertia that we believe perpetuates the continued use of animals in biomedical research—established researchers rely on the (animal-based) methods that they are comfortable with when teaching classes and students are led to believe that such animal-based methods are what are required to proceed/succeed. This must change if we are to move to a world where research is more human relevant and based on the best science with which to address the questions we need to answer to improve human health.

## *Dr. David DeGrazia*

David DeGrazia is the Elton Professor of Philosophy at George Washington University, whose faculty he joined in 1989, and a former Senior Research Fellow in the Department of Bioethics, National Institutes of Health, which he joined on a part-time basis in 2013.

DeGrazia earned a B.A. from the University of Chicago (1983), an M.St. from Oxford University (1987), and a Ph.D. from Georgetown University (1989), all in philosophy. His research interests focus primarily in applied ethics and ethical theory and secondarily in personal identity theory and the philosophy of mind/cognitive sciences.

DeGrazia is the author, coauthor or coeditor of eight books, including his scholarly monographs *Taking Animals Seriously: Mental Life and Moral Status* (Cambridge University Press, 1996), *Human Identity and Bioethics* (Cambridge University Press, 2005), and *Creation Ethics: Reproduction, Genetics, and Quality of Life* (Oxford University Press, 2012). He was an editor through four editions of *Biomedical Ethics* (McGraw-Hill), one of the most widely used bioethics anthologies. With Tom Beauchamp he is the coauthor of *Principles of Animal Research Ethics* (Oxford University Press, 2020).

In addition to books, DeGrazia has published 120 or more journal articles, book chapters, review essays, and shorter writings—most of them solo-authored—in such journals as *The Hastings Center*

**Dr. David DeGrazia**

*Report*; *Ethics, Philosophy and Public Affairs*; *Public Affairs Quarterly*, and *ILAR Journal*. His research has been supported by major grants from the American Council of Learned Societies, the National Institutes of Health (before he became an employee), and the National Endowment for the Humanities (twice).

In 2012, he worked part-time as Senior Advisor to the staff of the Presidential Commission for the Study of Bioethical Issues. He also served, at GW, a three-year term as Chair of the Philosophy Department. Outside of GW, he has served as Co-Chair of the 2000 Program Committee for the American Society for Bioethics and Humanities and Chair of the Committee on Philosophy and Medicine for the American Philosophical Association.

He is currently a member of the editorial boards of *Public Affairs Quarterly* and *The Journal of Applied Ethics*. In 2018 he was named a Fellow of the Hastings Center and the recipient of GW's Office of the Vice President of Research Distinguished Scholar Award.

## *Dr. Stacy Lopresti-Goodman*

Stacy M. Lopresti-Goodman earned her B.S. in psychology from Kutztown University in May 2000, and earned her Ph.D. in experimental psychology from the University of Connecticut in August 2009. She is a Professor of Psychology and the Honors Program Director at Marymount University, in Arlington, Virginia. She teaches a variety of courses, including *Abnormal Primate Psychology*, which educates students about the harms of captivity on nonhuman primates, and teaches a required Honors seminar on *Food, Ethics and Society*. She has led five study abroad programs to primate sanctuaries in Kenya and Spain.

**Dr. Stacy Lopresti-Goodman with George, a rescued research dog**

Dr. Lopresti-Goodman actively engages in research. Her work is aimed at understanding the enduring negative impact that confinement and usage in research laboratories has on the psychological well-being of nonhuman animals, including chimpanzees, monkeys and dogs. She also conducts research on alternatives to the use of animals in psychology education.

She has presented her research at academic conferences nationally and internationally, including meetings of the American Association for the Advancement of Science, the World Congress on Alternatives and Animal Use in the Life Sciences, the International Primatological Society, the American Society of Primatologists, and the National Institute on the Teaching of Psychology. She has published in peer-reviewed journals such as *Neuroscience Letters, Behavioral Sciences, Journal of Trauma and Dissociation, Psychology and Education*, and the *Journal of Animal Ethics*, and has been featured in media outlets such as the *Washington Post, Nature*, National Public Radio and *Science*.

## *Justin Goodman*

Justin Goodman is the Vice President of Advocacy and Public Policy at *White Coat Waste Project*, a 3-million-member taxpayer

**Justin Goodman**

watchdog group working to end $20 billion in taxpayer-funded animal experiments.

For more than 15 years, Goodman has led successful grassroots and lobbying campaigns to expose and stop experiments on dogs, cats, primates, and other animals. He has also helped pass local, state and federal laws and policies to curb animal tests. For these and other wins, Goodman was awarded the 40 Under 40 award by the American Association of Political Consultants in 2017 and his team at WCW was awarded the 2018 LUSH Prize for Public Awareness.

Goodman earned his bachelor's and master's degrees at the University of Connecticut. He lives in Washington, D.C., with his wife and rescued cat Mr. Littlejeans.

## *Kathleen (Katie) M. Conlee*

Katie Conlee is Vice President for Animal Research Issues with the Humane Society of the United States (HSUS) and has worked for the organization since 1999.

Her work focuses on the long-term goal of replacing the use of animals in harmful research and testing and the ongoing development and implementation of non-animal alternatives. These efforts involve educating the public about the plight of animals in laboratories, reaching out to the scientific community, regulators, policymakers, and legislators to spur change; engaging in dialogue with corporations; publishing technical papers; and representing the animal protection community on scientific and other committees.

Katie Conlee

Conlee led the HSUS efforts to essentially end the use of chimpanzees in research and is now focused on retiring chimpanzees from laboratories to sanctuaries, including by serving on the board of directors for Project Chimps, a chimpanzee sanctuary in Georgia.

Prior to joining HSUS, she spent several years at a primate breeding and research facility in South Carolina as the behavioral manager for more than 3,000 primates, applying environmental enrichment and other strategies to reduce stress and help emotionally disturbed animals. She also worked as the supervisor of care at the Center for Great Apes, a sanctuary for chimpanzees and orangutans. Conlee has a bachelor's degree in zoology and a master's degree in public administration, with a specialization in public policy.

# Part 1

# Dogs in Science

# 1

# Early History of Using Dogs in Research

"...[N]o creatures, I believe, have been of more eminent service to the healing tribe than dogs. Incredible is the number of these animals, who have been sacrificed from time to time at the shrines of physic and surgery. Lectures of anatomy subsist by their destruction ... and in general, all new medicines and experiments of a doubtful nature are sure to be made in the first place on the bodies of these unfortunate animals."

—Francis Coventry (1752)[1]

## *Vivisection*

The practice of cutting into or using invasive techniques on live animals. Derived from the Latin *vivus,* or alive, vivisection is commonly called animal experimentation, and includes the use of animals for research, testing and education.

## *Anti-vivisectionist*

Someone who is opposed to experimentation on living animals, especially when considered to cause pain or distress to the subject.

Dogs' relationship with humans has been documented as far back as 20,000 years.[2] Cave art in present-day Saudi Arabia depicts ancient desert dwellers leading dogs on leashes, hunting gazelles and ibexes with bows and arrows.[3] For most of their history dogs have herded, hunted, kept guard, assisted solders in war, and provided companionship, and sometimes were even a source of food for humans.

For all the ways dogs have served humans, there is one way that has caused enormous controversy: vivisection. While many animal species, including rats, mice, birds, rabbits, pigs, monkeys, and others, are used for scientific research, this chapter addresses the history of using dogs in research, including vivisection.

Most people don't realize that mankind has used dogs for centuries to help advance the understanding of diseases of the human body, and the effects of chemicals, and drugs. Most people are also unaware of the often obscured descriptions of the experiments for which millions of dogs have lost their lives, often cruelly.

While public concern about vivisection on dogs has waxed and waned over time, the global scientific argument for the continued need to use dogs in research has remained exactly the same: that it saves human lives. As we will explore later, this is a debatable claim with many credible arguments to the contrary. Nonetheless, it has perpetuated the use of dogs in research experiments to the present day.

As efforts to regulate dogs' pain and suffering in research have been attempted decade after decade, supporters of animal research and animal welfare advocates still find themselves sitting on opposite sides of the table in regard to the ethical treatment of animals, unable to shed their veils of resentment and mistrust.

To end research on dogs means changing cultures, mindsets, beliefs, systems, and laws (all facets of animal experimentation) that have existed for hundreds of years—a gargantuan task that must be undertaken on a global scale. To continue research on dogs means facing increasingly stringent laws and unprecedented public scrutiny—a reason for the scientific community to build up strong defenses. In the meantime, the dog remains a commonly used mammalian model for scientific research in most developed nations in the world.

## *Villains or Heroes?*

It may be difficult to imagine dogs being used for vivisection for such a long period of time in human history, yet this is where our journey must begin. Why were dogs first used? How were they used, and who used them? And most importantly, how has history prepared us to finally begin to move away from the need to use dogs in vivisection?

As with any compelling saga, there are characters portrayed as villains and heroes, and the issue of vivisection in history has both, depending on one's point of view. If animal experimenters were described as villains, they never thought of themselves that way; in their minds they were heroes of science. On the other hand, scientists thought anti-vivisectionists were the villains who were trying to stop their experiments and human progress, while anti-vivisectionists saw themselves as heroes saving animals and preserving human morality through compassionate treatment of animals.

Regardless of who was right or wrong—that is for the reader to determine—one can get a glimpse of the complexity of the issue surrounding vivisection, especially as it pertains to dogs.*

## *A Dog's Purpose: Early Thoughts*

Written texts depicting the use of live animals for scientific experiments date back as early as the third century BCE. For most ancient Greeks, using live animals in experiments did not raise any relevant moral questions, since they believed humans were higher ranking than animals.[4] At the same time Greek philosophers such as Aristotle (384–322 BCE) established that mammals, in particular, resembled humans to the extent that they could act as stand-ins.[5]

Throughout history, dogs in general were not recognized as the companion animals they are today. A dog's purpose was basically utilitarian, meaning they had to work to earn their place with people. In spite of that, humans still formed emotional attachments with dogs. Excavations in the coastal Israeli city of Ashkelon uncovered a cemetery from the fifth century BCE that contains more than one thousand dogs. The dogs appear to have died of natural causes, and the careful arrangement of their bodies suggests that people held them in high regard.[6]

During the Middle Ages (500–1500 CE) debates about the human-animal relationship emerged among influential Christian theologians, including Augustine of Hippo and Thomas Aquinas. Augustine argued that animals were part of a natural world created to serve humans, so humankind did not have any obligations to them. Thomas Aquinas condemned cruelty to animals, because he believed it could lead humans to develop feelings and actions of cruelty towards other humans.[7] Today, Aquinas's theory holds true. It has been proven that animal abuse often leads to violent behavior against other humans.[8] As Aysha Akhtar states in her book *Our Symphony with Animals*, "How we define cruelty to animals is very dependent on our fickle views about them."[9]

---

*Some of the following pages contain graphic descriptions of early science experiments on dogs. It is not my intention to upset readers; it is also not my intention to hide the truth. I have omitted the most gruesome medical notes. While I urge readers to read the stories through to fully understand this topic, it is not necessary to read them in order to follow the progress of this book.

Many people still believe that humans have a right to use animals as we please to advance ourselves as a species. This has been, and continues to be, the argument surrounding dogs used for vivisection. Ethical lines become blurred when dogs are seen as "tools" versus intelligent beings with emotion. While dogs' loyalty to humankind has remained steadfast, our views on a dog's purpose in our lives is still evolving.

The French philosopher René Descartes (1596–1650) argued that "animals lacked a rational soul," using their lack of speech as proof, and he further claimed that "therefore they were merely automata [machines] who lacked the mental capacity to experience pain." It is unclear whether Descartes believed animals feel no pain or only that they cannot cognitively perceive it the same way humans do. While few early scientists believed that animals could not feel pain, they nonetheless believed painful experiments were justified for the greater human good.[10]

## *Why Use Dogs?*

Using dogs for vivisection began in earnest around the 1600s to help scientists develop new treatments for a wide range of human maladies and diseases.[11] Dogs were used then for the same reasons they are used today: They were readily available, easy to work with, and scientists believed they had biological systems and health conditions that were similar to humans.

According to Dr. James Serpell, Professor of Ethics and Animal Welfare at the University of Pennsylvania School of Veterinary Medicine, it is the *hypersociability* of dogs, which is defined as "enhanced motivation to engage socially with humans combined with extreme willingness to comply with human direction," that may also account for the popularity of dogs as research animals dating back in history.[12] Only in the first decades of the 20th century did rats become a preferred tool in research.[13]

## *Europe: The Scientists and Their Dog Experiments*

Our historical journey of vivisection begins in Europe, where scientists and medical men in Great Britain and France often disagreed on the ethicality and validity of animal experiments, especially in regard to the cruel manner in which they were performed at that time.

French scientists were known for their controversial and public demonstrations of painful and often fatal operations on dogs, known as Continental-style vivisection.[14] These gruesome dissections on dogs occurred in a time when anesthesia (for humans and animals alike), or opiate-based pain relief such as morphine, were not yet available. This made the infliction of pain during animal experiments a central ethical issue.[15]

Morphine was not developed until 1805.[16] Furthermore, anesthetic agents, including ether and chloroform, were not discovered until the 1840s. Even then, scientists often chose not to use anesthesia during dog experiments, fearing it would alter desired outcomes.[17]

The following stories represent some historical examples of science experiments using dogs. Whether the characters in these stories were villains or heroes depended on what a person deemed to be important at the time. Even within the medical field, there was a great divide between those who felt that pain and suffering inflicted upon animals in the name of science was wrong, and those who felt it was necessary for advancing human knowledge. It is interesting to note that this same divide continues today, over two centuries later.

## François Magendie (1783–1855)

François Magendie may be portrayed as a pioneer in the early study of human physiology. However, due to Magendie's cruel use of dogs in his experiments, he was also considered by many to be a heartless villain. Still, his discoveries about the spinal cord remain respected to this present day.

Magendie was a Professor of Medicine at the Collège de France and head of one of the first laboratories devoted to experimental physiology—the branch of biology that deals with the functions of living organisms and their parts. Magendie established the importance of direct experiments on living animals—mainly dogs, cats, and rabbits.

One of Magendie's most famous discoveries was the Law of Spinal Roots, also known as the Bell-Magendie Law, which identified nerves along the back and skull (dorsal), and belly or lower side (ventral) of the animals he studied. Magendie never used anesthesia during his animal experiments, perhaps because of their depressing effect on nervous functions, the very thing he was trying to study.[18] It is estimated that the discovery made by Magendie of the anterior root of the spinal cord driving motor impulses, and the posterior root driving sensory impulses, required the use of 4,000 to 9,000 dogs.[19]

The published accounts of Magendie's experiment in 1824 at London's Windmill Street anatomy school, in which he nailed a greyhound to the dissecting table before cutting it open, provoked a vigorous anti-French outcry that marked the start of the organized anti-vivisection movement in Britain. As a medical eyewitness who attended Magendie's demonstrations in Paris reported: "...he really likes his business ... when loud screams are uttered, he sometimes laughs outright."

At the time of Magendie's arrival, vivisection in Great Britain was rare. It has been estimated that in the 1820s, fewer than a thousand experiments on live animals were performed each year in the whole of the British Empire, and English medical men were said to have a particular "horror" of them.[20]

## Claude Bernard (1813–1878)

> A physiologist is not a man of fashion, he is a man of science, absorbed by the scientific idea which he pursues: He no longer hears the cry of animals, he no longer sees the blood that flows, he sees only his idea and perceives only organisms concealing problems which he intends to solve.
>
> —Bernard, 1927[21]

Bernard was the founder of modern experimental physiology and, like Magendie, was one of the most famous French scientists of all time. Bernard was a student of Magendie's, and he eventually took over Magendie's laboratory to do his research. Among Bernard's most known experimental discoveries were the glycogenic function of the liver, the role of the pancreas in digestion, effects of poisons and chemicals on the body, and the nerves that control blood vessels and heart function. Most of Bernard's work was done early in his career, between 1843 and 1858, in a small damp cellar and with little funding.[22]

Like Magendie, Bernard preferred not to use anesthesia on his experimental animals, which often included dogs. His experiments with curare were especially cruel. Curare, traditionally used by South American indigenes in tandem with arrows or darts as a weapon, is a poison that causes asphyxiation as respiratory muscles became paralyzed and fail to contract.[23] Bernard's research often included cutting open conscious animals under the paralyzing effects of curare.

George Hoggan, a doctor who spent four months as an assistant in Bernard's laboratory in Paris, published an extraordinarily powerful letter describing the experiments, such as those conducted in Bernard's laboratory. Hoggan's belief was that not one of those experiments was justified. He described dogs being brought up from the cellar where they were kept before vivisection, seized with terror upon entering the laboratory. Hoggan's letter also described animals being slapped when writhing through a painful vivisection.[24]

The public effect of Hoggan's letter was immense, because it was a recent eyewitness account of vivisection (and few anti-vivisectionists could claim to have ever actually observed the process), and because the witness had a medical degree.[25] It was akin to an undercover investigation and revealed the realities of the pain and suffering animals endured in vivisection.

Claude Bernard's line of work would have a heavy personal cost. In 1845, near the beginning of his career, financial difficulties led him into an arranged marriage with Fanny Martin, the daughter of a wealthy physician. The marriage was a disaster from the start, and Bernard's habit of bringing home opened up and dying animals with various tubes inserted was the final straw for Fanny. Tired of her husband's atrocious experiments, Fanny divorced him—taking with her his two daughters, who grew to hate him. She joined the anti-vivisection movement and set up a rescue shelter for stray dogs and cats.[26]

Bernard would, however, die a national hero, being given the first state funeral ever to be granted to a scientist in France.[27] He collected more honors than any other French scientist, and was elected to the Academy of Science, the Academy of Medicine, and became president of the French Academy. A bronze statue of Bernard engaged in vivisection was even set up in front of the College de France after his death.[28]

Scientists like Magendie and Bernard, despite their disregard for animal suffering, did not see themselves as evil villains but rather as humanists who believed that animals did not deserve the same moral consideration as humans. As Bernard wrote: "...the science of life can be established only by experiment, and we can save living beings from death only by sacrificing others.... I do not admit that it is moral to try more or less dangerous or active remedies on patients without first experimenting with them on dogs ... it is essentially moral to do experiments on an animal, even though painful and dangerous to him, if they may be useful to man."[29]

## Louis Pasteur (1822–1895)

Pasteur is one of the most famous scientists in the world, known for his research and discoveries around microbes, the diseases they cause, how heating can kill harmful bacteria in liquids or foods, and his development of vaccines. His work led to huge medical advances that protected people, livestock, and industry.

It was Pasteur's work in France to discover the origin of a mysterious bacterial disease in silkworms that was destroying the silk industry in 1853 that led him to propose the germ theory to explain the basis of all infectious diseases. In the scientific community, this germ theory triggered a hunt for pathogens that within the next twenty years led to the discovery of the bacteria responsible for most infectious diseases, including leprosy, tuberculosis, diphtheria, cholera, and bubonic plague.[30]

Pasteur went on to study the spread of devastating epidemics in farm animals, such as fowl cholera that was killing chickens, and anthrax, a widely spread plague of cattle and other animals. By 1894, Pasteur's anthrax vaccine reduced the cattle mortality rate in France to 0.3 percent. By all accounts, Pasteur saved the lives of millions of farm animals during his lifetime. But what Pasteur may be most known for is the vaccination against rabies he developed in 1885. By this time, he was 63 years old and handicapped by a permanent paralysis in his left arm due to cerebral hemorrhage. His first successful use of the rabies vaccine in a human was on July 6, 1885, on a nine-year-old boy who had been severely bitten by a rabid dog. A few months later in October 1855, Pasteur successfully vaccinated a 15-year-old shepherd dog that was also bitten by a rabid dog. By 1886, mortality rates of French patients affected by rabies went from 40 percent to 0.5 percent after vaccination.[31]

Pasteur's work required the experimental infection of numerous animals, including dogs. This made him a prime target of anti-vivisectionists. While he was reportedly uneasy with the experiments conducted, Pasteur maintained that the use of dogs was both humane and justified in the interest of mankind. Pasteur would often receive hate letters, mostly because of his infection studies on dogs, although he also used chickens, rabbits, rodents, pigs, cows, sheep, and monkeys. However, Pasteur was described as being more sensitive to animal suffering than other French scientists in his field, and he always insisted that animals be anesthetized whenever possible to prevent unnecessary suffering.[32]

## Ivan Pavlov (1849–1936)

> "The dog is irreplaceable; moreover, it is extremely touching. It is almost a participant in the experiments conducted upon it, greatly facilitating the success of the research by its understanding and compliance."
>
> —Ivan Pavlov (1893)[33]

Pavlov is known for experiments with dogs on "conditional" reflex, where he noted that dogs began to drool as soon as they saw a stimulus they associated with food, like the sight of person in a lab coat. However, it was for his overall study of the physiology of digestion that he received

Monument to Ivan Pavlov's dog at the Institute of Experimental Medicine, St. Petersburg, Russia. Photograph from Catriona Bass Russian Images. Reproduced by permission of Alamy Stock Photo.

the Nobel Prize in Physiology and Medicine in 1904.[34] Pavlov's research focused on the ways in which eating excited salivary, gastric, and pancreatic secretions. To do that, he developed a system of "sham" feeding. Pavlov would remove a dog's esophagus and create a surgical opening in the animal's throat, so that, no matter how much the dog ate, the food would fall out and never make it to the stomach.[35]

The dog, left hungry from the night before, would be harnessed to a wooden stand and presented with a bowl of raw meat. No matter how much it ate, it never got full. The dog chewed and swallowed, but the masticated meat would erupt from its esophageal opening and dribble back into the bowl, whereupon the dog would lap it up all over again. In the meantime, a glass tube attached to the animal's stomach opening allowed its gastric secretions to drip into a collecting bottle, so they could be filtered, analyzed, and sold to the public as a remedy for indigestion.[36]

In 1935, just before his death, Pavlov approved the design for a monument to his canine subjects, erected on the grounds of the Institute of Experimental Medicine in Saint Petersburg, Russia. A bronze plaque on one side depicts the dogs on laboratory tables, tied to their wooden frames.[37]

## *Other Discoveries Using Dogs*

Diabetes: In 1889, Joseph von Mering and Oskar Minkowski showed that removing the pancreas from a dog produced diabetes. This was the first demonstration of an anti-diabetic factor (later discovered to be insulin), produced by the pancreas which enabled the body to regulate sugars in the blood. In 1922 insulin from cow pancreas was tested in dogs and then on human patients.

*First intravenous injection:* Dogs were the first animals to receive an intravenous injection. Sir Christopher Wren developed a system involving a quill and a pig bladder to inject alcohol into a dog's veins. Over the years this developed into blood transfusions; dogs were used as test subjects for many of the advances in the procedure.

*Cardiology:* Ventricular fibrillation, a common cause of cardiac arrest, was first described in dogs in the 1840s, when scientists discovered it could be induced by closing off a dog's coronary artery or applying an electric currant. In 1899, Jean Louis Prevost and Frederic Batelli in Geneva demonstrated that electrical currents could also be used to restore normal rhythm to a dog's heart, thereby inventing the first electrical defibrillator.[38]

# 2

# The Debate Begins: Researchers Meet Public Outcry

It is true that dogs have contributed to many medical advances in human history. To say that nothing useful has been learned from dogs would be false, and also a failure to recognize the dogs themselves who above all should not be forgotten for their sacrifices. It can also be argued that just because a particular discovery was made through vivisection on dogs, does not mean that it was the only way that discovery could have been achieved, as was often claimed.

If ethics and morality had played more of a part in the early days of vivisection, would scientists have taken a different route to these discoveries? If recognition of dogs as emotional and intelligent beings had been factored into the scientific equation, would researchers have acknowledged that causing pain and suffering in dogs and other animals was not an acceptable means of gaining knowledge? We may never have the answers to these questions; however, we can see, as history has progressed, that the ethical treatment of animals in research has become a central issue, and therefore, difficult to ignore.

To fully understand the growing discontent among the general public toward the treatment of animals—especially dogs—in science, we must first explore the debates surrounding vivisection and the complications surrounding each point of view.

For vivisectionists, the justification for their experiments was that the benefits to medicine outweighed any animal suffering, and they saw anti-vivisectionists as tender-hearted but profoundly ignorant.

On the other side, anti-vivisectionists proclaimed anyone who experimented on living animals to be callous and insensitive.[1] A good, moral society included the respectful treatment of both people and animals, and anyone who could mistreat animals, as they did in vivisection, was a poor reflection on society.

In the 19th century, 70 percent of anti-vivisectionists were women.

The anti-vivisection movement came to be seen as feminine, and men who took it up were subject to accusations of unmanliness. Experimenters faced the opposite criticism: that they were "dispassionate and wanting in normal human feeling."[2]

## *Queen Victoria: (1819–1901)*

> "...[animal experimentation is] horrible, brutalizing, unchristianlike ... one of the worst signs of wickedness in human nature."
>
> —Queen Victoria[3]

In 2016, the cable channel PBS released the television series *Victoria*. The series is based on true events and follows Queen Victoria's life from her first moments in the monarchy as a teenage girl in 1837. A central character in the first few seasons is Dash, Queen Victoria's beloved King Charles spaniel. In the film series—as in real life—Dash was Queen Victoria's constant and loyal companion and best friend. When Dash died, he was buried with an epitaph on his grave at Windsor reading:

> Here lies Dash, the favorite spaniel of Her Majesty Queen Victoria, in his 10th year. His attachment was without selfishness. His playfulness without malice. His fidelity without deceit. Reader, if you would live beloved and die regretted, profit by the example of Dash.

Queen Victoria's dogs were her cherished companions, and in her lifetime she owned more than a hundred dogs of 28 different breeds. The Queen greatly prized her dogs and promoted their care in the royal kennels. Queen Victoria's public display of dogs as her companions started the social trend of keeping dogs as pets.[4] One can understand why the Queen so detested the practice of vivisection.

By 1874, Queen Victoria's personal anxieties about the suffering of experimental animals had been publicly conveyed to the Royal Society for the Prevention of Cruelty to Animals (RSPCA). Her repugnance of animal experiments and teaching them to students was further expressed in a letter written by her private secretary to Joseph Lister, a Professor of Surgery at Edinburgh University and Surgeon to the Queen, stating, "The Queen has been dreadfully shocked at the details of some of these practices and is most anxious to put a stop to them."[5]

However, given the growing reliance on vivisection for medical progress and its increasing list of staunch supporters, Queen Victoria

**Queen Victoria. Photograph by W. and D. Downey for the Hulton Royals Collection. Reproduced by permission of Getty Images.**

was not able to stop vivisection on dogs, even in her position. Still, her outspokenness was not for naught, as the tides of unregulated animal experimentation were starting to turn in a curious chain of events.

## Frances Power Cobbe (1822–1904)

Frances Power Cobbe is known as the most high-profile anti-vivisectionist of the 19th century. She was born in Dublin in 1822 into an upper-class family. After the death of both her parents, Cobbe embarked on an 11-month tour of Europe and the Middle East, a journey which would shape the rest of her life.[6] It was through a series of events during her travels across Europe in 1863 that Cobbe first became aware of the practice of vivisection. One of these events happened when Cobbe was visiting Florence, Italy.

An acquaintance, Dr. Appleton of Harvard University, drew her attention to the experiments being performed on animals there by Professor Moritz Schiff. Appleton told Cobbe how he had seen dogs and other creatures in a "mangled and suffering" condition in Schiff's laboratory. Cobbe promptly drafted a petition that was sent around Florence and was eventually presented to Schiff with 783 signatures. While Schiff ignored the petition, it had put his experiments into the public light, making Florence an unpleasant place for him work. He eventually retreated to Geneva in 1877.[7]

Upon her return home, Cobbe became increasingly interested in advocating for animal rights, and began writing avidly on the topic. In 1875 she founded the Society for the Protection of Animals Liable to Vivisection, later renamed the Victoria Street Society, which is now known as the National Anti-Vivisection Society (NAVS)—the world's first organization campaigning against animal experiments. With Cobbe in the lead, NAVS published many leaflets and articles opposing animal experiments, and gathered many notable people of the day to support the cause.[8] Later, in 1898, Cobbe also founded the British Union for the Abolition of Vivisection (BUAV), now known as Cruelty Free International.

Cobbe believed that human's relationship with animals was based on moral grounds. She did not deny that vivisection had provided mankind with knowledge in the past, or that it was possible it might again in the future. But she did not believe this should be accepted as a basis to allow the practice to continue. She believed that the good of mankind did not justify the "torture of beasts."[9]

## The Absinthe Scandal and the Regulation of Vivisection

One event in particular set the stage for Great Britain's early attempts at regulating vivisection, as the necessity of certain experiments on dogs came under question. In 1874, Valentin Magnan, a French psychiatrist who did research on the effects of absinthe (a distilled, highly alcoholic beverage), was invited to lecture at the annual British Medical Association meeting in Norwich. His lecture was to include actually inducing epilepsy in two dogs by injecting them intravenously with absinthe.

As the first dog was brought in, strapped to a board with legs extended, and the absinthe was injected, chaos among the audience ensued. A great "scene" followed as medical men vehemently protested the unnecessary experiment. Magnan was questioned on why the experiment was performed, as the effects of alcohol on the human system were already well known.[10] This protest resulted in one of the dogs' being set free. While the absinthe experiment continued on the second dog, this turn of events demonstrated the deep divide that had formed in Great Britain regarding vivisection on dogs—even among men of science.

Two months after the barbaric absinthe dog experiment, the Royal Society for the Prevention of Cruelty to Animals (RSPCA) charged Magnan with unjustified cruelty to a dog. While the prosecution failed, since Magnan was already back in France and did not appear, the publicity the case generated ensured that vivisection remained in the press. Two bills to regulate vivisection were subsequently put before parliament.[11] In 1875 the government set up a royal commission on the matter, resulting in the 1876 Cruelty to Animals Act, also known as the Vivisection Act.[12] With this Act, Britain became the first country to pass legislation regulating vivisection before the 20th century.[13]

The Cruelty to Animals Act mandated that vivisection be performed only for an original, useful purpose. This put an end to the public Continental-style demonstrations, but left open the private use of animals for medical research and teaching. It required all vivisectionists to hold a license, but these were liberally bestowed. By 1891, more than 600 scientists had been granted such a license, a large proportion of whom were given "special" certificates dispensing them from the need to use anesthesia.[14]

## *Vivisection in the United States*

The first animal experimentation laboratories in the United States opened in the 1860s and 1870s. From the start, anti-vivisectionists such as Henry Bergh, who founded the American Society for the Prevention of Cruelty to Animals (ASPCA) in 1866, began trying to regulate the practice of vivisection. The ASPCA tried several times to pass federal legislation regulating animal experimentation, but failed.[15]

In the late 19th and early 20th centuries, a period known as the Progressive Era in the United States, Americans were increasingly engaged in reform movements aimed at uplifting the downtrodden and improving society. Women were central to Progressive Era reforms. Mainly representing the "elite" class, women joined reform movements to act as the "moral compass" of American society and to care for the voiceless. Accordingly, American anti-vivisectionists were predominantly urban and female.

In 1869 Caroline Earle White and Mary Frances Lovell, both from Philadelphia, founded the Women's Branch of the Pennsylvania Society to Prevent Cruelty to Animals (WBPSPCA), known today as the Women's Humane Society. They both believed the humane treatment of animals was a moral issue that Americans could not ignore. With the increasing use of animals for experimentation and research, they realized that their efforts were needed on this front.

Inspired by Frances Power Cobbe, White traveled to London to meet Cobbe. In 1883, White returned to Philadelphia and called a special meeting of the WBPSPCA during which the American Anti-Vivisection Society (AAVS) was formed, the first anti-vivisection society in the United States, which still exists today.[16]

## *"Zoophil-psychosis": Anti-vivisectionists Said to Be Afflicted by Mental Illness*

In 1909, the *New York Times* printed an article about Charles Loomis Dana, a neurologist who diagnosed a new nervous disease which he described as being "...developed from a preposterous love of pet animals—dogs, cats, and horses—pushed to the verge of insanity." This odd proclamation was the result, the article said, of a newly identified mental illness he called *zoophile-psychosis* that people, particularly women, with a heightened concern for animals succumbed to.[17]

Dana coined this term in 1909, a time of great controversy over the practice of vivisection. Advocates of animal experimentation immediately accepted Dana's diagnosis in vivisection's defense, claiming that anti-vivisectionists were fanatics, ill-balanced people, cranks, and perverts.[18]

Neurologists believed that women were inherently inferior, an assumption deeply rooted in late 19th-century science. Women were said to have smaller brains and weaker nervous systems than men, predisposing them to nervous exhaustion. Mental activity or emotional trauma that men could master women could not.[19]

Dana believed that experiments on animal nervous systems could play a crucial role in understanding the weakness of nerves. Dana predicted "catastrophe" should anti-vivisectionists succeed in regulating labs.[20]

His own poor opinion of women became clear when he wrote that concern for animals was a form of female laziness, it being "much easier to pet a dog or nurse a kitten" than to "nurse the sick, provide thoughtfully for the poor, or ... make a household comfortable." Dana claimed that zoophilists cared nothing for human suffering, only animal suffering.[21]

Even as late as 1966, amid the controversy over the passage of the U.S. Laboratory Animal Welfare Act, at least one vivisection advocate tried to use the zoophile-psychosis diagnosis to oppose the Animal Welfare Act.[22]

## *Riots, Dog Thieves and Increased Public Scrutiny of Vivisection*

In the early 20th century, American and British history regarding vivisection and animal welfare in experimentation began to move in almost parallel motion. Members of the public became braver in speaking out against research on animals. Research institutions became more brazen and secretive. Perhaps more than ever before, the use of dogs in research was being boldly scrutinized.

### The Brown Dog Affair: London

A physiological demonstration to medical students at University College in London became national news in 1903, when the physiologist William Bayliss was accused of animal cruelty after an experiment he performed on a brown terrier dog in class. This demonstration, which included vivisecting an anesthetized dog to show pancreatic secretion, was infiltrated by two Swedish anti-vivisectionists, Louisa Schartau and Louise Lind-af-Hageby, who were posing as medical students.

When these women witnessed the vivisection, they noticed that the dog had an unhealed abdominal wound, which indicated that it had recently been used for another experiment. They both made a record of the incident in their diaries. Louisa and Louise also claimed the dog had struggled throughout the course of the demonstration and was still alive when it was taken from the lecture room.

The ladies took what they had written to Stephen Coleridge at the National Anti-Vivisection Society (NAVS). Coleridge immediately saw that if what they had recorded was correct, then there had been a serious infringement of the 1876 Cruelty to Animals Act. Under the Act, a vivisected animal could not be revived after one experiment and used for another: It had to be destroyed.

Coleridge publicly charged the physiologist Bayliss with having broken the law. Bayliss then sued Coleridge for libel in order to protect his reputation. The case was heard in November 1903. The jury found for Bayliss, and Coleridge was fined two thousand pounds to the delighted cheers of University College medical students who packed the court throughout the trial.[23]

Louise Lind-af-Hageby was outraged by the Bayliss verdict, but was not ready to admit defeat. She met with the secretary of the Church Antivivisection League, and the two women decided to present the Battersea Council, a district near University College, with a radical idea: to erect a strongly-worded memorial statue in Battersea, designed to be a drinking fountain for dogs, with a sculpture of a dog on top. The mayor of Battersea welcomed the statue and all that it stood for. Along with the Battersea Council, he approved both the design and the inscription on the base of the statue:

> *In memory of the Brown Terrier Dog Done to Death in the Laboratories of University College in February 1903 after having endured Vivisections extending over more than two months and having been handed over from one Vivisector to another till death came to his Release.*
>
> *Also in memory of the 232 dogs vivisected in the same place during the years 1902–3.*
>
> *Men and Women of England*
> *How Long shall these things be?*[24]

It was agreed that the statue should be placed in the Latchmere Recreation Ground. There was a large crowd on September 15, 1906, when the statue was unveiled. Beginning in November 1907, several violent attacks on the statue took place by University College medical students armed with sledgehammers and crowbars. While they did not succeed in destroying the statue at first, they tried again and again over the years. Police had to guard the statue day and night, and often intervene to stop students from destroying it.[25]

It was finally determined that the statue was more trouble than it was worth. On March 10, 1910, at the request of the newly elected Battersea council, the monument was carried away by four Council workmen guarded by 120 police in the dead of night.[26] It was said to have been handed over to a blacksmith to be melted down.[27]

Ten days later, more than three thousand people assembled to hear the leaders of the anti-vivisection movement demand the return of the brown dog statue. More scuffles broke out between medical students and police. However, the medical community regarded the removal of the statue as a victory for progress and science.[28]

In 1985, a new brown dog statue, funded by the British Union for the Abolition of Vivisection (BUAV) and National Anti-Vivisection Society (NAVS), was unveiled in Battersea Park. The bronze statue, sculpted by Nicola Hicks, was accepted by the Greater London Council on condition that the organizations had libel insurance to cover the wording of the inscription, which remained the same as on the original statue.[29]

## Dog Thieves Strike London: Selling Pets for Research

Just three years after the brown dog statue was removed, University College would once again be involved in controversy surrounding its research activities using dogs. University College was first linked to dog stealing for experiments in 1913. At this time the college's professors included some of Europe's most distinguished physiologists. Their students were receiving over 300 hours of practical teaching in experimental physiology—around ten times more than in any present-day medical school.

Obtaining sufficient animals for research and teaching at this scale was challenging, and while London, like any big city, had plenty of stray dogs, it was illegal to give or sell them to a laboratory. Dogs for vivisection had to be purchased from dealers; however, dealers found it easy to break the law and often stole dogs to be sold to the college for research.[30]

## Mr. Smythe and Bob

On November 19, 1926, a wolfhound mix named Bob had been taken from his home near University College. His owner, Frederick Smythe, had informed the police and visited the local dog shelter without success in finding him. Knowing that dogs were being stolen for research by University College, Mr. Smythe met Professor Verney at the University and gave him Bob's description. Professor Verney told Smythe that nothing could be done without first consulting the provost and told him to return the next day. On his return Mr. Smythe was reunited with Bob. Bob hadn't escaped without injury, though; a large lump on the base of his skull suggested a blow to the head.

Both the suspected dog thief and Professor Verney were charged with theft. The BUAV provided legal help and financial assistance for the case, and Mr. Smythe and Bob became celebrities. Their appearance at a public meeting in January 1927 was "greeted with much applause." Both the dog kidnapper and Professor Verney were acquitted. While the BUAV expected this defeat, it had achieved much in the way of publicity. The issue of using dogs in medical research was reported in national newspapers long after the court case concluded.[31]

One story, reporting on the fact that University College had used 1,147 dogs for research over a two-year period, resulted in the college's receiving a flurry of letters from anti-vivisection ladies and from owners of lost dogs pleading for professors to look in laboratory cages.[32]

## Stealing Dogs for Research in the United States—A Despicable Business:

As in Great Britain, dog theft by dog dealers selling to research laboratories was a problem in the United States. Even into the 1950s and 60s, the United States still had no regulations for animal welfare in research, and an illicit underground world of dog trade for research had been festering in neighborhoods across the country. Outraged residents posted signs on trees in their towns with the messages like, "Dog nappers, beware. We are on to you!"

## Pepper the Stolen Dalmatian

Perhaps the most famous dog theft case involved Pepper the Dalmatian, a beloved family pet whose disappearance and subsequent death in a research laboratory made national headlines. In the summer of 1965, Pepper disappeared from the Lakavage family farm. Pepper was known for her gentle disposition and was Julia Lakavage's favorite out of all the dogs they owned. Julia, her husband Peter, and their four children lived on an 82-acre farm near Slatington, Pennsylvania. Pepper especially loved car rides and visiting the nursing home where Julia worked.

On the night of Tuesday, June 22, 1965, the Lakavage children let Pepper out onto the back porch for her usual evening walk around the house. When they opened the door half an hour later, Pepper wasn't there. A loyal family dog, this was very unusual for her. They called and called into the darkness for Pepper to no avail. By the following morning, the Lakavages knew that Pepper was officially missing. They desperately launched a search that included scouring the local woods, posting signs in the neighborhood, and talking to neighbors. Someone they talked to had seen a man loading a Dalmatian into the back of a truck near their farm.

Pepper had indeed been stolen and was then sold to an animal research laboratory in New York. It was later learned that medical researchers there had tried to implant her with an experimental cardiac pacemaker but the procedure failed and Pepper had died.[33]

## Vivisection Regulation in the United States: Ending One Era, Beginning Another

The Humane Society of the United States (HSUS) was aware of this problem of dog theft for some time and had been actively investigating dog dealers around the country. Frank McMahon, HSUS director of field services at the time, had been preparing to carry out an intensive campaign to expose this system of funneling dogs from random sources—such as people's backyards—into medical or commercial laboratories.

On a cold winter morning in late January 1966, a raid of known animal dealer Lester Brown's White Hall property in Maryland finally revealed the dirty and secret world of dog dealing for the research industry. State troopers accompanied the HSUS in the raid, as did *Life* magazine photographer Stan Wayman. The photos Wayman took that day disturbingly showed dogs outside in the freezing weather, chained to boxes and barrels, or jammed into chicken crates and wire pens. According to the HSUS report, "The dogs were starving and emaciated, unable to stand on their own feet, frantically licking at frozen water pans in futile attempts to drink...."[34]

When *Life* published its photo exposé called "Concentration Camp for Dogs" in the February issue, the piece elicited a tremendous response from an outraged public. Americans sent more than 80,000 letters to their congressional representatives, demanding action to protect animals used for research and to prevent pet theft.[35]

In August 1966, President Lyndon Johnson signed into law the Laboratory Animal Welfare Act, now known as the Animal Welfare Act, which criminalized the theft of dogs for research and required the humane treatment and care of animals in laboratories.[36]

The photographer Stan Wayman was given the Albert Schweitzer Medal for outstanding achievement in the advancement of animal welfare. He was also given a great deal of credit for the passage of the 1966 Animal Welfare Act, since it was through his images that Americans were enlightened to the plight of dogs in research at last.[37]

This turn of events marked a new era for dogs used in scientific research in the United States. While dogs could no longer be snatched from people's backyards, the need for dogs in science was growing. This need would be met by purposefully breeding dogs that could be shipped from large-scale breeding operations right to a research laboratory's doorstep—perpetuating the use of dogs on an even larger scale.

# 3

# Dogs in Research—Stories and Statistics

When a small dog named Laika was blasted into space in 1957 aboard a Russian rocket ship, scientists knew she wouldn't survive the journey. It was not known how long she would live, only that she would not return to earth alive. Laika was testing the waters, so to speak, for human space travel. Scared and physically overcome by the side effects of the experiment, Laika suffered and perished. Laika's story is told in more detail below. It is an example of how deeply reliant we have become as a society on dogs to test many things we may use or come into contact with. Even outer space.

With new animal welfare protections now in place in the United States, the United Kingdom, and other nations, one might think that life for dogs in research had become better. More humane perhaps. That again is for the reader to decide.

## *Human Drug Tragedies Call for More Dogs in Research*

Several public health disasters struck the United States in the late 19th and early 20th centuries, a time when pharmaceutical research and large-scale product development was burgeoning. In 1901, 13 children died from a commercial diphtheria antitoxin that had been contaminated with tetanus. This tragedy led to the adoption of the U.S. Biologics Control Act of 1902, which mandated annual licensing of establishments that manufactured or sold vaccines, serums or antitoxins.

Another tragedy struck in 1937 when (absent a requirement for toxicity testing) 105 people died of kidney failure after receiving an antibiotic that had been formulated in a toxic solvent. In response to this episode, Congress passed the 1938 U.S. Food, Drug, and Cosmetic Act, followed by the 1962 Kefauver Harris Amendment, which required drug sponsors to demonstrate that their products be both effective and safe before being granted marketing approval.

By 1965 it had become standard regulatory practice to conduct product toxicity testing in multiple animal species—one rodent and one non-rodent (often dogs)—before approving it for human use.[1] It was the hope that this two-species paradigm, which included dogs as the second test species, would provide sufficient data to pick up drug side effects or toxicity not observed in rodent species.[2]

From here on, dogs were used in all types of research to ascertain the effects of potentially toxic elements and products on a living body system. The stories below are just a few examples of these experiments on dogs over the decades.

## *Heatstroke Experiments*

Heatstroke experiments on dogs have been taking place since the 1800s. Even though published results of these studies were widely available, such experiments continued in 1927, 1971, 1973, and 1984. The experiments caused great suffering, with the major findings seeming to be the advice that the heatstroke victims should be cooled—something that seems to be common sense.

However, when the U.S. Federal Aviation Administration (FAA) carried out a heatstroke study on beagles in 1984, researchers claimed the study was done because "animals occasionally die from heat stress encountered during shipping in the nation's transportation systems."[3] In the experiment, FAA experimenters subjected ten beagles to heat. Dogs were isolated in chambers, fitted with muzzles, and exposed to 95 degrees Fahrenheit combined with high humidity. They were given no water and were kept in these conditions for twenty-four hours.

The behavior of the dogs was then observed and recorded: "deliberate agitated activity such as pawing at the crate walls, continuous circling, tossing of the head to shed the muzzle, rubbing the muzzle back and forth on the floor of the crate, and aggressive acts on the sensor guards." Some of the dogs died in the chambers. When the survivors were removed, some vomited blood, and all were weak and exhausted. The experimenters refer to "subsequent experiments on more than one hundred beagles."[4]

The title of the published paper that resulted from this study was "Tolerance Endpoint for Evaluating the Effects of Heat Stress in Dogs."

Ironically, as of 2019 there were 31 states in the United States and the District of Columbia that had some kind of "hot car" law, which makes it unlawful to leave a dog confined in a car on a hot day.

## *Laika (Barker): The First Living Creature to Orbit the Earth*

The story of Laika, depending on one's point of view, is either a heroic tale of bravery or an unnecessary, inhumane operation for forcing animals to precede humans into space. Laika's story is worth mentioning for at least two reasons. First, it is an example of how far-reaching, literally, biomedical research on animals can be. Second, since space exploration is still in its infancy, Laika reminds us—when looking ahead (or above)—to contemplate weighing the value of human progress against the value of the animal lives that we decide to sacrifice.

Before humans went into space, one of the prevailing theories of the perils of space flight was that humans might not be able to survive

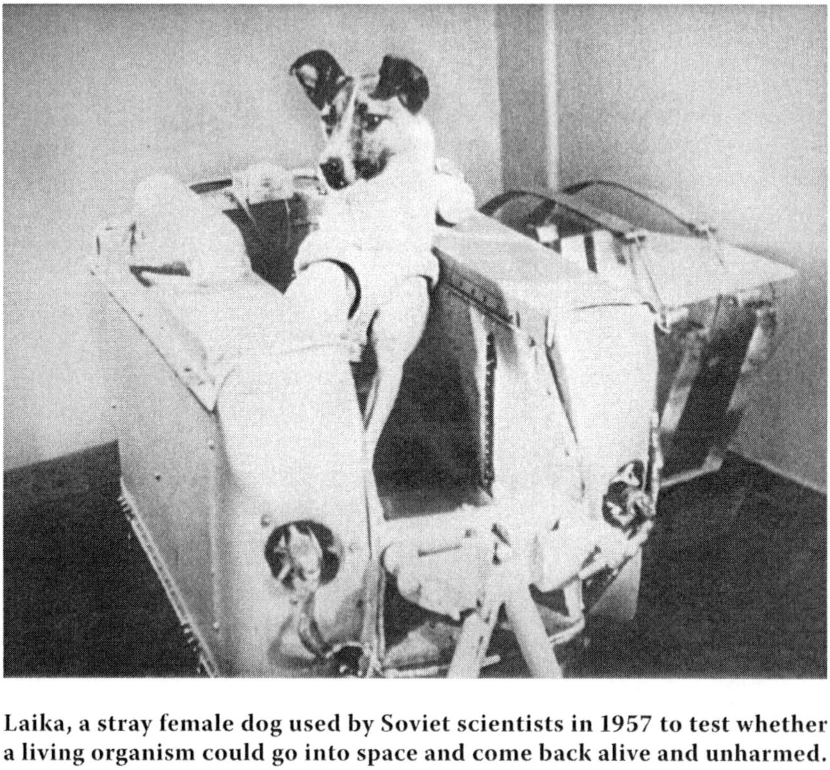

**Laika, a stray female dog used by Soviet scientists in 1957 to test whether a living organism could go into space and come back alive and unharmed. Reproduced by permission of the Smithsonian National Air and Space Museum (NASM 75–10226).**

long periods of weightlessness. American and Russian scientists utilized animals—mainly monkeys, chimpanzees, and dogs—to test whether a living organism could go into space and come back alive and unharmed.

Basing their experiments on American biomedical research, Soviet scientists used mice, rats, and rabbits as one-way passengers for their initial tests. However, they needed to gather additional data to design a cabin to carry a human being into space. Eventually they chose small dogs for this phase of testing. Dogs were chosen over monkeys because it was felt that they would be less fidgety in flight.[5]

Soviet canine recruiters chose to work with stray female dogs because they were smaller and more docile than male dogs. Initial tests on the dogs assessed their obedience and passivity, two requirements of a "space dog."[6] Canine finalists lived in tiny pressurized capsules for days and then weeks at a time.

The training of "space dogs" included being confined in ever smaller cages and being spun in centrifuges to accustom them to conditions inside a space capsule.[7] Testers also fitted candidates with a sanitation device connected to the pelvic area. The dogs did not like the devices, and to avoid using them, some retained body waste, even after consuming laxatives. However, some adapted.[8]

Eventually, the team chose a calm three-year-old dog named Kudryavka as *Sputnik 2's* dog cosmonaut. Introduced to the public via radio, Kudryavka barked while on the air, and thereby became known as Laika, which means "barker" in Russian. Doctors performed surgery on Laika, embedding medical devices in her body to monitor heart impulses, breathing rates, blood pressure, and physical movement. Russian scientists fully expected Laika to die from oxygen deprivation—a painless death within 15 seconds—after seven days in space.

One of Laika's keepers, Vladimir Yazdovsky, took Laika home shortly before the flight because "I wanted to do something nice for the dog," he later recalled. Three days before the scheduled liftoff, Laika entered her constricted travel space that allowed for only a few inches of movement. She wore a spacesuit with built-in metal restraints.

On November 3, 1957, at 5:30 a.m., the space ship lifted off with G-forces reaching five times normal gravity levels. The noises and pressures terrified Laika: Her heartbeat rocketed to triple the normal rate, and her breath rate quadrupled. She reached orbit alive, circling Earth in about 103 minutes. Unfortunately, loss of the rocket ship's heat shield made the temperature in the capsule rise unexpectedly, and Laika died "soon after launch."[9] The exact mode of Laika's death was not publicized by the Soviet government until 2002, when secret material about the mission was declassified. The Soviets initially claimed that Laika had been euthanized after five days in space, before her oxygen ran out—although how such a claim could have been accomplished is a mystery.[10]

While the United States primarily used mice and monkeys for space flight experiments, the Soviet Union continued to use dogs throughout the 1960s. The dogs Veterok ("Breeze") and Ugoyok ("Little Piece of Coal") were launched aboard *Kosmos 110* on February 22, 1966. The flight was an evaluation of prolonged effects on animals of radiation during space travel. Twenty-one days in space still stands as a canine record and was only surpassed by humans in June 1974 with the flight of *Skylab 2*.[11] It has been suggested that the use of animal testing in spaceflight was essential to prepare for manned spaceflight.[12]

## *Radioactive Beagle Dog Studies*

The Argonne Beagle Dog Experiments were comprised of 15 distinct experiments conducted between 1961 and 1991 on 4,900 beagles at Argonne National Laboratory in Illinois. Beagles were chosen for their ready availability, easy management, optimum size and lifespan, and presumed physiological similarities to humans. The studies focused on the safety risks of radioactive elements.[13]

The dogs involved in the studies were exposed to whole-body external beam radiation while housed in one-dog kennels.[14] A nuclear reactor was located in the center of the experiment room, with the dog kennels lining the wall, around it, stacked three high. This ensured that dogs were exposed to a consistent dose of radiation for 22 hours a day.[15] After all exposures were complete, the dogs were transferred to outdoor kennels where they lived with two other dogs who had been exposed to radiation. The dogs were given regular medical care which focused on maintaining the dog's health, but not on treating pathologies as they developed.[16]

In one of the experiments, all 72 dogs exposed to high doses of radiation suffered acute deaths from septicemia (inflammatory response to bacterial infection) less than 100 days after their first exposure. Experiments also showed that acute deaths were not observed in dogs exposed to lesser doses. Instead, they suffered from late-effect toxicities, high tumor counts, and lifespan reduction.[17]

The materials and results, including dog tissues from the Argonne Beagle Dog Experiments, have been preserved by the Woloschak Laboratory under a grant from the U.S. Department of Energy. It is hoped that such archival efforts may reduce or remove the need for new animal studies in radiation and preserve the findings of researchers who participated in the studies.[18]

## *Smoking Beagles*

On February 6, 1970, the *New York Times* headline read, "12 Dogs Develop Lung Cancer in Group of 86 Taught to Smoke." The purpose of the study was to determine whether smoking cigarettes with an efficient filter is less harmful than smoking cigarettes without the filter, and to ascertain whether smoking cigarettes for two years or longer would produce lung cancer in dogs.

Researchers bought 97 male beagles from breeders in upstate New York. Once the study began, the researchers cut a small opening through the front of each dog's neck into the trachea, a procedure known as a tracheotomy. A hollow tube, used to keep the tracheostoma open, was connected to a cigarette holder. Eighty-six of the dogs were trained to gradually smoke up to a maximum of nine cigarettes a day. All were the same brand of cigarette.

The dogs varied considerably in weight. The 38 heaviest dogs were put in one group "with the intention of keeping them smoking until all

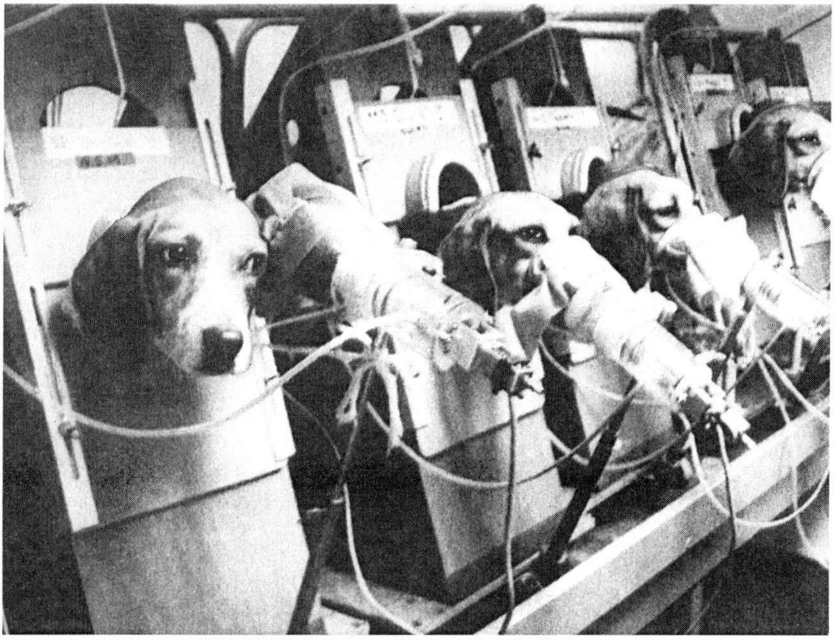

**Beagles used for smoking tests at Dog Toxicity Unit, Alderley Park, Cheshire, United Kingdom, in 1975. The dogs were forced to smoke up to 30 cigarettes a day to help in tests for a new, safer cigarette for humans. Photograph by Mirrorpix. Reproduced by permission of Getty Images.**

eventually died," according to one of the researchers. Other dogs were divided into groups smoking filter tip or non-filter-tip cigarettes, with some beagles smoking as many as 6,143 cigarettes within an 875-day period. During the 875 days, researchers reported that "death rates were in alignment with dosage of tar and nicotine relative to body weight." Twenty-eight of the smoking dogs died of lung diseases rarely seen in dogs. At day 875, the researchers began putting to death the remaining dogs, and autopsies were performed on all the dead dogs, revealing that 12 of the heaviest-smoking beagles smoking non-filter cigarettes had developed lung cancer.[19]

## *Narcoleptic Dobermans*

Dogs were first identified as suffering from a form of narcolepsy in 1972, and thus were of interest as a model for humans, because humans also suffer from narcolepsy. According to the National Institute of Neurological Disorders and Stroke, anywhere from 135,00 to 200,000 people have narcolepsy. Symptoms of the disease include excessive daytime sleepiness; loss of voluntary muscle control triggered by sudden, strong emotions such as laughter, fear, anger, stress or excitement; sleep paralysis; and hallucinations.

Attempts to establish breeding colonies of narcoleptic poodles and beagles failed. It was in the Doberman pinscher that the first genetic transmission of canine narcolepsy was demonstrated in 1976. From 1977 to 1997, canine narcolepsy was well studied, with the majority of research performed on colonies of Dobermans and Labrador retrievers. During that period, genetic studies linked narcolepsy to a single autosomal recessive gene. However, as scientific understanding of narcolepsy has advanced, it was discovered that the cause of narcolepsy in dogs is different from humans. In dogs, narcolepsy is caused by a mutation at the level of the orexin receptor, whereas the human disease is due to a deficiency in orexin-producing neurons. Therefore, while dogs played an early role in understanding narcolepsy, genetically engineered mice are now the animal of choice to study this disease.[20]

* * *

As we leave the past behind, remembering all that dogs have sacrificed for us, we may reflect on one verifiable truth: History does not need to repeat itself. We have the opportunity to change the future for dogs in research. The goal, in fact, should be to end the need to use dogs in harmful scientific research and replace dogs with better, and safer methods more relevant to humans. First, we must understand some important facts and figures.

## Dogs in Research Today: Global Statistics

While the number of dogs used in research in the United States has declined by more than 70 percent since their peak use in 1979, the U.S. Food and Drug Administration (FDA) still specifically references dogs as a preferred "non-rodent species" to fulfill safety testing requirements for regulated pharmaceutical and medical devices. While most use of laboratory dogs today is carried out to satisfy regulatory requirements related to product development by private industry such as pharmaceutical companies, investigators in a limited number of biomedical fields continue to perform research using dogs as well.[21]

Globally, an estimated 207,700 procedures involving dogs are conducted every year, with China and the United States being the biggest users of dogs. This figure, compiled by Cruelty Free International, one of the world's leading organizations campaigning to end animal experiments, is the first global figure ever compiled on dogs in research.[22]

### United States

Approximately 330 research facilities in the United States use dogs for testing and research each year. According to 2019 data from the U.S. Department of Agriculture, more than 49,000 dogs were used in research, 32 percent of which were used in harmful experiments—meaning there was pain involved for which the dogs either did or did not receive pain relief drugs. Approximately 6,000 additional dogs were being held in laboratories.

The most common use for dogs is for product testing—such as for drugs, pesticides, and medical devices—but they are also used by private and public sectors for a wide range of research areas, including cardiac, neurological, respiratory, and dental studies.[23]

**U.S. Facilities with the Largest Number of Dogs Used in Harmful Experiments (2019)**

| *Facility Name* | *Number of Dogs* |
|---|---|
| Covance Laboratories Inc. | 1,251 |
| Charles River Laboratories Inc. | 958 |
| Louisiana State University System | 565 |

| *Facility Name* | *Number of Dogs* |
|---|---|
| WVC (Viticus Group) | 523 |
| University of Pennsylvania | 419 |

**United States facilities with the largest number of dogs being used in harmful experiments as of 2019. For more information on animal usage by research facility by year, visit the USDA's website at www.aphis.usda.gov and search for "Research Facility Annual Summary and Archive Reports" (The Humane Society of the United States).**

## What Breeds of Dogs Are Used in Research?

Beagles are the breed of choice for chemical, pesticide and drug companies (as well as for contract laboratories that carry out tests for these companies), public and private universities, community and technical schools, and government-owned facilities. Of the estimated 55,000 dogs being used in research labs in the United States, a majority are beagles. Other dogs used are usually larger hounds (also known as mongrels), and more rarely, other breeds of dogs.[24]

## Where Do Research Dogs Come From?

Large-scale commercial breeding operations supply dogs to research laboratories. The locations of these facilities are not publicized. Research activities using dogs are generally kept out of the public eye. For example, even if universities have a large number of dogs being used for research on campus, students may not be aware of the dogs, or they most likely are not given access to the rooms where the dogs are kept. Overall, the entire research dog industry is conducted behind closed doors.

The U.S. Department of Agriculture (USDA) identifies several classes of dog breeders for research including: Class A dealers and Class B dealers. Class B dealers are individuals who obtain dogs and cats from pounds, auctions, or individuals like private breeders and hunters and then sell them to laboratories These types of dealers have long been considered controversial. While there were hundreds of random source Class B dealers operating across the U.S. in the 1970s, today there are only around five. In fact, the U.S. National Institutes of Health stopped funding research studies using dogs from random sources in October 2014.[25]

The majority of dogs in laboratories today are "purpose-bred." Facilities that breed dogs for this purpose are called Class A dealers and are licensed and inspected by the USDA. The following are the largest Class A dealers in the United States that provide dogs to laboratories, according to figures for 2019.

**U.S. Class A dealers with largest numbers of dogs (2019)**

| *Institution* | *Number of Dogs* |
|---|---|
| Marshall Farms Group Ltd. | 23,354 |
| Covance Research Products Inc. | 4,795 |
| Ridglan Farms | 3,153 |

**The number of dogs reported in Class A breeding facilities in the United States as of 2019. Class A facilities breed animals specifically to be used in research. This information was gathered from USDA-licensed breeders' 2019 inspection reports containing inventory numbers (The Humane Society of the United States).**

## Research Dogs in the United Kingdom, the European Union (EU), and Beyond:

In the United Kingdom, dogs were used in 4,227 experiments in 2019, with 96 percent of these experiments using beagles. Across the rest of Europe the same year, dogs were used in 21,369 experiments.

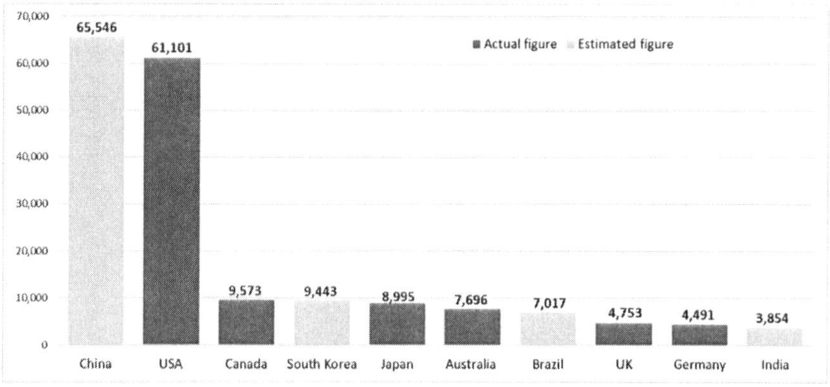


**The top ten users of dogs in research by country, based on actual or estimated figures. Reproduced by permission of Cruelty Free International. Derived from Taylor, K. and Rego Alvarez, L. (2019) "An Estimate of the Number of Animals Used for Scientific Purposes Worldwide in 2015," *Alternatives to Laboratory Animals*, 47(5–6) 196–213.**

Of a total of 16 EU member states using dogs, the top three users were France, the United Kingdom and Germany.

Globally, most experiments on dogs are done to satisfy regulatory requirements for product testing such as drugs, pesticides, and medical devices.[26]

# 4

# Dogs and Drug Development

In 2016, a Portuguese pharmaceutical company was testing a new pain-killing drug called BIA 10–2474. Per regulation, the drug was first tested successfully in several species of animals—including dogs—before entering human trials. The path forward seemed clear, until the trial took a terrible turn. Five human volunteers involved in the drug trial started to bleed deep inside their brains. One volunteer was declared brain dead and the other four had irreversible brain damage.

What happened? Why was this drastic, catastrophic effect not seen in the previous animal tests, and why didn't the dogs in the drug study bleed internally? What had everyone missed that could have averted this human tragedy? The short answer is, in most cases biological reactions in dogs do not coincide with biological reactions in humans.

Later in this chapter we'll delve into the details of the research for the pain-killing drug that led to the tragic outcomes for the volunteers. But first, we will examine some of the most recent science behind how animal testing may be contributing to skyrocketing drug failure rates for many diseases we face today. We will discuss how studies using dogs may no longer be ethically acceptable or offer the most effective tools to ensure human safety and health.

One thing we know for certain: The use of dogs in biomedical research is deeply entrenched in a multi-billion-dollar industry of human drug development. This fact adds even more complexity to the debate surrounding animal research, and in this case, dogs have been caught in the middle.

## *How Much Does It Cost to Approve a Drug?*

Economically speaking, dogs' continued use is an important discussion point, especially if the health benefit to humans is not consistent with the amount of money being spent. Even if we may not agree on the ethics surrounding the use of dogs in research, economics may be a point of common ground.

The drug development process is largely the same in the United States as in other countries. Preclinical research, typically in animals, is a regulatory requirement to gather safety information before a drug is tested in clinical trials in humans.

The U.S. National Institutes of Health (NIH) is the largest biomedical research organization in the world. With a budget of $39.2 billion in 2019, the NIH also provides most of the funds for animal research.[1] Adhering to governmental regulations, which are in place to prove safety and efficacy, makes the process for developing a single drug immensely expensive. This makes drug failures—like BIA 10–2474—financially disastrous for all the stakeholders involved. For example, the average pre-approval cost of research and development for a successful drug is estimated to be $2.6 billion.[2]

A 2018 article in *Drug Discovery Today* reported that despite the investment of billions of dollars by the NIH and other funding organizations, the number of new drugs approved per billion dollars spent in the United States has halved approximately every nine years since 1950. What this means is that now more than 90 percent of drug candidates entering clinical (human) trials fail to gain regulatory approval, mainly as a result of insufficient efficacy, and/or unacceptable toxicity, because of the limited predictive value of preclinical (animal) studies.[3]

## How Much Are We Spending on Animal Testing?

Statista, a global data portal for market and economic sector statistics, estimates the global markets for animal testing in 2018 at $7.4 billion for drug discovery, $11.2 billion for preclinical development and safety studies, $58.5 billion for clinical development, and $2.3 billion for central laboratory testing. It is estimated that annual U.S. biomedical and agricultural research and development investments involving animal research exceed $26 billion.[4]

While these figures represent all animals, not just dogs, it helps us understand how financially lucrative animal research really is. Class A dog breeders, such as Marshall Farms Group and Covance, are major stakeholders in the biomedical industry, as are universities that promote animal research, professors who design research, and laboratories that conduct animal research. In short, there are many players in the debate surrounding dog research, and each has a stake in the argument.

## *Lost in Translation: Dog Models Have Limited Accuracy in Predicting Human Toxicity*

> "...[It] seems clear that there is something gravely wrong with the way in which drugs are developed and tested: More than 90% of the drugs that appeared to be safe and effective in animals went on to fail in human trials between 2006 and 2015. It has been claimed that this simply is 'a reflection of normal design process,' but would this failure rate be thus described as acceptable for airplanes, car brakes, or nuclear power stations?"
>
> —Dr. Jarrod Bailey, Director of Science at *Animal Free Research UK*, and Fellow of the Oxford Centre for Animal Ethics (U.K.)[5]

A significant challenge that medical research is facing today is the understanding and possible treatment of chronic, complex human diseases, many of which are not well understood.

In 2013, Cruelty Free International, in conjunction with the Fund for the Replacement of Animals in Medical Research, conducted a study that showed that using dogs in experiments to predict how humans will respond to drugs is not scientifically justifiable. The authors of the study analyzed data from 2,366 publicly available toxicological studies. The results clearly showed that safety tests on dogs contribute almost nothing to learning about the probability of safety in humans.[6]

For example: Say a drug has a 70 percent probability of no adverse reactions in humans, a figure based on non-dog evidence such as data from related drugs or in vitro studies. Adding a dog test that shows dogs have no adverse reactions to the drug raises the probability of no adverse reactions in humans to 72 percent. This is a difference of only 2 percent—statistically insignificant, giving no added evidence of safety in humans. This makes the dog test, at great ethical and financial cost, not worth doing.[7]

According to the U.S. Food and Drug Administration (FDA), adverse drug reactions cause about 100,000 human deaths annually, making adverse drug reactions the fourth leading cause of death in the United States.[8] These deaths reflect a high failure rate in drug development across all disease categories that is based, at least in part, on the inability to adequately model human diseases in animals, and the poor predictability of animal models. Some may even conclude that animal research is more costly and harmful, on the whole, than it is beneficial to human health.[9] One research area that still actively uses dogs has recently come into question: cardiac research.

## Cardiac Research Using Dogs:

According to the World Health Organization, ischemic heart disease—problems caused by narrowed heart arteries—is the world's biggest killer. From the late 20th century to the present, dogs have been used to develop cardiac treatments for humans. Dogs have played a role in the development of the pacemaker, stents, transplants, and many other treatments and procedures. While the use of dogs for cardiac research has decreased since the 1980s, the laboratory dog is still a preferred model for studying cardiovascular disease and also atrial and ventricular arrhythmias.[10]

In 2020, the U.S. Department of Veterans Affairs (VA) assembled a committee to investigate the areas in which dogs are still necessary for VA research, the first study of this kind conducted for dogs by the VA. While the committee concluded that several areas of research no longer benefited from using dogs—such as diabetes, narcolepsy, most imaging studies, and pharmacological research—it concluded that dogs are still needed for several areas of cardiac research.[11] However, cardiac research on dogs doesn't necessarily equate to better treatments for humans. In fact, treatments for cardiovascular diseases have one of the lowest likelihoods of approval, according to an analysis carried out in 2015. Only 6.6 percent of cardiovascular drugs that enter phase I clinical (human) trials reach the market. One of the reasons cited for this is "the failure of translation between animal models of disease to humans."[12]

In addition to cardiovascular disease research, dogs are used to assess drug-induced cardiotoxicity, a condition causing damage to the heart muscle. Cardiotoxicity remains one of the main causes of the withdrawal of drugs during development. Identifying drugs that may cause adverse cardiac effects in humans is still a major challenge. But this situation is improving. While current animal models in cardiac research, including dog models, raise ethical and translational questions, and have limited accuracy in human risk prediction,[13] other human-relevant, computational models are proving to be very useful. The work of Blanca Rodriguez at the University of Oxford, for example, is very promising in terms of developing computer models to predict possible cardiotoxicity.[14]

## Invasive Cardiac Experiments on Dogs Revealed

The ethical questions regarding dogs in cardiac research are profound, since the procedures the dogs must endure are extremely invasive, with often limited justification. In a rare instance, the details of some of these experiments became public knowledge in 2019, when a report surfaced about cardiac research being conducted on dogs at Wayne State University in Michigan.

Through Freedom of Information Act requests, the Physicians Committee for Responsible Medicine (PCRM), a nonprofit research and advocacy organization based in Washington, D.C., was able to obtain thousands of veterinary records and official protocols from Wayne State, revealing their decades of heart failure and hypertension experiments on dogs. These were ongoing as of 2019. According to the documents obtained, the cardiac experiments on the dogs involve numerous surgical procedures, implanting up to nine medical devices in each dog's heart and near major blood vessels, and drastically increasing the dog's heart rate with surgically implanted electrodes to induce heart failure. To control the devices and collect data, up to nine cables and wires are surgically "tunneled" between the shoulder blades of each dog, and the dog is fitted with a restrictive vest.

According to the PCRM report and official Wayne State records, the surgeries are so intensive that up to 25 percent of the dogs are expected to die during or shortly after the procedures—in other words, before any data are collected that might benefit humans.[15] The limited usefulness of deeply invasive cardiac experiments on dogs raises the question, Is such research ethical?

## *Drug Disasters*

Failure rates in drug development are also leading to serious questions about whether dog and other animal testing accurately predict toxicity in human trials. The following human drugs successfully passed pre-clinical tests in dogs, as well as other species, only to cause much harm to humans in subsequent clinical trials. It is important to note that even drugs that survive clinical trials and attain market approval may still be recalled later due to toxicity identified only after months or years of human use, as was the case with a drug called Vioxx.

### Vioxx

Vioxx caused serious heart problems in many people who took the drug—a problem that was not detected in the dogs on which it was tested. Vioxx, also known as rofecoxib, was approved by the U.S. Food and Drug Administration (FDA) in 1999 for the treatment of osteoarthritis and pain. In clinical trials, Vioxx was shown to be an effective analgesic for dental pain as well as an effective fever reducer. Vioxx was developed and marketed by Merck, a pharmaceutical company based in Rahway, New Jersey.

Two animal species were used in the toxicological evaluation of Vioxx: rats and dogs. Male beagles weighing 20–22 pounds were obtained from Marshall BioResources, a large breeder of laboratory dogs, located in New York. Dogs were surgically prepared with a tube in the jugular vein and/or bile duct for sample collection. Doses of Vioxx were administered to dogs via ten-minute infusions through their veins and by oral gavage (a tube inserted through the mouth, down the throat and into the stomach). All the procedures performed on the dogs were approved by the Merck Research Laboratories Institutional Animal Care and Use Committee.[16]

Even though Vioxx passed as being safe in dogs and rats, it was found after release into the human market to significantly increase the risk of cardiovascular morbidity and mortality, costing Merck more than $8.5 billion in legal settlements alone. An estimated 88,000 people suffered heart attacks after taking Vioxx and 38,000 died.[17] By the time Vioxx was pulled off the market in 2004, more than five years after it was approved, about 25 million Americans had taken the drug. Merck withdrew Vioxx from the market in more than 80 countries.

Merck also pleaded guilty to one misdemeanor count of illegally introducing a drug into interstate commerce and promoting Vioxx to treat rheumatoid arthritis before the FDA approved it for that purpose in 2002. This illegal marketing caused doctors to prescribe Vioxx when they otherwise would not have.[18]

## Two Drugs.... Two Tragedies

Thalidomide, a sedative drug developed at the end of the 1950s, caused devastating phocomelia, a rare congenital deformity in which the hands or feet are attached close to the trunk, the limbs being grossly underdeveloped or absent. This deformity, that affected an estimated 20,000 to 30,000 infants, was a side effect of the drug's being taken during early pregnancy.

Animal tests had failed to reveal the drug's capability of producing fetal malformation, despite testing in two breeds of dogs; ten strains of rats; eleven breeds of rabbits; three strains of hamsters; eight species of primates; and various cats, armadillos, guinea pigs, pigs and ferrets.

In 1993, Fialuridine, for the treatment of hepatitis B, caused the deaths of five volunteers during phase II clinical trials despite being shown as safe in dogs, mice, monkeys and woodchucks in doses that were hundreds of times higher. Two other volunteers survived only after receiving liver transplants.

In the first decade of the 21st century, approximately one-third of FDA-approved drugs were subsequently cited for safety or toxicity issues, or a combination of both, including human cardiovascular toxicity and brain damage, after remaining on the market for an average of four years.[19]

## BIA 10–2474: Another Painkiller Gone Wrong

In January 2016, a tragic mishap occurred in Phase I of the clinical trial for BIA 10–2474, a drug developed for a range of disorders, including pain, hypertension, multiple sclerosis, and obesity, by Portugal's Bial Pharmaceuticals. The five volunteers who were subjected to multiple doses of the test drug were all adversely affected with deep brain hemorrhages and necrosis and admitted to the hospital. One volunteer was declared brain dead and the other four had irreversible brain damage.[20]

BIA 10–2474 had been found to be safe in dogs who were given doses 400 times stronger than the doses given to the human volunteers.[21] Bial had performed studies on four animal species: rat, mice, dog and monkey. Dog toxicological studies were carried out for 13 weeks. Safety studies in animals predicted the drug to be safe for human use, but because of species variation, the adverse effects were not predicted.[22]

## What Happens When Animal Tests Identify a "Safe" Chemical as "Toxic"?

When animal tests falsely identify a "safe" chemical as "toxic," the almost certain outcome is abandonment of further drug development. Undoubtedly many potentially beneficial drugs that have failed animal testing due to animal toxicity have been lost to human patients, even though they would have been both safe and effective. A few examples of highly beneficial drugs that would have failed animal testing and would never have been brought to market, except that they were developed before animal testing was required, include:

Penicillin (fatal to guinea pigs)
Paracetamol—also known as acetaminophen—(toxic in dogs and cats)
Aspirin (embryo toxicity in rats and rhesus monkeys).[23]

## *Hearing from the Experts: Views on the Relevance of Dog Research*

Several experts on the topic of biomedical research were interviewed for this book. These experts will in the next several chapters offer their opinions on how we can best meet the human health challenges we are facing today—and how dogs and other animals may not be the best tools for this job. Below, two of these experts, who have spent much time in biomedical research, share their professional views on using dogs to test drugs and medical devices for use in humans.

***Dr. Jarrod Bailey:*** Director of Science at *Animal Free Research UK*, and Fellow of the Oxford Centre for Animal Ethics in the U.K.

***Dr. Lindsay Marshall:*** Biomedical Science Advisor for Humane Society International (HSI) and the Humane Society of the United States (HSUS)

**Question: Why should we be reevaluating our historically-based, continued use of dogs in biomedical research?**

**Dr. Marshall:** We have to acknowledge that we're working on a platform of animal data, and we have no choice in that, because that's how it's always been done. Victorian scientists worked out that if you gave a dog carbon dioxide, then you could cut off its ear it wouldn't squeal. That's the kind of historical background we're looking at.

It doesn't mean that this data isn't valuable, but it also doesn't mean that we should continue. Historical use doesn't justify continued use. That just doesn't make any sense at any level. We can acknowledge the fact that dogs have contributed [to science], but that doesn't mean that they're still important and that we haven't moved beyond it.

Animals are not evolving anymore. So, if you're using an animal as a model for a human, you can't change it to be more like a human. You can't make it any better than it is because fundamentally it's an animal. There's an insurmountable species difference that exists that you cannot get over. And it doesn't matter what genetic modifications you make to it—it's still an animal, and not a person.[24]

* * *

**Dr. Bailey:** When I was looking at the history of vivisection and how it came about and got traction, I could kind of understand how it happened because we all have the same gross biology. We have eyes, and ears, a brain and limbs, and a spinal column, and so on. The problem is that as [the study of] biology has caught up, we've realized that we're largely a product of our genes, and our genes are very different. Even when we share genes they're often expressed differently. All of that difference is at the root of how you cannot reliably extrapolate any data from any one species to another. So, from rats to cats to mice to dogs to macaques to marmosets to chimps to humans, you can't do it.[25]

**Question: In terms of trying to obtain beneficial human data from dog experiments, what makes dog and human data *incompatible*?**

**Dr. Marshall:** What always shocks me about animal research is it's not really done on a scientific basis. It's not done because the dog's heart is exactly the same as a human's, and it's not done because a dog has exactly the same physiology as a human—because it doesn't.

Dogs have four legs. Their backs are in one position [horizontal] and our backs are in another [vertical]. These are obvious differences. You only have to measure a human's blood pressure while they're standing up, compared to when they're lying down, to realize what a difference that change in position has.

There's not a good physiological match between a human and a dog, but we're told there is because in comparison to a mouse, then it's better. Or in comparison to a rat, it's better. The horrible arguments we're getting now is that pigs might be a better replacement for dogs because of the size of the heart.

There are many fundamental differences that tend to get brushed aside because the physiological similarity is "good enough," which it really isn't. It's [animal research] not from a scientific basis, it's from a practical basis.[26]

* * *

**Dr. Bailey:** There's a growing frustration among enough scientists who are saying, "We know scientifically that data from dog experiments apply to human biology very rarely and very unreliably." Many animals in labs are chronically stressed, and that means whatever results you're getting from those animals don't even apply to the same animals outside a lab. Look at things like heart rate and blood pressure, and look at things more deeply in terms of the impact of stress on immune function. What does stress do to metabolism?—These are two of the biggest research areas in animals—infectious diseases and the testing of new drugs.

The course of infectious diseases depends on what your immune system is doing. Testing a new drug or the toxicity of a chemical looks at how you're metabolizing things. If you look at the expression of thousands of your genes—just because of stress—it's all over the place.

On the whole, your dog model is either good and reliable or it isn't. There's a huge amount of evidence that it isn't good and it isn't reliable. So the fact is that, if you are using such a demonstrably poor model with poor human relevance that doesn't predict human safety, then yes, some things [drugs] will get through. But that's in *spite* of the dog testing, not *because* of the dog testing.[27]

**Question: You state that there are human ethical consequences if animal testing of human drugs is not sufficiently predictive of human safety, which may result in significant human suffering, pain, and death. Can you expand on this thought?**

**Dr. Bailey:** When new drugs look bad in dogs, then the development of those drugs is often terminated. It's widely accepted that we will have lost really good drugs because they look toxic in dogs. The easy way to illustrate that is "dogs and chocolate." You don't want your dog eating chocolate because it can get sick. So, something very different metabolically is going on.

There are some scientists, maybe more moderate, who have the humility to accept what's going on, who realize that science hasn't got a choice for its future direction. It has to move away from animal use and onto something better and more human specific, not just for the sake of the animal but for humans as well.

We're still floundering and trying to understand all types of cancers, Alzheimer's, etc. and ... haven't gotten to the bottom of them because we're using the wrong models. That's why all of the treatments and cures we've been testing for people are just falling down—because we're using the wrong model. We have to begin, and end, with human biology—and what's really frustrating is we can do this, but we're not doing it nearly enough.[28]

# 5

# The Welfare of Dogs in Research

## *The Beagle—The Breed of Choice for Research*

> "In toxicology, pharmacology and other fields of science, the Ridglan Beagle, has earned its reputation of superiority."
>
> —Ridglan Farms, Inc.[1]

Beagles are known for their kind and gentle temperament, big floppy ears, uncanny sense of smell and a huge baying that can carry for miles when hunting rabbits in the countryside. Weighing anywhere from 20 to 30 pounds, beagles make great companions for young children and families because of their docile nature. According to the American Kennel Club (AKC), beagles were the seventh most popular dog in America in 2020.

The AKC officially recognizes two beagle varieties: those standing under 13 inches at the shoulder, and those between 13 and 15 inches. "The Beagle's fortune is in his adorable face.... Beagles are loving and lovable, happy, and companionable—all qualities that make them excellent family dogs," states the AKC on its website. "No wonder that for years the Beagle has been the most popular hound dog among American pet owners."[2]

The beagle's small stature and happy-go-lucky, easy-going temperament also happens to be the breed's greatest misfortune. Chosen for their docile nature and small size, beagles are the breed of choice for research laboratories worldwide.

Of the estimated 55,000 dogs being used in research labs today in the United States, the majority are beagles.[3] In fact, there are even a few "secret" breeds of beagle known only to the scientific community. They are known as the *Marshall Beagle*®[4] produced by Marshall BioResources, and the *Ridglan Beagle*[5] produced by Ridglan Farms, Inc. These breeders, known as Class A Dealers, supply beagles by the thousands to research institutions in the United States and around the world. These enormous breeding operations—housing anywhere from 500 to over 20,000 dogs each and operating in stealth mode—represent the largely hidden economy of the animal research industry.[6]

Dealers like Marshall and Ridglan breed what are known as "purpose bred" dogs. Sold by Class A Dealers as "research models," dogs bred into the world of laboratories most often die there as well. Experimental side effects, as well as a lack of priority given to re-homing healthy dogs after the research project has ended, make these dogs tools that are used and discarded. As tools, research dogs are not usually given names. They receive a number tattoo on the inside flap of an ear, which is how they are identified by research staff. Most research dogs spend their entire lives in wire cages or kennels, never seeing the outdoors. As they are sold to labs all around the world, their cages are moved between trucks and planes. But the stark reality of their research life follows them wherever they go.

## *Undercover Videos Reveal Experiments and Deaths*

In March 2019, Corteva Agriscience found itself immersed in a public relations nightmare. An undercover investigation by the Humane Society of the United States (HSUS) at the Charles River Laboratories in Michigan revealed video footage of several dozen beagles being poisoned and killed as part of a one-year pesticide study Corteva Agriscience had commissioned for a new fungicide. Any dogs that survived until the designated end of the study in July 2019 would be euthanized and their organs assessed for damage done by the fungicide. The video also showed workers carrying out experiments on dogs on behalf of Paredox Therapeutics and Above and Beyond NB LLC.[7]

### Harvey

Footage of one of the beagles went viral. He was number 1016, and against usual practice was also given a name—Harvey—because laboratory workers thought he was "a good boy" and stood out as friendly and "adorable." In the undercover video, Harvey, a beagle with soft brown eyes being used for a study for Paredox, was recorded being taken out of his stainless-steel cage. A big surgical scar is visible where his chest had been opened and two chemical substances poured in. When another beagle from the same study is being carried to a room for euthanasia, one of the lab workers remarks about Harvey, "He's gonna die."[8] Harvey

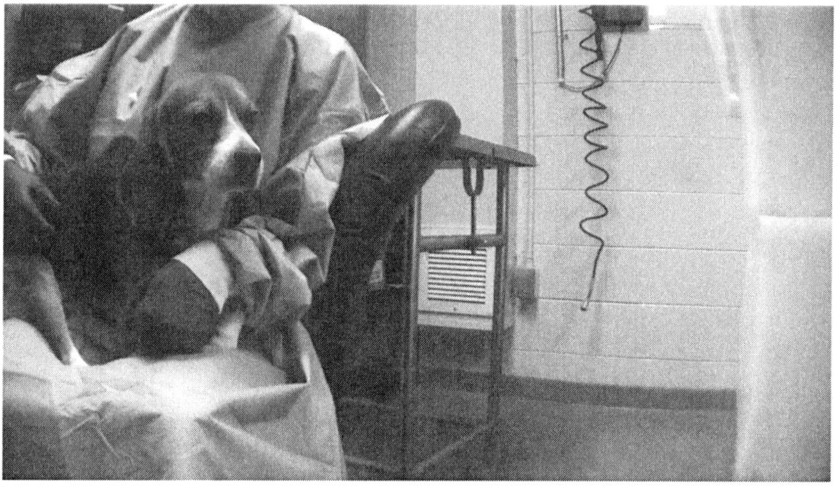

**Harvey the beagle getting last minute snuggles before being euthanized in the laboratory. He was being used for a study for Paredox Therapeutics. This photograph is a screen grab taken from undercover video footage in 2019 of Harvey while he was in the laboratory. Unseen in this photograph is a surgical scar where his chest had been opened and two chemical substances poured in (The Humane Society of the United States).**

did die. On the day Harvey was euthanized, he was let out of his cage for a few minutes to run around on the floor. That day was "the best life he knew," one lab employee observed. The employee sat Harvey in her lap and asked if he wanted some "last minute snuggles" before handing him over to be euthanized.[9]

It was no different for most of the other dogs who were part of studies at Charles River Laboratories. The HSUS investigator, who spent nearly 100 days at the facility, documented the dogs cowering and frightened in their cages, marked with surgical scars and implanted with large devices. Using crude methods, employees force-fed or infused dogs with drugs, pesticides and other products, many that were unlikely ever to be used in humans.[10]

Charles River is not a "bad" lab. They were operating entirely within the law and regulations governing animal use in the United States. So, everything that happened to those dogs—all that horrific footage—was absolutely legal.

## The Public Responds

While most of the dogs the investigator encountered were killed at the end of the studies, 36 beagles in the Corteva Agriscience study remained and were still undergoing the testing. When HSUS released the undercover investigation in March, more than 500,000 people signed a petition and called on the company to demand the release of these beagles. Public outcry was so immense that Corteva Agriscience announced a week later it had ended the test and later released the surviving 32 dogs to the Michigan Humane Society, an HSUS shelter and rescue partner. More than 800 people applied to adopt one of the beagles. Within weeks, all 32 beagles were adopted.[11]

## *Discoveries in Dog Cognition: A Case for Making Welfare a Priority*

> It makes sense that dogs, as a species being so sensitive and attuned, and cognitively and emotionally capable, suffer when they are kept in a laboratory and subjected to experiments. You don't have to be Sherlock Holmes or a rocket scientist to work out that dogs are going to be damaged by this.
>
> —Dr. Jarrod Bailey, Director of Science at *Animal Free Research UK*, and Fellow of the Oxford Centre for Animal Ethics in the U.K.[12]

Dogs are smart. Well, just as smart as a young human toddler at least. According to Dr. Stanley Coren—a psychology professor, neuropsychological researcher, and writer on the intelligence, mental abilities and history of dogs—the mind of a dog is equivalent to the mind of a human two- to three-year-old child. As such, a dog most likely has all the basic emotions of a two- to three-year-old child as well, including empathy.

As Dr. Coren explains, someplace within the age range of two and three, human children begin to show acts of empathy. One child may wander over to another child who is distressed, and although they are not very good at it, they seem to be trying to offer some kind of comfort. It's not surprising then, that that same type of empathy may come from dogs as well, as when a dog seems to want to comfort someone who is crying by sitting with them or licking their face.[13]

In 2016, Hungarian researchers discovered a type of memory in dogs that was previously thought to occur only in humans—*episodic memory*. Episodic memory involves the ability to recall personal events and specific episodes in one's life, and it is thought to be linked to self-awareness. The study found that dogs were able to recall past events as complex as human actions.[14]

This trailblazing study on dogs was highly praised in scientific circles and represented the first evidence of episodic-like memory in a non-human species. While self-awareness in dogs and humans may not be expressed in exactly the same ways, the fact that dogs are capable of complex memories is an important part of the ethical debate surrounding dogs in research laboratories. If dogs are capable of self-awareness and are as emotionally capable as a two- or three-year-old human child, how does that change how we treat them in laboratories? Some may say that it changes everything, to the point where it is no longer ethically acceptable to use dogs at all.

Carl Safina, the famous ecologist and author, gained national attention when he suggested in his book *Beyond Words: How Animals Think and Feel* that animals can feel empathy. *National Geographic* magazine and the *New York Times* both interviewed Safina about this growing human understanding of the animal world. Safina, who has spent most of his life watching animals—including his own dogs—doesn't question the fact that animals are conscious and have mental experiences much like humans.

In a July 2015 interview with *National Geographic*, Safina brought up animals in research laboratories as an example of why denying that animals have emotions or feel pain is no longer a valid argument:

> It's very obvious that animals are conscious to those who observe them. They have to be in order to do the things they do and make the choices that they do, and use the judgements that they use. However, in laboratories the dogma persists: Don't assume that animals think and have emotions—and many scientists insist that they do not.
>
> With the public, I think it's quite different. Many people simply assume that animals act consciously and base their belief on their own domestic animals or pets. Other people do not want animals to be conscious because it makes it easier for us to do things to animals that would be hard to do if we knew they were unhappy and suffering.[15]

## Learning More About How Dogs Think

Animal neuroscience has perhaps always been debated, mostly by those who might not want to believe that non-human mammals (and very likely many other animal species) are capable of rich emotional lives. Being privy to such knowledge of how animals think and feel might make certain current practices seem wrong, therefore jeopardizing so much of what we use animals for in agriculture and industry, including scientific research. More and more science is pointing to the fact that dogs have feelings very much like we do.

In 2012, Gregory Berns, a professor of psychology at Emory University, undertook a ground-breaking study on dog cognition called the *Dog Project,* the result of which would become a *New York Times* best-selling book called *What It's Like to Be a Dog.* Inspired by his own dogs—a pug named Newton and a terrier named Callie—Berns began wondering: Are dogs capable of loving us? Why do dogs like to learn new things? How does the dog mind actually work?

To answer these questions, Berns and a team of researchers at Emory University and Comprehensive Pet Therapy began training dogs to lie still in an MRI machine—completely voluntarily and without sedation, in order to understand more about how a dog thinks and processes information. Several policies guided the *Dog Project.* First, the dogs used were owned by people who loved and valued them in their household. Second, only positive reinforcement was used to train them. And third, the dogs were never forced to participate.

The brilliance of the project was that dogs who chose to participate were never physically restrained and were never sedated in the MRI machine (almost all dogs are sedated for veterinary MRIs due to fear of the procedure and the need to hold completely still). Dogs were provided with steps into and out of the MRI machine, and they were given the choice to voluntarily leave the experiment at any time.

Initially, two dogs were trained, using positive reinforcement. The dogs learned to hold an extended down-stay on a custom-made chin rest inside a simulated MRI. They also learned to wear ear protection to guard against the noise an MRI makes and to become acclimated to the sounds. Within a few months, Berns and his team performed the first such scans in the world, demonstrating that the reward system of the dog's brain could distinguish between hand signals that meant the presence or absence of a food reward. For example, in anticipation of treats, the dogs' brains responded much as a human's would to anticipating a pleasurable experience.[16]

The *Dog Project* revealed one major insight: that the same basic structures for emotion could be found in both dog and human brains. While many readers may have already come to this conclusion through their own personal experiences with dogs, dog consciousness and emotion continues to be hotly debated in science. As this debate has continued, dogs are still considered to be "property" and "equipment" in research institutions. At the same time, there have been efforts to help ensure that they are treated humanely. Given what we know now about dog cognition, are these efforts to ensure dog welfare sufficient? Let's take a look.

## *Laboratory Animal Oversight in the United States*

Who is tasked with ensuring the humane treatment of research animals in the U.S.? Are there any laws and restrictions placed on how dogs may be used in research experiments? The answers are yes, there are laws and committees entrusted with ensuring the welfare of animals in research. However, the fact is that these laws *permit* continued pain and suffering. That is what the laws are there for—to allow dog use in laboratories. And, with no upper limit on severity of pain in research animals in the United States, it stands to reason that these laws are *not* protective. One of these laws is known as the U.S. Animal Welfare Act.

### U.S. Animal Welfare Act (AWA)

The first federal law regulating animal research in the United States is known as the Animal Welfare Act, originally enacted in 1966. The U.S. Department of Agriculture (USDA) enforces this act by inspecting laboratories and monitoring compliance with the Act.

A quirk of the AWA is that it does not cover the most common species of laboratory animals, namely rats, mice, and birds.[17] Although the AWA does set minimal requirements for the care of certain animal species used in laboratories, including dogs, ensuring they have water, food, and shelter, according Dr. Sarah Kenehan, a Professor of Philosophy at Marywood University, it fails to protect animals from suffering in research experiments. Dr. Kenehan explains the AWA shortcomings:

> ...simple adherence to the AWA is not an appropriate tool for gauging if an animal's interest in not suffering has actually been respected. To begin, the Act only demands adequate food, shelter, and water to be provided outside the demands of the experiment; that is, as a matter of experimentation, animals can be denied these things and, worse, for sustained periods of time.
>
> It is not uncommon for animals to be subjected to radiation exposure; shock therapy; exposure to nerve gas; mutilation; social isolation; drug overdose and addiction; starvation and dehydration; oxygen deprivation; surgery without anesthesia; poisoning; deprivation studies; toxicity tests; and immersion and injection studies.
>
> The Act presumes that experimentation on animals is actually acceptable, thus subordinating the interests of animals from the outset.... Clearly then, simply adhering to the AWA (or similar rules in other countries) does not guarantee that a company has rightfully considered the interests of its animal test subjects.[18]

While the AWA does provide some special provisions for dogs, such as daily exercise, these provisions are limited to "certain conditions." Not surprisingly, the AWA is a source of contention between the research industry, which purports its high standards, and others who maintain that it doesn't adequately protect animals in research.

Dr. Lindsay Marshall, Biomedical Science Advisor for both the Humane Society International and the Humane Society of the United States (HSUS), lives in the United Kingdom. While her work is global in reach, she also has acknowledged the weak protections offered to laboratory animals in the United States compared to other countries. In an interview for this book, she relayed her concerns:

> One thing that bothers me is the way that dogs are treated now. And while there's this "necessity," while there is this apparent "requirement," what can we do to try and improve their [dogs] lives? With HSUS we really struggle with this because we don't want the dogs there at all. But while they're in there, the least we can do is let them outside once a day.
>
> The US regulations are frankly disgusting for that. You don't have to take a dog out. The room [cage size] that the dogs have in the US is one third of the size they are given in the EU [European Union]—that is the space given per individual dog.
>
> In terms of keeping a dog alone in a cage, a recent publication came out in the UK that said for toxicity testing there is no impact on the data if you keep dogs together, so you could have a pair of dogs in a cage to comfort each other. There's no need for that kind of isolation and that madness you're instilling in these dogs. They deserve a lot, lot more. We should be pushing for that—at least until we can get all dogs out of labs.[19]

## How Do Dog Experiments Get Approved?

How do experiments like the one Harvey was subjected to for Corteva Agriscience and other companies get approved? How is animal welfare measured in these experiments? Kathleen Conlee, Vice President of Animal Research Issues at the Humane Society of the United States (HSUS), explained in an interview for this book, "We know how basic and minimal those [AWA] standards are. These standards are not the ceiling—they are the floor. It [the AWA] talks about cage sizes and access to water and things like that, but it doesn't prohibit any type of research from happening. As long as an Institutional Animal Care and Use Committee *(IACUC)* approves it, it can move forward."

This IACUC requirement, according to Conlee, is an often-biased animal research approval process that might not always have the animals' interests at heart as it claims.[20] Perhaps the most important revision of the AWA was in 1985 when IACUCs were required for institutions that used animals in research. These committees are charged with reviewing all animal research at institutions that receive federal funding.[21]

An IACUC is established at each institution to review all proposed animal experiments. Each animal protocol must include: 1. A justification for using animals, the number of animals to be used, and the species chosen; 2. The procedures or drugs to be used to eliminate or minimize pain and discomfort; 3. A description of the methods and sources used to search for alternatives to painful procedures; and 4. A description of the search used to ensure that the experiment does not unnecessarily duplicate previous research.

An IACUC typically has at least five members, one of whom must be a Doctor of Veterinary Medicine responsible for animal care at the institution. The committee must also include at least one scientist experienced in animal research; a professional whose primary concerns are not scientific (e.g., clergyperson or lawyer); and a member who is not affiliated with the institution in any way and who is meant to represent the interests of the community at large.[22]

Conlee of HSUS pointed out a major flaw of the IACUC, mainly that the majority of its appointed people are affiliated with the research institution (such as a university), with the exception of one spot. She also explained that many universities have a financial investment and interest in getting grant funding for animal research.[23]

Biomedical research is particularly lucrative for universities in the United States which charge overhead (facilities and administrative fees) on every research dollar, typically at a 50 percent rate.[24] In short, in many cases IACUCs can be heavily skewed towards animal researchers whose livelihoods depend on animal research—and perhaps not so much toward the animals that it should protect.

## University of California, San Diego: An IACUC Falls Short

In 2001, hundreds of San Diego physicians signed a petition urging the University of California, San Diego (UCSD) Medical School to end dog experiments and exercises for teaching euthanasia in a freshman pharmacology course. These physicians knew from professional experience that killing dogs was unnecessary to becoming a doctor and so filed an appeal to the University's IACUC, pointing to federal guidelines requiring a good-faith effort to replace animal labs in education and research, once alternatives became available.

The official response of the UCSD IACUC was that experiments and euthanasia of dozens of dogs in those labs raised no animal welfare issues. Public protests followed. Finally, after sufficient adverse publicity, the UCSD Faculty Council and School of Medicine department chairs ended the unnecessary dog experiments, accomplishing what the IACUC should have done, which was "respect society's concerns regarding the welfare of animal subjects."[25]

## Other Guidelines for Animal Protection

Several other guidelines have been put into place in the United States to protect animals in research. The *Public Health Service (PHS) Policy on Humane Care and Use of Laboratory Animals* applies to all institutions that use live vertebrate animals in research supported by any component of the PHS, including the Centers for Disease Control and Prevention, the Food and Drug Administration, the National Institutes of Health, and other national health organizations.[26] Also, the *Guide for the Care and Use of Laboratory Animals,* first published in 1963, promotes the humane care of animals used in biomedical research, teaching, and testing. PHS policy requires research institutions to base their programs of animal care and use on the *Guide*.[27] Finally, the Association for Assessment and Accreditation of Laboratory Animal Care International (AAALAC International), a nonprofit organization founded in 1965, promotes uniform standards of animal care in U.S laboratories, although accreditations are on a voluntary basis.[28]

However, none of these committees, laws, or policies protected Harvey and other beagles from the fatal experiments commissioned by Corteva Agriscience and other companies at Charles River Laboratories.

## *Refining Experiments to Reduce Suffering: Are We Doing Enough for Dogs?*

> "I've worked in labs long enough to know there are dogs who very readily come and accept whatever you're going to do—take a blood sample, give them a dose, whatever it is—and they're happy to get a pet on the head."
>
> —Former lab worker[29]

This statement by a former laboratory worker, speaking at a Public Workshop on the Uses of Dogs in Biomedical Research at the National Academies of Science in 2019, deserves contemplation. Is this the prevailing thought process of people who work with dogs in research labs? Is a dog's "apparent" acceptance of research procedures a sign of happy willingness, or a sign of something much worse: learned helplessness, a condition in which animals feel helpless to avoid negative situations and so have no choice but to comply? Many experts point towards the latter, and it is a serious welfare concern for dogs in laboratories.

For example, according to Kathleen Conlee, Vice President of Animal Research Issues at the Humane Society of the United States (HSUS), there are chimpanzees and monkeys in laboratories who will immediately give their thigh if they see a needle—even the ones who weren't formally trained, but knew the inevitable would happen. The same is often said of dogs who demonstrate similar behavior and offer their front paw for blood draws—an unusual act noticed by those who have adopted former laboratory dogs.

When W. M. S. Russell (1925–2006), a zoologist, and R. L. Burch (1926–1996), a microbiologist, published their book *The Principles of Humane Experimental Technique* in 1959, their aim was to guide researchers to improve treatment of laboratory animals while also advancing the quality of science in studies that use animals. In their book, Russell and Burch presented three principles, known as the "3Rs," which today supposedly govern ethics in animal research worldwide. The principals are:

> *Replacement*—to avoid or replace the use of animals in research;
> *Reduction*—to minimize the number of animals used per experiment; and
> *Refinement*—to minimize animal suffering and improve welfare.

Russell and Burch included mental states such as fear, anxiety, boredom, hunger, thirst, bodily discomfort, and any other significantly unpleasant feelings in their definition of *pain and distress*.[30]

Efforts to refine or improve a dog's welfare in a laboratory is a real problem because of the essence of the experiments themselves which they must endure. As Russell and Burch state, "...in so-called experimental neuroses, the animal is normally driven into a situation where flight is either impossible or blocked by conflict with other drives. In such circumstances, fear must become an acutely unpleasant state which, by human analog may be termed 'anxiety.'"[31]

Today, common refinements for dogs in laboratories can include modifying home pen design (the kennels where the dogs live) to make it more comfortable for dogs to move around and relax. Some labs try to provide enrichment activities to dogs in laboratories, such as chew toys, or play areas. Even further, some laboratory staff are being trained to be more "compassionate" toward laboratory animals. This may include understanding that certain procedures performed on dogs, such as oral gavage (administering drugs or chemicals through a tube down a dog's throat and into the stomach) may be particularly unpleasant for dogs. Attempts to refine techniques to prepare the dogs for such procedures are also sometimes part of lab protocol. However, it is unknown how many labs are incorporating refinements, and there are few guides available as to how to incorporate refinements successfully.

## Dr. Stacy Lopresti-Goodman and Justin Goodman: Refinements Are Not Enough for Welfare

Dr. Stacy Lopresti-Goodman is a professor of psychology at Marymount University and Justin Goodman is Vice President of the White Coat Waste Project, a nonprofit taxpayer watchdog group based in Washington, D.C., which advocates defunding animal experiments. They are husband and wife and together make an influential team advocating for the welfare of dogs, and other animals, in research laboratories. Here are their opinions, gained in an interview, on their formative experiences and whether dog experiments can be refined to eliminate suffering.

**Question: What inspired you to get involved in advocating for laboratory animals?**

**Goodman:** We've been together for over nineteen years. We cared about these issues when we met, but it wasn't part of our daily life. It was in graduate school that we saw that we could combine our passion for advocating for animals with what we were deciding to do with our lives. Specifically, the reason we got involved was learning there was a monkey lab at the University of Connecticut where we were both graduate students. No one had ever tried to stop it. Basically, the two of us started a student group [to protest the monkey lab] and a few years later the lab was shut down. The lab had to give money back to the government, and they never opened again.

We saw the power a few individuals could have when they dedicated themselves to fighting injustice against animals. That really empowered us to look for other ways we could use our skills, whether in academia or otherwise, to help chip away at the problem.[32]

**Question: Is it possible to refine procedures used in dog experiments, such as oral gavage, to improve dogs' welfare?**

**Dr. Lopresti-Goodman:** In terms of refinements, my argument is that they're not enough. Maybe, if you can train the dogs, their distress and discomfort might go, on a zero to 10 scale, from a 10 to an 8. You've reduced some distress, and that matters for that dog, but is that enough? No. We shouldn't be doing it at all. At a conference I attended where everyone was talking about "refinement" and how great it is, I came in and said, "No ... these animals are still traumatized. We need to add a fourth R—Retirement."

**Goodman:** In any video you see of dogs being oral gavaged, they are always fighting for their lives. Just put yourself in the same predicament. It's not just about the discomfort of the procedure. It's that it's going to make the dogs sick. It's the fear of the person coming to get you, and the force-feeding large doses of a drug or chemical intentionally to make you sick or kill you.

So, making oral gavage a little less traumatic is ridiculous and more window dressing from people who are willing to throw good science out the window.... They say, "We're trying to do better." Well, doing better is not having dogs there in the first place. It's still torture by any standard. If anything they did to dogs was happening outside of a lab—if they did it on the outside front stairs of the lab—they would be arrested for animal cruelty.

**Dr. Lopresti-Goodman:** When I talk about the percentage of dogs being used in painful and distressing procedures, we're talking about physical pain and distress. Most people are not thinking about the emotional and psychological pain and distress.

Regarding Post Traumatic Stress Disorder (PTSD), it isn't just that you have experienced an event which was threatening your life, or you thought was threatening your life, it is also (in revised PTSD criteria) if you witness someone else experience a life-threatening event. Not only are dogs in labs having horrible things happening to them, but they are also seeing the person in white or blue walk down the hall and do it to their cage-mate, or the dog across from them. And that is also psychologically traumatizing. So, it's all day, every day, happening to them or other dogs around them.[33]

# 6

# The Ethics of Dog Research—A Human Perspective

## *The Lab: Voices from the Inside*

> "In my experience, the welfare of dogs living in lab colonies or kennel environments is not good, and one of the main reasons for it is that we have studies that show that one of the things dogs value more than anything else is human social contact, and they get very little of it. They get very short periods of rather indifferent contact with lab staff who don't have time to socialize with the dogs. And this is a big ethical issue that needs to be addressed."
>
> —Dr. James Serpell, Professor of Ethics and Animal Welfare at the University of Pennsylvania School of Veterinary Medicine[1]

How can anyone work in a research lab where they experiment on dogs? Why do lab workers continue to do their jobs, watching dogs suffer and die, day after day? Many of us who own dogs and love dogs cannot fathom a job in a dog lab. Indeed, being a laboratory technician in a dog lab cannot be an easy job. People might take jobs in dog labs because they are told—and believe—that dogs are essential for testing drugs and products that save human lives. They might take this job because they believe they are doing a good thing for society. They might also take this job because they actually love taking care of animals. However, the reality is often much different than they expected.

In his book *What It's Like to Be a Dog*, Gregory Berns recounts a poignant story of his own early experience in a medical school course known as "dog lab," in which he and his classmates learned how various drugs affected the heart of a live, anesthetized dog. After experimenting with the various drugs on the dog, whose chest had been surgically opened, the final steps included injecting potassium chloride directly into the dog's heart and then severing the blood vessels behind it to make the heart deflate and stop beating, killing the dog. Berns, now a professor of psychology at Emory University and a ground-breaking researcher in the field of dog cognition, remembers that experiment with great regret. This excerpt from *What It's Like to Be a Dog* describes how the dog lab affected him:

> It is one of the deep regrets of my life, and I wish I had been strong enough to boycott the lab. The thought had crossed my mind, but I justified participating with the standard reasons: the dogs came from the pound and would be killed anyway, and doctors needed to see how real living systems worked. In retrospect, I realized neither was true. The dogs wouldn't necessarily have been killed and the laboratory exercise only confirmed what we had been taught in class. Seeing how drugs worked on a live animal didn't impart any additional knowledge. The lab didn't make me a better doctor, and it diminished me as a human being.[2]

Another scientist, Lynda Birke, talks about her personal experience dissecting a rabbit in preparation for dental school in her book *Feminism, Animals and Sciences: The Naming of the Shrew,* in the chapter "Into the Laboratory." While Birke is talking about a rabbit, not a dog, the message she imparts is one directed more toward humanity. It is not so much about the animal as it is about her own feelings toward using the animal in a certain way. She writes:

> Emotionality and empathy are qualities that ... a trainee dentist must learn to suppress; they get in the way of the quintessential "objective pursuit of truth." Somehow I knew, as a 17 year old, that I had to swallow my disgust when confronted with a white rabbit with pink ears for dissection; after all, I wanted to be a dentist, didn't I? Learning to be objective means learning to distance yourself from those feelings. To become a scientist I had to leave emotion behind and learn to construct a façade of scientific authority. That is not to say that I no longer felt those emotions ... but I had learned not to admit them.[3]

Birke also talks about the social relationships in the lab between the scientists, the animals, and the technicians. Within this division of labor, there are different relationships with the laboratory animals, she says. While scientists generally do the experiments on animals, it is the technicians who care for the animals and are thus closer to the animals than most scientists. Most technicians see themselves as caring people, who come into the job because they like animals. She says, "While there is no doubt truth in the images of terrified beagles, and of uncaring people force-feeding them, many other people in laboratories seek to ensure the animals' welfare."[4]

## From Lab Work to Animal Advocacy: Inspired to Change

Perhaps one could conclude that many of today's most ardent animal advocates have evolved to become advocates precisely as a result of their life experiences on the opposite side of the tracks, so to speak. In an interview for this book, Kathleen Conlee, Vice President of Animal Research Issues at the Humane Society of the United States, revealed how one of her early jobs working at a primate research laboratory changed her life and professional goals profoundly:

> I worked at a primate breeding and research facility. Among the three sites were about 8,000 primates. We'd breed them and universities would call and say they needed five females who are "this old" and weighed "this much." I would literally fill orders to send monkeys out to laboratories. We did some research studies onsite, but it was mainly breeding.
>
> I was in charge of the behavioral team. When I found out what was really going on, I became afraid to leave because of the animals. I thought, if I don't stay here, who is going to advocate for them? It ended up that the facility I was working for was illegally importing animals and lying on government forms. It got pretty bad.
>
> Twenty years later, I'm still having nightmares about trying to get back to take care of the animals. I don't think I'll ever get over it. I cared a lot about the animals. I truly believe there are people who care. A lot of times it's the researchers who don't care. They are not in there every day taking care of the animals. They are disconnected....[5]

Today Conlee is leading one of the nation's most targeted campaigns to end research and testing on dogs. Conlee's team was responsible for exposing the beagles being used in the Corteva Agriscience fungicide studies, getting the research project shut down, and transferring the surviving dogs to a rescue organization. Conlee can be seen on a social media video, emotionally greeting one of the fungicide study survivors named Teddy for the first time. In tears, she says in the video, "I knew if we kept pushing hard enough there would be a good outcome. And it happened, so now we need more. We need every dog who is experiencing this to not have to suffer like that anymore."[6]

## Emotion in the Research Laboratory?

Emotion has little place in a research laboratory. Yet emotion is difficult to stifle, especially around animals. Animals have a way of unlocking deep, even hidden emotions and bringing emotions like happiness and confidence to the surface. It is one of the reasons why animals are used for emotional support and therapy. Although it's been a hush topic for decades, evidence is emerging that many laboratory workers who directly handle and experiment on animals suffer deep emotional trauma. They report experiencing guilt, grief, sadness, anger, anxiety, headaches, sleeplessness, despair, overeating and rage. Support groups, publications, and conferences are becoming more common to assist lab workers traumatized by their profession.[7]

For her book *Animal Ethos*, Lesley Sharp—a professor of anthropology and senior research scientist in the field of sociomedical sciences—spent time in several research labs interviewing researchers and lab workers. According to Sharp, "For animal technicians, laboratory labor is a moral project." She points to job burnout, or "compassion fatigue," as dimensions of moral lab work. Sharp explains that compassion fatigue is associated with enduring the emotional trauma caused by regularly euthanizing animals, working in an environment where one is undervalued, and assisting those who regard animals merely as "resources" or "data points."[8]

Naming animals is widely regarded as officially taboo within laboratories, because the personalization of animals evokes emotion and signals attachment.[9] Workers often name animals anyway, as was the case with the with the aforementioned beagle Harvey, who was given the name by lab staff at Charles River Laboratories.

Animal care technicians also often possess the deepest wisdom about the habits, preferences and needs of the dogs, yet they may have little power to instigate change. As Sharp discovered in her interviews with lab workers:

> Whereas the childhoods of caretakers and veterinarians are typically overrun with all sorts of house pets or farm animals ... my interviews reveal that, surprisingly, the vast majority of lab researchers had no personal, sustained contact with animals prior to entering their professions. These divergent histories subsequently inform affective responses to lab animal subjects.[10]

Social media today are rife with comments denigrating anyone who works at a dog research laboratory. It seems that lab workers are "guilty" by association of torturing and killing dogs, even though they are not the ones who designed or are carrying out the research projects.

Justin Goodman of White Coat Waste Project, who often interacts with laboratory workers who contact him to report animal abuse, agrees that dog caretakers in labs are often not in power positions to change research protocols, and that has serious ethical and personal repercussions for them. In a discussion for this book, Goodman elaborated:

> I don't want to paint everyone who works in a lab with a broad brush, like these are "bad" people. You can never say that. I do think some of the lab

> technicians are the people who buy into it; that this research has to happen, so I'm going to try and help the animals. The premise is false from the get go. But if you are there, then try and do the best you can. Lab animal caretakers don't have a voice. They are the least powerful person in the lab, but maybe they can help get these animals out.
>
> We work with lab techs who are whistleblowers. They are not the ones standing to benefit the most from this work. The scientists are. They are the ones getting big grants and getting the big salary and have the prestige. It's not the lab techs making $12 an hour and who decapitate mice all day, traumatizing themselves, [who benefit]. These are people who want to help animals and they believe working with animals in labs is a way they can do it. They are forced to do all the dirty work.
>
> I think if these scientists had to do the dirty work of harming and killing animals all day long, we'd have fewer scientists wanting to do animal research. A lab tech's job is often designed to watch an animal slowly die, and these are the people who care about them the most.[11]

As Lesley Sharp writes, "...the repression of emotional responses shifts an often unbearably heavy burden of responsibility onto those charged with the care of the dying and the dead, and they then feel embattled or devalued in the workplace; in some instances, they may even cease to care."[12]

## *Public Opinion: Voices from the Outside*

At a 2019 Public Workshop on the Uses of Dogs in Biomedical Research, Dr. James Serpell, Professor of Ethics and Animal Welfare at the University of Pennsylvania School of Veterinary Medicine, presented on the topic "The Unique Role of Dogs in Society." Alluding to how the growing value we place on dogs as a society today is threatening their public acceptability as research tools, he concluded:

> So, we're caught between a rock and a hard place. These traits we have selected for in the dog have made it both a desirable animal to use, but also a desirable animal to be a member of your family, or to be a replacement for a child, and that creates this very, very profound moral tension. And, there is no sign that this is going to go away anytime soon. In fact, I'd say probably the pet owners are winning the argument at the moment. I don't see that reversing itself.[13]

In fact, the public seems to be turning against animal research more strongly than ever, historically speaking, especially when it comes to animals we identify with strongly, such as dogs.

A Gallup poll released in 2017 revealed that only 51 percent of U.S. adults find such studies morally acceptable, down from 65 percent in 2001.[14] Further public opinion polling informs us that most people occupy an ethical middle ground, with approval of animal research contingent upon animals not suffering too much, and only in the service of research likely to benefit human health. A poll in the U.K. found that only 16 percent of people there approve of using dogs for research.[15]

In 2018, *Science Magazine* published Gallop Poll results tracking 17 years of United States public attitudes about animal research. Beginning in 2001 and going to 2017, polls showed that public support for animal research declined almost every year and is projected to continue in this direction.[16]

While surveys can measure public opinion among people who are aware of animal research, many people are not even aware that animal research still exists, or that their tax dollars help pay for much of it. Sometimes, in fact, they can't know, because the research is hidden from the public. When undercover investigations reveal the truth of animal experiments, members of the public are often outraged.

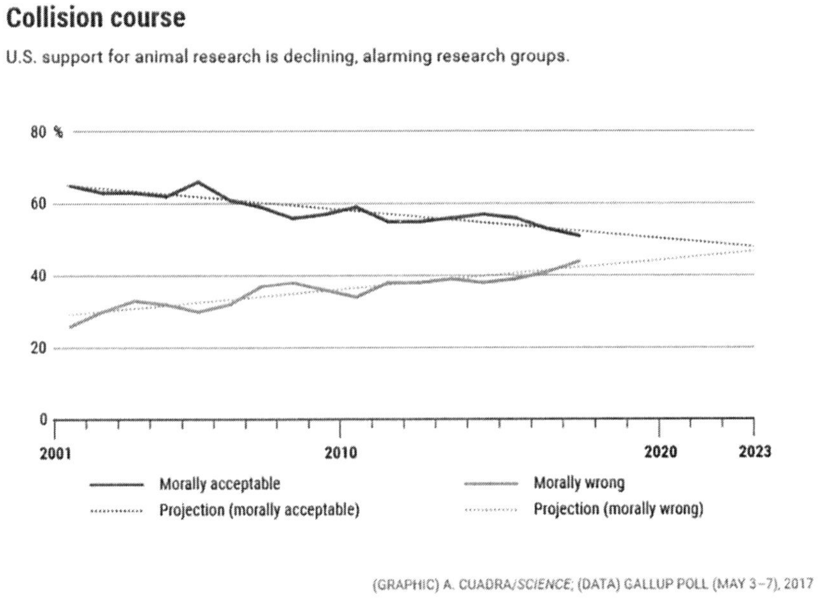


**Gallup polls tracking the past 17 years of United States attitudes about animal research. As time ticks by, a "morally acceptable" line creeps downhill, while a "morally wrong" line climbs higher. The lines are expected to intersect in 2023. From Grimm, David. "Opening the Lab Door."** ***Science*****, June 29, 2018. https://science.sciencemag.org/content/360/6396/1392.long. Reprinted with permission from AAAS.**

### Protesting Golden Retriever Studies: Celebrities Join In

In 2017, Texas A&M University found out how ethically controversial their dog experiments were perceived to be by the general public. In experiments led by Dr. Joseph Kornegay, golden retrievers were bred to develop different types of muscular dystrophy, including Duchenne muscular dystrophy—a particularly severe form of the disease that causes progressive muscle wasting and weakness. Results of these experiments were caught on undercover video by an anonymous Texas A&M employee. The videos show disabled golden retrievers struggling to walk and eat, and drool dripping from the mouths of dogs whose jaw muscles had weakened as a result of the disease.

Two Texas A&M students started a petition to end the experimentation, getting over 200,000 signatures. The university continued to stand behind the testing, stating that "there is not another way" to study the disease.[17] Almost two years later, noted animal rights activist and Beatles member Paul McCartney implored Texas A&M to end its use of dogs as laboratory test subjects. In a published letter, McCartney asked University President Michael Young to halt muscular dystrophy research with golden retrievers and to release them for adoption.[18]

In 2019 James Cromwell, the actor and animal rights activist, also stepped up to publicly decry Texas A&M's golden retriever experiments. Cromwell was arrested during a protest at the University's Board of Regents meeting, while calling on the school to shut down its laboratory where golden retrievers and other dogs are used for medical research. After two years of battling lawsuits and fending off unfavorable media coverage, in September 2019 Texas A&M finally halted its breeding of sick dogs for canine muscular dystrophy research. While the university has stopped breeding dogs, it continues its research into the disease using dogs.[19]

## *A Difficult Question: How Do We Balance Human Benefit Versus Harm to the Dog?*

Ethics is defined as moral principles that govern a person's behavior or the conducting of an activity. *Animal ethics* is a branch of ethics which examines human-animal relationships, the moral consideration of animals, and how animals ought to be treated. Animal research ethics currently falls somewhere in the middle—between human ethics and animal ethics. This is where the argument for or against animal research gets tricky. However, given the current public sentiment toward dogs and awareness of dogs as sentient beings, research ethics can no longer stand as applying to humans alone.

In his book *Principles of Animal Research Ethics*, Dr. David DeGrazia—Elton Professor of Philosophy at George Washington University—suggests that the animal research and animal protection communities can and should converge on three pivotal claims:

1. Sentient animals have moral status and therefore are not merely tools of research;
2. The only possible justification for (non-therapeutically) harming animals with moral status, including animal research subjects, is the prospect of substantial and otherwise unattainable social benefits;
3. Any permissible harming of animals in research is limited by considerations of animal welfare.[20]

## An Interview with Dr. David DeGrazia

In an interview for this book, Dr. DeGrazia discussed where the research community's attitudes stand and the public's right to know about animal research.

**Question: What are your thoughts on the ethical treatment of animals in biomedical research?**

**Dr. DeGrazia:** Over the years a lot of people in the research community haven't really understood the ethical issues involving animals—which are very complex and include hard issues concerning animals' moral status. Many have treated the issues as purely political—where they just have one side and they want to win. And that's unfortunate.

But I think there is starting to be more communication across sides. There are more people who are in both the animal protection community and biomedical research community.

Maybe, there is more openness to the real ethical issues that are here, and not pretending that they are trivial or that it's obvious that we should go full steam ahead with biomedical research. That position just isn't sustainable anymore. Especially if you consider how much of this research doesn't produce valuable results. It's a good time for reconsideration, change, and progress.[21]

**Question: In a public workshop, you stated, "To the extent that animal research is largely a public enterprise, the perceived moral status plays a role because one of the stakeholders here is the public**

**who is paying the bill for most of the research that is done." Can you expand on this statement?**[22]

**Dr. DeGrazia:** So, if there are kinds of research that are being hidden from the public, that's like smoke. It's a signal that makes someone think, "Maybe the public wouldn't be too happy if they did know." If what you're doing is really good science and ethically acceptable, you should be able to explain it to the public without hiding anything. The public has a stake and a right to know. I would think we should work toward a day in which whatever animal research is judged to be important enough, irreplaceable, and ethical, that it never be hidden. There would be transparency.

The public should be able to know exactly what kind of animal research is going on, the methods, and so on, because there should be nothing to hide. Transparency is an appropriate goal for all research. Again, the public is a stakeholder. This sets a tough standard in a way, but it's an appropriate standard.[23]

## *What About Us: What Is Our Part in Animal Research?*

Animal welfare will continue to be a source of controversy in research labs until our society, industry, educational system, and governmental organizations can agree on what value animals actually have in relationship to humans. In her book *Our Symphony with Animals,* Aysha Akhtar states that, "Most animal abuse occurs not by rogue killers, violent spouses, or drug gangs, but by industry and government." Research labs are an example. Akhtar writes:

> These institutionalized forms of violence are more treacherous than any other kind because they have become normalized. By ... experimenting on them [animals], we have embedded the practice of violence into our everyday routines. With our tax dollars, our purchases ... we have told our governments and businesses to go ahead and hurt animals. We just look the other way.
>
> We have to look the other way, otherwise our natural empathy for animals will be confronted. These institutionalized practices are hidden from our view precisely because the suffering they cause distresses us. We tuck these forms of animal cruelty away from our day-to-day reality in order to feel comfortable.[24]

Perhaps a first step in advocating for dogs in research is to understand how we can help. Usually, it is a feeling of *helplessness* that makes us turn our backs—and not a lack of empathy for the animals themselves. The next chapter on future technologies, which may one day replace dogs in research laboratories, is a very promising place to start a change.

Children, young scientists, students, teachers: this is the future. You may be leading the charge.

# 7

# Future Technologies

Imagine fitting a human lung neatly into a two-inch computer chip. Visualize treating a person who just had a heart attack using a three-dimensional, simulated computer model of their own heart to quickly and accurately determine the safest form of treatment. The biomedical toolbox of the 21st century—human-specific tools and technologies—is growing, and they are as practical as they are futuristic. Descriptions of 3D tissue models, organs-on-chips, stem cell platforms, *in silico* tools, and cell imaging dominate the non-animal biomedical technology dialogue.

For most of us, this is simply industry jargon and these terms mean little. However, upon closer examination, these new technologies in reality make quite a bit of sense. Certainly, an entire book may be written on this topic of human-specific technologies. This chapter provides only a small glimpse into this ever-evolving world of biomedical research. While the overarching goal remains to improve human safety in drug and product development, these emerging technologies also provide us with something more: a compelling reason to finally move away from using dogs and other animals for this purpose.

## *Lung-on-a-Chip*

### Wyss Institute Award

In February 2013, a revolutionary piece of new technology won a prestigious international design award. This technology, a small device the size of a memory stick, is called *lung-on-a-chip*, and it is exactly that: a tiny, fully functional human lung on a computer chip. While it doesn't look like a lung, it has all the functional units that behave like a lung. Created by the Wyss Institute, a research institute at Harvard University, lung-on-a-chip is made using human lung and blood vessel cells.

It is an exciting new alternative approach to animal testing, which also has the potential to change how drug development is carried out in the future.

The award for lung-on-a-chip came from the National Centre for the Replacement, Refinement, and Reduction of Animals in Research (NC3Rs), an independent scientific organization based in the United Kingdom. This organization was set up by the government to lead the discovery and application of new technologies and approaches that minimize the use of animals in research and to improve animal welfare.

The lung-on-a-chip offers a new outside-the-body way to screen drugs by mimicking the complicated mechanical and biochemical behaviors of a human lung. The small device is composed of a clear, flexible polymer that contains hollow channels fabricated using computer microchip manufacturing techniques. Two of the channels are

**A sample organ-on-chip. Two microfluidic channels have been filled with a red and blue polymer, respectively. In a functional organ-on-chip, the red channel would be lined with blood vessel cells and perfused with a blood-mimicking medium, while the blue channel would be lined with organ cells and perfused with whatever medium is most appropriate (e.g., air for lung cells). There is a semipermeable membrane between the channels so that nutrients and oxygen can diffuse between them, and mechanical forces like cyclical stretching and relaxing are applied to the flexible chip to mimic the body's movements. Reproduced by permission of the Wyss Institute for Biologically Inspired Engineering.**

separated by a thin, flexible, porous membrane that is lined on one side with human lung cells taken from air sacs. Human capillary blood cells from the lung are placed on the other side with a medium flowing over their surface to mimic blood flow. A vacuum applied to the side channels deforms this tissue-to-tissue interface to recreate the way human lung tissues physically expand and retract when breathing.[1]

## Chlorine Gas Research Using Lung-on-a-Chip

Perhaps, one small step at a time, the ways in which human lung disease treatments are developed may be changing. In 2019, the Biomedical Advanced Research and Development Authority, a division of the U.S. Department of Health and Human Services, awarded a $24 million grant to the Wake Forest Institute for Regenerative Medicine (WFIRM) for lung-on-a-chip studies. Specifically, the grant funded a five-year study on the effects of chlorine gas on human lungs in order to develop treatments for chemical injury.

Chlorine gas was used as a weapon during World War I and was used repeatedly during the civil war in Syria. It is also one of the most-used industrial gasses in the United States and causes multiple deaths and injuries due to accidental leaks and household exposure. In addition, the large volume and ready availability of manufactured chlorine make the chemical a potential national security threat in the hands of terrorists.

The WFIRM lung-on-a-chip technology is used to model normal and diseased tissue, innate immune system response, and reaction to drugs and toxins. It uses human cells to create tiny 3D organ-like structures called *tissue equivalents* that mimic the function of the heart, liver, lung, blood vessels, and other organs. Placed on a two-inch chip, these structures are connected to a system of fluid channels and sensors that provide online monitoring of individual organs and the overall organ system. A circulating blood substitute keeps the cells alive and can be used to introduce chemical or biological agents, as well as potential therapies, into the system. The long-term goal of this research is to reduce the overall burden of testing in animals and to speed up the development of safe and effective human treatments for lung injuries.[2]

## *The Living Heart Project*

As noted in Chapter 4, in June 2020, the U.S. Department of Veterans Affairs (VA) announced that several areas of VA research on dogs were no longer necessary, such as diabetes and pharmacological studies. However, the VA deemed cardiac research on dogs to be still a necessity.[3] Universities and other institutions also still perform cardiac research on dogs. Cardiac research, which may involve multiple surgeries to implant test devices, most often ends in death for the dogs in these experiments.[4] In addition to the ethical controversy surrounding these experiments, dogs may not be the best model going forward in advancing cardiac care for humans.

Scientists around the world, as well as government institutions, have known for some time that insights gained from experimenting on dogs often do not provide the accuracy required for successful use of medical devices in human hearts. This is indeed an urgent problem, as heart disease is the leading cause of death in the United States and other developed countries, and spending on heart-related conditions constitutes the largest portion of United States healthcare expenditure. However, a central problem in medical device simulation is the need to model not just the mechanical behavior of the device, but also its physical and physiological interaction with the *human* body.[5]

A ground-breaking international initiative called the Living Heart Project may change how cardiac research is conducted in the future, and might one day eliminate the need to use dogs, or other animals such as pigs, to test devices for the human heart. The Project is an ongoing collaborative research initiative between Dessault Systèmes, a software company based in France, and the U.S. Food and Drug Administration (FDA). Their computer-based Living Heart Model is gaining worldwide recognition.

It has been acknowledged that the biomedical industry has been lagging on its adoption of computer aided engineering, in part because of the lack of accurate models. The Living Heart Project is uniting leading cardiovascular researchers, educators, medical device developers, regulatory agencies, and practicing cardiologists on a shared mission to develop and validate highly accurate, personalized, digital human heart models.

So, what does a Living Heart Model look like? Also known as the *Simulia* Living Heart, it is a computerized reproduction model of a healthy, four-chamber adult human heart and all its occurring processes and systems, including valves, coronary arteries, veins and muscle fibers. Just like a real human heart, the *Simulia* heart also models blood flow inside the heart chambers.[6]

## Simulated Treatment of a Heart Attack

In 2015, researchers used data from an actual human heart attack to first induce a heart attack into the *Simulia* Living Heart model, and then to experiment with implanting a new heart device, called a novel annuloplasty ring with a sub-valvular component, to determine the device's effectiveness in treating the blockage that caused the heart attack.[7] In other words, without ever needing to experiment with this device on a dog, for example, the Simulia human heart model enabled researchers to know how a specific human would respond to this new human heart device.

The Living Heart may also be used to help improve pacemakers and simulate the effects of heart disease. Efforts to identify solutions customized for patient-specific heart geometries and cardiac pathologies are also being developed.

By creating simulated 3D human heart models, the project's ultimate goal is for physicians and surgeons to be able to virtually analyze their patients' health and plan therapies and surgeries using the same advanced simulation technology that the automotive industry uses to test cars before they are ever built.

In fact, besides its Living Heart Model, Dessault Systèmes is well known for helping automotive companies design cars. Using Simulia technology, automotive engineers can model a full vehicle consisting of hundreds of parts and connections and complex tire-road interactions—all in a single simulation.[8] In short, engineers can test drive thousands of vehicle designs on a computer, with virtual people sitting behind the wheel, before selecting the best one to create in the real world. Testing everything from slick road performance to accidents and crashes, this technology makes today's cars safer than ever to drive.

This same technology applied to cardiac medicine may open doors to what we never thought was possible—"test driving" patient-specific human hearts to determine what the best treatments are, and what reactions a human may have to certain drugs, implants, and other influences. Just as Simulia technology in the automotive industry helps make better cars, the Living Heart Project may be paving the way for better and safer human hearts.

## *Human-Derived Organoids*

Treatments and cures for some of our world's most confounding health challenges—such as cancer, infectious disease and brain disorders—might be somewhere in the distant future, but they're on their way. In fact, the answers to these medical mysteries are being delivered in surprisingly small packages called "mini-organs," which are being hailed by scientists as the possible future of human disease research and drug development. Mini-organs are finding their way onto the global biomedical stage, modeling many human diseases in ways that animal models have historically been unable to. Professionally known as *organoids*, these mini-organs are giving scientists a unique view of human organs in remarkable detail.

Human organoids are tiny, three-dimensional tissue cultures that are derived from human stem cells. Organoids can range in size from less than the width of a hair to five millimeters. They grow from stem cells—cells with the potential to develop into many different types of cells in the body. Scientists have learned how to create the right environment for stem cells to follow their own genetic instructions to self-organize (interact with their surroundings) to form tiny structures that resemble miniature organs. While organoid technology is still in its infancy, so far researchers have been able to produce organoids that resemble the brain, kidney, lung, intestine, stomach, and liver, and many more applications are on the way.[9]

The benefit of human organoids is that they are highly similar to actual human organs. In some cases, when studied under a microscope, organoids are indistinguishable from actual human organs.[10] Scientists at Harvard University who have been studying human organoid models believe that the pharmaceutical industry could greatly benefit from this technology. They believe that using human cells rather than animal models could make the drug discovery and development process both faster and more effective.[11] This theory is well on its way to being proven in other areas of research as well, for example, for diseases that affect the human brain.

## Zika Virus

The human brain is the most highly developed brain in the animal kingdom and is the most complex organ in the body. Because of this complexity, it has been difficult to model human brain development using animal systems. Human brain organoids, however, are now being successfully used to model the development of the human brain and its diseases.

The first brain disease studied using organoids was microcephaly, a congenital condition in which a human's head is abnormally small. Microcephaly became well-known during the Zika virus outbreaks of 2015 and 2016. Zika fever, an infection transmitted by a certain genus of mosquito, carried with it a terrible birth defect: pregnant women who were bitten by the mosquito gave birth to babies with abnormally small heads. Zika fever affected thousands of people in more than twenty countries and territories in the Americas, and many more in Africa in previous outbreaks.

Using human brain organoid models, scientists were able to reveal the effect of Zika infection on human brain development. Further studies also revealed different strains of Zika virus. For example, scientists identified a Brazilian strain of Zika that was more virulent than an African strain. In addition, in testing various chemical compounds on human brain organoids, it was discovered that gene mutations of Zika virus could be alleviated.[12]

## *Who Is Making Non-Animal Technology a Priority?*

These human-specific technologies sound so great and useful that it might come as a surprise that they are not already being used in place of animals in drug research and product development. Historically, animals have always been used in scientific research—dogs perhaps longer than any other species. Therefore, the next question is: How do we change long-held traditions, regulations, programs, operations, and laws to embrace these new technologies? Unfortunately, the answer is: Not quickly or easily.

First, new human-specific technologies are currently limited in their advancement due to a lack of funding. It has been suggested that non-animal technologies need to be funded at the same level as climate change initiatives; in other words, by the billions of dollars. Current investments are not enough to push the technology to the level required to change regulations on a global scale. More investors are needed to help ramp up the growth and financial support of these technologies.

Second, global harmonization and collaboration will need to be prioritized to make a true impact on the reduction of animal use. Academic and industry sectors must increase their communication and collaboration to improve their understanding of these technologies and the capabilities of the technology developers.

Another major barrier to global harmonization in accepting non-animal technology includes skepticism in some sectors of the scientific community who support animal research. Changing this perception is not an easy task, especially when many researchers may feel that they would be losing something they are acclimated to—using animals for research. Also known as *loss aversion*, the fear of losing something can be a much more powerful motivator than the hope of gaining something, in part because once we have something, we start to value it much more highly.[13]

Perhaps we can use a process known as diffusion as our guide for establishing a timeline for when the balance of research will tip toward non-animal technologies. Diffusion is the process by which something new is spread through society over time. In sociology, successful diffusion is described as following an s-shaped curve, where at first, a tiny number of people change, and very gradually that number increases. Theory holds that when 10 to 25 percent of a society has adopted the change, acceptance suddenly and dramatically increases.[14] We have not yet arrived at the 10 percent mark. But we may not be far off. Only time will tell how and when animal testing—in this case, on dogs—will be phased out of biomedical research. What is certain is that diffusion has already begun.

The following initiatives represent collaborative efforts on a global scale to reduce and replace animals in research. In some cases, dogs have been in the spotlight as a species that needs to be, for ethical and scientific reasons, urgently replaced with more effective technologies. While this is not an exhaustive list, these are some prominent examples of where animal testing in the world may be headed.

## European Union Directive

All animal research in the European Union (EU) is regulated under Directive 2010/63/EU, which was revised in 2010 with more stringent goals for eliminating animals in research. In 2013, the EU instated a ban on animal testing for cosmetic purposes.[15] The final aim of the 2010 Directive is to replace all animal research with non-animal methods of research, such as organoids or computer simulations.[16]

## Biomedical Research for the 21st Century (BioMed21), Initiated by the Humane Society International

The Biomedical Research for the 21st Century (BioMed21) Collaboration was formed by an international group of stakeholders representing animal protection, research funding, academic, regulatory, corporate, and other communities. BioMed21 recognizes the human relevance and translational limitations of the current paradigm in biomedical research and drug discovery, and the need for change. BioMed 21 funds non-animal research projects, hosts workshops and conferences worldwide, and provides training for *Adverse Outcome Pathway*—a framework for improving drug development and chemical safety using knowledge of biological pathways or networks.[17]

## Toxicology in the 21st Century (Tox21), a United States Federal Initiative

Tox 21 is a collaboration among the National Institutes of Health (NIH), the Food and Drug Administration (FDA), the Environmental Protection Agency (EPA), and the National Toxicology Program at the National Institute of Environmental Health Sciences. The goal of Tox 21 is to achieve better assessment of the toxicity of substances by using faster and more efficient human-specific methods in high-throughput technologies. Two examples of Tox21 in action are:

*NIH Chemical Genomics Center: At the NIH Chemical Genomics Center, a major testing program has been underway since 2004, involving a robotic-arm system that tests thousands of chemicals, using patient donated cells. The high-throughput system performs approximately three million tests per week for different diseases. The success of the system (funded under the Tox 21 Initiative) in screening and identifying suitable candidate drugs has dramatically saved time, cost, and resources, resulting in human clinical trials starting in less time.*[18]

*EPA Decision—All Mammal Studies Will End by 2035: In a 2019 memorandum, Andrew Wheeler, the head of the EPA, announced that it would reduce its requests for, and funding of, mammal studies by 30% by 2025, and eliminate all such requests and funding by 2035. Wheeler announced the EPA's increasing use of computational toxicology methods, among other approaches, to predict toxicity without the use of animals.*[19]

## The Center for Alternatives to Animal Testing

The Johns Hopkins Center for Alternatives to Animal Testing (CAAT), founded in 1981, is part of the Johns Hopkins University Bloomberg School of Public Health, with a European branch (CAAT-Europe) located at the University of Konstanz, Germany. The CAAT promotes humane science by supporting the creation, development, validation, and use of alternatives to animals in research, product safety testing, and education. The Center seeks to effect change by working with scientists in industry, government, and academia to find new ways to replace animals with non-animal methods, reduce the numbers of animals necessary, or refine methods to make research methods less painful or stressful to the animals involved.[20]

# 8

# Interviews with Global Experts

## *Ending Dog Research ... How and When?*

In interviews for this book, four experts in the fields of biomedical science, psychology and ethics answered questions about the progress of non-animal technologies, the barriers to progress, and how we can end biomedical research on dogs. Their candid discussions reveal hopes, frustrations, personal experiences, and most of all, a profound desire to make the world a better place for people and animals. The experts are: ***Dr. Jarrod Bailey***, Director of Science at *Animal Free Research UK*, and Fellow of the Oxford Centre for Animal Ethics in the U.K. ***Dr. Lindsay Marshall***, Biomedical Science Advisor for the Humane Society International (HSI) and the Humane Society of the United States (HSUS). ***Dr. Stacy Lopresti-Goodman***, Professor of Psychology at Marymount University. Currently, her work is aimed at understanding the enduring negative impact that confinement, social isolation and physical abuse have on the psychological well-being of animals rescued from laboratories, including chimpanzees, monkeys and dogs. ***Dr. David DeGrazia***, Elton Professor of Philosophy at George Washington University.

**Question: How has your work as a research scientist led you to believe that dogs and other animals may not be good enough models for advancing human health?**

**Dr. Bailey:** I think back to when I was an undergraduate (and I'm almost fifty years old now), post-graduate, and post-doctorate doing research in a lab. We just couldn't have dreamed of some of the techniques that are now available to science that were not available ten, fifteen, twenty years ago.... With what we can do instead, it's completely astounding that we're still here—that we're still meeting so much resistance from people who think they have a reason to do dog research.

I spent seven years researching why some women have premature babies. Is there a genetic component to that? I was using human tissue from the hospital [from] women who were having hysterectomies, women who were not in labor, and women who were in labor, trying to see if the genes were doing different things. It was hard to make sense of it because people are different.

The variation even within our species is huge. We saw that with the coronavirus. People were saying, "We have to test new coronavirus treatments and vaccines on diverse people. We need more African Americans ... more women ... more younger people." People are different enough to affect immune response. So, if you accept the fact that there's this huge degree of intra-species variation, then how on earth can you argue [that dogs are good models for researching human disorders]?

Having said that, I believe now is really the time to concentrate on this. So, we've built the case against using animals—effectively, the "stick." Now we have to—use the "carrot" and say, "Look, this is what we can do instead." I think in the next five to ten years it's going to take off.... That's where science will go because that's where science has to go.[1]

* * *

**Dr. Marshall:** I did my Ph.D. in cell biology. I had a couple of post-doctorate positions looking at cystic fibrosis, which is a human disease. That was my first realization that animals weren't the same as people, medically speaking.... At the time I was doing my Ph.D. on cystic fibrosis, the first genetic mouse model for cystic fibrosis was generated with a massive fanfare. Everyone was saying, "Look at this! We've cured the disease! This is brilliant!" And then ten years down the line [there is still no cure for cystic fibrosis] they were thinking, "What happened there? We were all completely hoodwinked."

Mice don't get lung disease.... But in cystic fibrosis [people] get these chronic infections that are life threatening. Mice aren't bothered by that at all. It's kind of that light-bulb moment when you think a disease is more than just one gene. A disease is about *that* human and the lifestyle that *that* human has. I didn't see any need to use animals.

My research used human cells and creating human models and trying to look at what a human airway looks like. What are the bare minimum requirements that we need to re-create that airway in a lab, so that we could start to infect it to see what's going on in a healthy airway, versus what's going on in a cystic fibrosis airway? Then we can start to work out what's missing, why does it happen in cystic fibrosis ... and what can we put back to try to prevent these infections, or at least reduce the damage caused by these infections.

I did that for about nineteen years. We developed a beautiful model of the airways and had a lovely model of cystic fibrosis that responded like a cystic fibrosis patient would. We could infect it with bacteria, and then we developed methods to spray drugs on top of it to see whether or not we could knock out the bacteria.[2]

**Question: What barriers are you encountering to ending research on dogs and other animals in the biomedical field, and embracing new human-specific technologies?**

**Dr. Bailey:** We've never had a stronger argument to move on. But we're still fighting to do that. We're fighting because scientists involved don't want to admit they're wrong. They've built their careers on it.... All they have to do to defend animal research is to tell scare stories like, "If you don't let us do this, you will never have a cure for cancer, or Alzheimer's, or other diseases."

We're in a situation now where the default for the regulators who approve new drugs is pre-clinical data, largely based on animals. That's how it's been for a long time. That's what they know gives them protection if anything goes wrong, and things do go wrong. That will change when they're confident enough to change. The problem is that unreasonable validation criteria have been thrown at human-specific methods. There are a number of problems with the validation they [regulators] are requesting. The main one is that the animal tests have never been validated. They never had to pass any validation criteria. It's just what's always been done. Then you set up these really stringent validation criteria for the new tests, and largely you compare the new tests, not against the humans you're trying to benefit, you compare them against animal tests: the animal tests that demonstrably don't predict human toxicity or safety.

If you compare something that is going to be brilliant against a "gold standard" that's atrocious, then your new method is going to look poor because it won't correlate with the method you're using.

Why is it so difficult to get validation? And even when you've got it, to get it embraced, accepted, and used? It's because there's political wrangling and red tape that takes years to get through, and a number of other issues. Even when you have validation and acceptance, people are still driven by habit and won't use it.

In Europe as a whole, two-thirds of a million animal tests were done in the last year for which there were validated, accepted alternatives. That is unforgiveable. But that shows you the trouble we're having. We need to keep showing that the foundation of this new science is strong and giving regulators the confidence and the reason to move ahead.[3]

* * *

**Dr. Marshall:** A researcher had just been appointed to where I was working. They worked on asthma and was bringing their animal models to the university. I was told this person would be working close to me in the lab. I expressed my discomfort with that. Nothing personal, but I didn't really ... want to be near animal research in the lab. Nor did I want to share space with someone who was focused on, and continuing to use, animal models of disease when we know that animals are not naturally susceptible to most human diseases and do not respond to human diseases in the same way that people do. But I was told that this was my opportunity to work with someone like that—reinforcing the idea that the animal-dependent research is acceptable and the norm and that this was something that I, as a non-animal researcher, had to accept.[4]

I also tried to set up a virtual society within the university for finding replacements for animal research. We were going to try to look at where funding opportunities were, look at where the conferences were, and promote that through the university for everybody, including the biomedical research community. But we were told that we could not do that because it would make those people using animals uncomfortable.

It's shifting the mindset of the researchers [who believe] that a non-animal method is not an alternative. It [a non-animal method] is not second best, and it's not lower down the line. It's *better* able to answer your question, and we need to start appreciating that at every level.

* * *

**Dr. Lopresti-Goodman:** In terms of the way science works, when you go to graduate school, you apply to work with an individual professor. Once you get into grad school, you have to continue doing their research. They're not going to let you come in and say, "I know you've been doing this for thirty or forty years, but I don't want to use animals. I want to do it this other way." So, scientists are perpetuating these methods. It's going to take more and more young people coming saying, "No, I don't want to do that," to actually shift the culture, but that's a really slow process because you're challenging the status quo when you say you don't want to use animals.

The public has an implicit trust in science. If you hear a scientist, someone with some sort of credentials or letters after their name, say we need to do animal testing, you as a general member of the public are going to believe them. But if you can actually get the message out there that over 90 percent of drugs that work in animals don't work in the human population, then maybe that would also change the public's opinion.

Again, the problem is that there are systems in place that allow researchers at universities and government agencies to just keep rubber-stamping their research proposals, even when you're supposed to look for alternatives. At universities, when you propose an experiment with animals, there's a part of the application that asks, "Are there viable alternatives?" ... The researchers are always going to say, "No," even if there are. People just accept that.[5]

**Question: Even though there are barriers to cross, are there grounds for optimism? If so, at what point will non-animal technologies become a preferred model to animals in biomedical research and why?**

**Dr. Bailey:** There are real grounds for optimism, largely because we're going to have a plethora of scientific approaches that are human-specific, quick, cheap and humane, and there will be no reason to do anything else.

A lot of people involved in discovering and developing these human-specific research testing methods think that actually where the change is going to happen is not in regulatory toxicology (the regulators telling us how to test the drugs and the chemicals); change is going to happen in academic research where scientists at the bench are trying to find out why we get Alzheimer's, how cancer spreads, what the basis of Parkinson's disease is, multiple sclerosis, diabetes. Those basic bench scientists are going to want to use these human-specific methods instead [of animals] because they're easier, cheaper, quicker, data-rich and human-relevant. Then regulatory toxicology will be left out on the limb and they will be dragged along with the flow.[6]

* * *

**Dr. Marshall:** ...A regulator ... has got to say a drug is safe [based on] what it does to a whole-body system. These systems [human-specific technologies] are starting to show us that whole-body system.

There are projects that are building a human-on-a-chip that have ten organs connected together. What's even more exciting is they are building a patient-on-a-chip. Patient-on-a-chip uses stem cells. So you take skin cells from your patient with Parkinson's, let's say, and in the lab you can re-program skin cells into brain cells, kidney cells, liver cells, and lung cells, all of which retain the genetic information from that one individual patient. We're talking about an ethical way to get better science.

That's being used for neurodegenerative diseases, turning skin cells into brain cells. For cancer as well. Taking a bit of someone's tumor, putting it in a lab, putting drugs on that and seeing how to manipulate that cancer and stop it from growing. Both are having clinical success. It's human data using human cells. It makes sense to me. You've got a drug. You're not really sure what it's going to do. So you put it on a tiny bit of a person and see what happens.[7]

**Question: There are two sides of the debate: those for animal research and those against. What advice do you have for people on either side who are struggling to communicate effectively about this issue?**

**Dr. Bailey:** I was involved in a few meetings with Freagles of India [a rescue organization for laboratory beagles based in India]. [It's led by] some amazing women. I met with them and [with] some of the people who breed dogs and use the dogs in contract testing facilities. It's difficult to do, because you know what these people [who breed dogs and use them for testing] stand for and what they do, but increasingly you realize you have to engage the other side. You have to engage who you're working with, otherwise you'll never get anywhere.

What was interesting was that you sit opposite one another and there's suspicion and looks through narrowed eyes, and then you have a cup of coffee and the ice breaks a little bit. Later in the day, or the next day you're having conversations, and while it's difficult because you're on different sides, there's an appreciation that you are people and that you can talk to one another. You are human beings and you need to talk. Increasingly those barriers are being broken down in India... Now, whether that's going to happen quickly in the U.S., I don't know, but it's something to emulate because it's being done elsewhere.[8]

* * *

**Dr. DeGrazia:** I think about how prejudice operates and [how] mistrust often operates in human minds. And often it's from not getting to know people who are on the other side. Let's say you're an activist who is committed to ending canine research. You're not going to assume [the] people [doing this research] are evil. You might instead assume that they genuinely believe that the best thing to do for our society is to continue to use dogs in certain kinds of research. They are decent people who want to do good for society. But, the difference between you and them is that they think this is permissible, and you don't. So, where can you find common ground to communicate?

I'm trained as a philosopher, so I'm really interested in trying to understand things objectively and see all sides. There's nothing wrong with people who are highly motivated to present a particular view emphasizing certain things. Often that's what moves people. That's what is needed to demand change where change is called for.

In any instance of animal research that is justified, there has to be some social benefit that helps justify it.... Animal welfare has to be respected and taken into account in the way the research is pursued. And so, people can agree on those starting points, and they might be able to communicate better than if they assumed the individuals on the other side of the debate are badly motivated.... That kind of stuff leads to rhetoric at best and violence at worst.[9]

**Question: How can the general public play a part in helping to support new non-animal technologies and be a voice for laboratory animal welfare?**

**Dr. Bailey:** One of the most critical things we can do is communicate all of this to potential scientists in high school, undergraduates looking at science as a career, and post-graduates training for what sort of research they're going to go into. Quite often people don't set out wanting to do animal research.... They just fall into it. So what we need to do is support scientists in their early career, mid-stage, and even late career to open up this channel to ... these new technologies.

You need to educate as many people as possible.... There's no option but to get the message out. Make connections at your local newspaper. Give school talks. The more people are aware of all the factors, the more they can speak about it and spread the word, and put pressure on their politicians. If ... [we] keep pushing and keep building the case ... we will tip the balance. It will happen. All we can do, unfortunately, is accept that it's going to take some time. But try to shorten that length of time as much as we possibly can.

At the same time, we need to try to change how science is funded because still far too much money is going to animal research, and a relatively tiny amount is going to non-animal research.[10]

* * *

**Dr. Marshall:** The whole idea is to get people educated so they understand what's happening, and understand what medical research is, and how they might be a part of it. Volunteering for medical research doesn't mean you have to be injected with horrible things. It might just mean that you give a skin sample, or ... leave your body to science, or donate your organs when you die.

I think people have a very skewed idea of what animal research is.

They don't understand that animals are still used and what happens to them.[11]

* * *

**Dr. Lopresti-Goodman:** I was at a Zoom workshop in 2020 about being a science advocate. There were four different people talking about how to be a science advocate. One of the questions asked was, "Do you confront the people who are using animals in your field or who are your colleagues?" All four people on the call said, "No, not really. We don't talk about it. They haven't challenged me, so we respect what each other does."

I was thinking, "Are you kidding me?" I have had animal researchers yell at me at an academic conference, in a room full of a hundred people, stand up yelling at me, telling me that I'm a liar for pointing out how harmful standard laboratory practices are for primates. I had their science, numbers, and data backing up my argument. I've had so many negative interactions with animal researchers, but because ... I'm the minority, it's challenging.

So many other scientists who oppose the use of animals in research, even if they disagree with a researcher's experiments ... know they are in the minority and ... don't want to ruffle the feathers of their colleagues. They don't want the repercussions of their paper not getting published or a grant not getting funded, so they don't criticize, and they just do their work silently, quietly, and keep their heads down. You need to challenge them. It's the only way things are going to change. We need more people to speak up.[12]

* * *

**Dr. DeGrazia:** Change is slow. People get attached to their way of seeing things, and it can be pretty hard to change minds. I think sometimes meaningful change has to wait for the people who represent the old ways ... to retire.

In June 2020 I was part of a keynote panel at a Public Responsibility in Medicine and Research Conference. During the question and answer [period], Tom Beauchamp [who was before he retired as Professor of Philosophy, and Senior Research Scholar at the Kennedy Institute of Ethics, Georgetown University] called for a national commission on animal subjects research. I was delighted.

We have as a society been pretty neglectful. There should be a presidential commission studying the whole area of animal research. If the public gets interested and involved enough, it could happen.[13]

# 9

# Re-homing Laboratory Dogs

Research dogs are a largely forgotten population of dogs. Globally, hundreds of thousands of laboratory dogs have no identities other than as numbered research tools and they remain hidden away in undisclosed locations—far from public view. This book is an effort to change that reality. Saving laboratory research dogs involves many steps. Changing the science of research is one step. Changing laws is another. Supporting adoption programs and organizations that specialize in re-homing research dogs is also a crucial step along this journey.

While there is some concern that dogs who have been bred to be laboratory equipment may not adjust well to life in the real world, mostly there is evidence to the contrary. Research dogs can make great pets and they deserve that chance.

## *Re-homing Policies: Federal and State Efforts*

According to the Humane Society of the United States, there are few publicly available statistics that show how many dogs get euthanized versus how many get adopted from research labs. One reason for this may be that research institutions don't want to reveal how many dogs end up being euthanized—even healthy ones. While it is possible that a large number of dogs used for research experiments meet the criteria for potential re-homing, it may be that the majority of laboratory dogs deemed healthy enough for adoption are being killed instead of re-homed.

But the situation is changing. Following increasing pressure from the general public and advocacy groups such as White Coat Waste Project, a Virginia-based watchdog group whose mission is to stop taxpayer-funded animal tests, major federal agencies that conduct research using dogs now have dog adoption policies in place. These include the Food and Drug Administration (FDA), the National Institutes of Health (NIH), and the Veterans Administration (VA).

Individual states have also implemented adoption laws through legislation like the Beagle Freedom Bill. This bill mandates that research facilities in the state that utilize dogs (or cats) for scientific, educational or research purposes, and receive public funds for those purposes, must re-home healthy animals. In 2014, Minnesota became the first state to pass and successfully implement the Beagle Freedom Bill. Since then, California, Connecticut, Delaware, Illinois, Maryland, Nevada, New York, Rhode Island, Washington, and Oregon have all passed similar laws, with even more states planning to follow suit.[1]

**Torrey Smith, champion wide receiver, with Lucia, a beagle rescued from a research laboratory, pose for a photograph as part of *The Show Your Soft Side* media campaign featuring the Baltimore Ravens football team, whose members were helping to promote the Beagle Bill in Maryland. Billboards featuring Torrey Smith appeared throughout the city of Baltimore. The Beagle Bill in Maryland passed and was signed into law in April 2018. The photograph: © 2017 Leo Howard Lubow ("Lubow"). All rights reserved. Reprinted with permission. The poster: © 2017 Show Your Soft Side, Inc. (SYSS). All rights reserved. Reprinted with permission.**

## Do Former Laboratory Dogs Make Suitable Family Pets?

Having read all the details of the science experiments which dogs must endure, one might wonder how these dogs could ever overcome their traumas to become happy, family pets.

Another question potential adopters ask is: What health issues might arise from the type of research the dog was used for?

For the most part, only "healthy" dogs are released from research laboratories. Often, it is a laboratory's veterinarian who determines whether a dog is physically healthy enough to be re-homed. Not all research experiments are designed to be fatal to dogs. Still, unknown health issues are a risk any adopter must take when adopting a former research dog.

Rescue organizations that specialize in finding homes for former research dogs admit that the number of dogs they save each year is "only a drop in the bucket"—meaning that very few research dogs are ever released from laboratories. This may be because the dogs are too ill from the side effects of experiments, or a research facility lacks a re-homing policy, or dogs are euthanized so their organs and tissues can be further analyzed.

The dogs that are released by a laboratory and re-homed are often called the "lucky ones." While it may be a romantic notion to adopt a research dog and sweep away all past sufferings of its laboratory life, there are some things to keep in mind about a former laboratory dog's adjustment to life in a household. Besides the aftereffects of past traumas, often it is a research dog's uncertainty of all the unknowns encountered in day-to-day life outside the laboratory that are the greatest challenges of all.

Until a research dog's rescue day, he or she might have never:

lived outside a small cage
been outdoors
touched grass or dirt
seen sky or sun
eaten out of a bowl
been offered a dog treat
had a good experience with a human
played with a toy
been touched with love and kindness
heard common household sounds like television, microwaves, etc.
walked through a doorway

been in a vehicle
walked up and down stairs
been potty trained
walked on a leash
slept on anything but a hard surface

Yet, despite all of these challenges, studies show that owning a laboratory dog is an overall good experience for the people who adopt them; that research dogs are able to adjust well to living in a household; and that, remarkably, the dogs are able to form strong bonds with their human caretakers.

## *International Studies Confirm the Value of Re-homing Dogs*

A number of studies have examined how re-homed laboratory dogs have fared overall. The results are encouraging.

### United States

A United States study compared psychological and behavioral characteristics of 100 former laboratory beagles living in private homes to a "convenience" sample of 244 beagles with no known history of laboratory use. Results revealed that former laboratory dogs exhibited increased fearfulness, avoidance, attention and attachment behaviors, and more abnormal behaviors than the convenience sample. Yet they were significantly less aggressive. The study also found no significant differences on a majority of behaviors assessed such as trainability, leash-pulling, chewing and energy.

Findings show that despite some residual fear and anxiety from their early life experiences, these dogs can adjust to living in private homes, form strong bonds with their caregivers, and make equally good companions as their non-laboratory counterparts.[2]

### Germany

In Germany, many companies and universities have been helping to re-home laboratory research dogs for many years, and reports indicate mostly positive experiences. Most dogs in Germany are re-homed through specialized animal welfare organizations with experience in re-homing laboratory dogs. A study in Germany published in 2017 observed laboratory beagles in their new homes six weeks after adoption. The study was conducted with 145 purpose-bred laboratory beagles from a German pharmaceutical company (Bayer AG), which had given the dogs to two rescue groups: *Laborbeaglehilfe* and *Tierheim Wermelskirchen*.

During the study, the dogs were observed during specific interactions with their new owners and during a walk. Results indicated that the dogs adapted well to their new homes. The main behavior problems reported were separation anxiety and house soiling. The majority of owners (92 percent) said that they would adopt a laboratory dog again. Only nine of the dogs were returned by their owners, resulting in a 94 percent success rate.[3]

## Finland

A study published in Finland in 2020 yielded similar positive results. The study followed 16 laboratory beagles that were owned by the University of Helsinki and re-homed in collaboration with animal protection organizations and the University. The dogs had participated in animal cognition studies and had undergone minor procedures during the development of a veterinary drug.

The dogs were housed, trained and re-homed in two groups. The first consisted of older dogs that were re-homed at eight years of age, and the second group was comprised of younger dogs that were re-homed as two-year-olds. While the dogs were still in the laboratory, they participated in a socialization program for several months prior to being placed in adoptive homes.

Results of the study showed that the dogs adjusted relatively easily to their new homes. Besides minor problems with house-training, fearfulness and separation anxiety, all of the stakeholder groups—the animal caretakers, animal protection organizations, researchers and dog owners—agreed that the re-homing project was successful and would recommend it as an alternative to killing the dogs.[4]

PART 2

# To the Rescue

# 10

# Beagle Freedom Project

If someone were to ask Shannon Keith, director of the Beagle Freedom Project (BFP), to describe her rescue group's work she wouldn't hesitate to say, "We are an advocacy organization." That's because Shannon knows that change often starts by changing laws, and that's what the BFP has been busy doing—in addition to saving dogs from laboratories. For example, the *Beagle Freedom Bill* is BFP's signature state legislation. By 2020, the bill, which requires the re-homing of dogs (or cats) by research facilities that receive public funds, had been passed in 11 states and was being actively promoted in several others.

The Beagle Freedom Project does not shy away from speaking out

**Beagle Freedom Project Founder and Director Shannon Keith with a newly rescued laboratory beagle.**

against animal research and spurring passionate support from around the world. Its core mission is clear: To rescue and rehabilitate animals used in testing and research. Through its educational programs, campaign initiatives and lobbying efforts, BFP is striving to make the world a better, safer and healthier place for both animals and people.

As one of the world's leading organizations for rescuing and re-homing animals used in experimental research, the BFP has established a loyal following. There is no shortage of foster and adoptive homes for laboratory dogs, and the Project has supporters lined up in each state waiting to get a call about available dogs. Adopters of BFP dogs often refer to Shannon as a close friend. Many volunteers who have worked side-by-side with Shannon in the field during some of her toughest rescue cases have said they are in awe of her tireless efforts to help dogs in laboratories. For many, Shannon is certainly a hero and a role model.

## Beagle Freedom Project

*Headquarters: Los Angeles, California*
*Founder and Director: Shannon Keith*

### *An Interview with Shannon Keith*

***Ellie: When and why did you start the Beagle Freedom Project?***

**Shannon:** I started BFP officially in December 2010. I was practicing animal rights law and I had my own practice. I had started a nonprofit called ARME (Animal, Rescue, Media, and Education) in 2004 through which I rescued and cared for unwanted dogs that were part of my legal cases. In 2010 I got a call from somebody who said there was a laboratory in California and they were closing for the holidays. They didn't want to pay anybody overtime to care for the dogs throughout the holiday season, so they were euthanizing them.

Somebody who worked there begged the animal facilities manager to release them if she could find homes for them. And he said yes. By the time we got the information there were two beagles left and I jumped at the chance. We rescued our first two dogs on December 23, 2010, Freedom and Bigsby, and BFP was born.

* * *

***Ellie: How has Beagle Freedom Project evolved over the years?***

**Shannon:** It was easier in the beginning to establish relationships with laboratories, because we were not well known and we hadn't gone political yet. We were just about rescuing the dogs. When I brought Freedom and Bigsby home that night, I looked into the dogs' eyes and I could just envision people changing. I had been working in anti-vivisection my whole adult life and I'd never seen this kind of impact on people before [of meeting a rescued laboratory dog face to face]. To actually meet the survivors is the way to do it.

My ultimate plan was to lay low for two years, to just focus on rescuing, and not do anything else. Get as many animals out as possible, educate the public about animal testing, and get everyone on board. Then I would start introducing legislation and start getting some political campaigns out there.

I predicted that at that point, labs would not work with us anymore. I would probably never get another animal out, but that was okay with me. That's what happened, but they [the labs] were never really on board to work with us anyway.... Most labs wouldn't release [dogs]. So it's not like we had all these great relationships with laboratories. It was really, really hard to get them out.... What's crazy though, even though we're "public enemy number one" to the animal testing industry ... we're actually getting more animals out now than we ever have before. We're just going about it differently.

* * *

***Ellie: What challenges has BFP faced in maintaining trusting relationships with research laboratories? Are you still facing those same challenges?***

**Shannon:** In the beginning, we did a lot of media [publicity] every time we had a rescue. That really [upset] the labs, even though we never mentioned their name. There was one lab that said, "Because of the publicity, we're not going to release anymore. We're just going to kill all the dogs." I was devastated and implored them saying, "Oh my God, what can I do? I don't understand. We have this great thing going, and I didn't mention the name of your facility"—which by the way was in northern California where there are literally hundreds of animal testing facilities. The lab replied, "We don't care. The industry doesn't want people to know we test on dogs. And you're putting it out there and you're destroying our industry."

So, for years afterward, I thought this lab was euthanizing dogs instead of releasing because of this incident. Fast forward, I got a call from another rescue group in northern California a few years later asking for our help. It turns out they had been re-homing dogs from this one lab for years and didn't have enough fosters or homes. I asked for the name of the lab, and it was same one. The lab had lied to me. They ... made me think my media attention had caused the killing of all these dogs for so long, but meanwhile they were still releasing dogs to rescue.

Some of the labs we used to work with directly got angry at the language we use like "torture" because they think that their animals are treated well. Then they would stop working with us. Right now we have some really good relationships with labs. They love the work we do and they're grateful. But that's less than a handful of labs that we work with directly. I don't make these rescues public knowledge. You won't see photos of any of the dogs anywhere. It's an established relationship of many years. They see that we have been around for over a decade and have an amazing track record.

That's where these labs stand. We don't agree ethically or politically, but they know that we will place their dogs in great homes. The number of animals we rescue is increasing. We also have more information about facilities, so we can do more now than we could do before

* * *

***Ellie: Why isn't more information available online about BFP rescues?***

**Shannon:** Most of our rescues are confidential. That's why you won't see a lot of dogs on our website.... We have a disclaimer on the adoption page saying you're not going to see a lot of these dogs, but if you're interested, you can apply and when we have a rescue in your area we'll contact you privately. That's how we work. Some rescues are public, but very few.

* * *

***Ellie: What is the general condition of the dogs when they first arrive from labs, emotionally and physically?***

**Shannon:** In terms of their physical [condition], almost 100 percent of the time they need dental work. Even the puppies. They are given the most horrific diet called "lab chow," made to produce the least amount of waste. Dental [work] is very expensive and we always have to do dental work on these dogs.

In terms of where they were [which lab], it's always different. Ear issues, device implants, and mental issues.... The younger ones often do much better when they're released. Some you wouldn't even know were in a lab.

Some don't do well for a long time. They have severe PTSD.

***Ellie: How many animals have you rescued from labs? What was your largest rescue?***

**Shannon:** In ten years we've rescued over 3,000 animals from laboratories, but that includes dogs and cats, horses, goats, and pigs. The largest group of dogs we rescued was the Spanish 40 [40 beagles from a laboratory in Spain].

* * *

***Ellie: How much are you told about what type of testing the dogs have undergone?***

**Shannon:** I'm given barely any information, if any at all, from a lab about what a dog was used for. If there's medical information ... we always give that to the adopter because they need to know. We just redact the name of the facility.

Often ... we will get dogs from the research department [of a veterinary school].... The people who work ... there ... can't even get that information for me as to what the research department did to those dogs. Sometimes I need to know because the dogs are in really bad shape, but I can't get that information. We've gotten some [dogs] that are worse than others in terms of residual medical issues, but there's nothing that we can point to and say, "This dog got this illness as a direct result of the testing."

* * *

***Ellie: What was your most memorable rescue?***

**Shannon:** My first rescue was the most memorable for me, not just because it was the first one, but because of how it affected me. I had these fantasies in my head of what that rescue would be like. I've been an animal activist my whole life. I've been on the streets protesting. I've done all of it, especially as it involved my anti-vivisection work. This was a dream come true for me, and I couldn't believe we were going to get these dogs [Freedom and Bigsby] out.

In my fantasy, we meet the dogs and they are so happy to be free and be outside. This scenario was playing out in my head as we were driving up there [to pick them up]. It wasn't the case at all. The dogs were scared to death. It was the most bittersweet moment I've ever experienced in my life. They wouldn't come out of their crates, even though they were set on the grass with the beautiful sun shining. We were trying to coax them out with treats. They wouldn't come out.... I didn't realize that it would be so scary for them, because they'd never been outside.

So, just going through that with them did so much for me. When they did finally come out, they started slowly becoming dogs and sniffing and running.

I learned so much from that rescue. That's [also] where I learned why they use beagles [for research].... On the way home, one of the dogs kept giving us his paw, and we thought, "Oh, how cute! He knows how to give a paw!" [Later] I was speaking to the woman who got them released from the lab and she said, "Oh by the way, do you notice that they are giving you their paw?" I said, "Yeah, that's so cute," and she said, "No it's not. They are doing that because they are trained to give their paw for blood testing."

* * *

***Ellie: What special requirements do you have for adopters and why?***

***Shannon:*** We have a whole training process. We are an advocacy organization. It's not just about someone wanting to adopt a dog from a lab, or a beagle, it's about someone who wants to embrace all of this advocacy work as well.

Adoptive homes are required to be cruelty-free—they can only have products in their home that don't test on animals. If they don't, as long as they are willing to change, we help them with that. That's one of the reasons I developed the Cruelty-Cutter App, so it's easy to do. They don't have to be an activist, but we'd like adopters to be advocates.

These dogs are our ambassadors, and we ask adopters to be involved in legislation, events, and interviews when those arise. Adopters are often required to have another dog in the home to help teach an incoming lab dog. Preferably [they] don't have jobs that keep them away from home all day, and don't care about peeing and pooing in the house—maybe for the rest of that dog's life. Adopters must be patient and loving and give these dogs everything they deserve.

* * *

***Ellie: What do you see as the biggest barriers to ending research on dogs today?***

**Shannon:** The biggest barrier is the mentality of the biomedical industry. I have no doubt that soon in the United States we'll be able to stop testing cosmetics on animals. But the biomedical industry has a completely different attitude. The problem is money. [It's costly] to implement ... the alternatives that are already available and much more successful than testing on the anatomy of a dog. In the end, it's going to be much less costly, because you don't have to take care of animals. But they [biomedical industry] don't want to put the money in to make that initial change.

It's hard enough to pass minimal animal welfare legislation like [re-homing dogs] ... after testing is over. You would think that would be easy, but it's not. We've had so much opposition to that and lost [the Beagle Freedom Bill] in so many states. Labs don't want to release dogs even though they have no use for them anymore. So, getting them to stop testing is huge. It can't happen overnight. You have to work on education, like [for] future scientists. Put the money there.

* * *

***Ellie: What is your advice to members of the general public who want to help?***

**Shannon:** There are so many ways to help. Everyone has their own gifts that they can contribute to this change. I believe that we are all spokes in the wheel. We've got to focus on coming at this from several prongs. From street activism to rescue to legislation and to outreach programs for children, which I think is critical. There's not one thing.

Seeing the reaction of people who have met the survivors was the single most important change I ever saw. I think that if we can get more of our survivor dogs out there, and people are able to meet them, that they really will make that change—a shift in consciousness ... will happen.[1]

# 11

# Kindness Ranch Animal Sanctuary

A far cry from the stress of laboratory life, Kindness Ranch Animal Sanctuary is a special place where research animals come to heal. On this 1000-acre ranch located in a remote area in southeastern Wyoming, the residents are mostly dogs, cats and horses, although there are other critters such as pigs, sheep and cows to be found—all rescued from research and testing facilities. As one of the only sanctuaries in the United States devoted to research animals, Kindness Ranch is a first step for dogs from laboratories to experience life outside of research.

**A winter view of Kindness Ranch Animal Sanctuary in Wyoming. This photograph was taken from one of the guest yurts located on the ranch property. The dirt road leads to more yurts where the dogs, cats, and other animals rescued from research laboratories are housed and get to experience freedom. Photograph by author.**

Yurts, which are custom-made for the dogs and cats at the ranch, dot a grassy hillside along the ranch property's dirt road. Each yurt houses staff members who give the rescued dogs 24-hour care and teach them how to live in a home environment. Outdoor play areas are ample, as are toys, healthy food, exercise, and lots of one-on-one attention from Kindness Ranch staff. The goal is to re-home the dogs and make room for more dogs to rescue.

Another unique feature of Kindness Ranch is that potential adopters and volunteers may stay in guest yurts located on the property, which are just a short walk away from the dog yurts. Here adopters can socialize with the dogs, or if they are interested in adopting, they may take the time to get to know a dog and make sure that he or she is a good fit for their family.

Under the big blue Wyoming sky, where sunshine is plenty, as are friends and new adventures, Kindness Ranch is an inspirational place where research dogs can find their courage—and a family of their own.

## Kindness Ranch Animal Sanctuary

*Headquarters: Hartville, Wyoming*
*Founder: Dr. David Groobman;*
*Director: John Ramer*

### *Kindness Ranch Beginnings*

Kindness Ranch first opened its doors to research animals somewhere in the early 2000s. Founded by Dr. David Groobman, a retired clinical psychologist, Kindness Ranch was founded on one main principal: to rescue as many animals as possible from research.

In the 1990s, Dr. Groobman founded a company called Senior Counseling Group that provides behavioral health services to residents in senior care facilities. When he had accumulated enough financial security to take care of his family, Dr. Groobman started putting aside all the profits from his company to start a nonprofit—although he wasn't sure what kind of nonprofit he wanted to start. As Dr. Groobman recalled, the moment he decided to help research animals began with a chapter in a book he was reading:

> I was reading a book by Peter Singer [a professor of bioethics with a background in philosophy; well-known for his book *Animal Liberation*] at this time. The chapter [in *Animal Liberation*] on vivisection ... really shook me

up. I wasn't aware of the extent of it [experiments on animals]. That was it. I wanted to rescue as many animals as possible from research.

After that pivotal moment, Dr. Groobman spent two years looking all through Colorado and Wyoming to find land pristine and isolated enough, and with minimal zoning requirements, to build an animal sanctuary on. Finding the land he knew would work in Wyoming, the sanctuary took one year to build.

Part of the building included guest yurts. Dr. Groobman felt it was important for people to visit Kindness Ranch, have someplace to stay onsite, and then go back to their communities and describe the experience to other people who would want to adopt a research dog, too. From the beginning, Dr. Groobman insisted that the dogs coming out of the labs would live in a home environment at the sanctuary, so that they could adjust to it. He was also personally responsible for contacting laboratories at the very beginning. "We started with dogs, then horses and cats. A lot of labs wouldn't talk to me," Dr. Groobman remembers. "Then there were some that would, and that is where our dogs came from."

## An Interview with John Ramer

The following is an interview with John Ramer, director of Kindness Ranch. In charge of running day-to-day operations at the ranch, he describes his experiences on the job and his views of the largely hidden world of laboratory dog rescue.

***Ellie: What made you want to work at Kindness Ranch?***

**John:** I became director of Kindness Ranch in November 2019. I have been working in animal sanctuaries since 1998. I worked at a primate sanctuary in Florida, where I was able to work with the first-ever primates released from a federal research lab, including 27 squirrel monkeys that were used in nicotine studies. This [position at Kindness Ranch] opened up a whole new direction of rescue for me.

* * *

***Ellie: What is your general impression of the laboratories you've worked with through Kindness Ranch?***

**John:** Labs are definitely not equal in their treatment of dogs. Even though there are so many USDA mandated guidelines, how all of the labs operate is vastly different and the [mindset of] staff also changes vastly between each facility. You can tell at each place—when the [animal] caretakers, who are usually not involved in doing any of the research, are allowed to build relationships with the dogs, or if they're told not to [build relationships] and keep that professional detachment. It's just so eye-opening....

When I came on [as director], there were two labs that we ... had existing relationships with. One we've been working with almost since the beginning of Kindness Ranch. With the other we are still trying to repair a broken relationship.

...A few years prior, one of the Kindness Ranch caretakers, who was made privy to some sensitive information, shared it with one of the adopters. The adopter decided to ... put together a group of people and they picketed the lab that their dog came from. That got us blacklisted for a little while. That was right when I came on board. I've been working really hard at rebuilding that trust and putting ourselves back in good standing with several labs.

* * *

***Ellie: What are some challenges you face when working with labs?***

**John:** It's really challenging to cold-call labs and ask them for their animals. As you can imagine, they are not very willing to part with them for just anybody. It's been a slow, slow process. We have dialogue with ten to fifteen labs at any given time. Out of all of those, it's everything from horses, to cats, to dogs, to pigs.

Confidentiality is the most important part of a relationship with a laboratory. Even though we try to put as many precautions as we can in place, as far as legal documents and nondisclosure agreements, the caretakers, depending on what research the animals were used in, ... have to be privy to some of that information in order to provide the correct level of care for the dogs.

If a dog was used in flea and tick studies, then chances are the dog will probably not have any long-term withdrawal symptoms or neurological problems or be prone to seizures. But if they're used in narcotics research, then there's a detox period that the dogs have to go through, and the caretakers need to know what to be on the lookout for. This is a tough wire to walk.

* * *

***Ellie: What was one of your most challenging rescues?***

**John:** This lab was told about Kindness Ranch and ... called us and left a voicemail. It was a strange chain of events because they simply introduced who they were and asked if we could take in some animals. But they didn't leave a phone number.... Then, I got an email asking if we could pick up some animals in three days. I responded to the email and my email was rejected. We played phone and email tag for two days and then I actually contacted [someone] from another lab to ask if he had heard of this facility. He said yes, and he called the owner of the lab with me in the room and introduced me. Less than 24 hours later I was picking up animals.

That lab wouldn't tell us what research the dogs were used in. When they refused to disclose that, it was a red flag. It was quite the risk because there's part of us that questions everything that the lab does, just as the lab questions everything we do and what our motives are. ... Imagine having a relationship based on trust when there's never that complete trust between you. It's a strange bed fellow for sure.

When our staff arrived at the lab to pick up the animals, we were rushed through the hand-over process in a way that seemed scripted and sterile. Although the people we interacted with claimed to be concerned about the wellbeing of their subjects, you would have been hard pressed to see it from the appearance of the beagles once we got back to the ranch.

The ten beagles were extremely timid. Most of them were malnourished and emaciated; ribs showing, eyes murky. One beagle was missing toes on his back feet. Another was missing part of his tail. All we were told was that these things "happened while in the lab." According to our vet, they appeared to be trauma injuries from catching toes in wire cages and tails getting slammed in doors. This is speculative, of course, though it often happens to animals who spend their lives in cages.

I named every one of those dogs after 2020 Grammy winners or Golden Globe winners. We had a dog named Joaquin Phoenix and we had another dog named Billie Eilish. They ended up with a really slow rehabilitation process, but [were] fantastic dogs with the most amazing personalities. We picked them up in early February 2020 and we got them all adopted by the last week of April 2020.

* * *

***Ellie: What's the process of picking up a dog from a laboratory? What's the general vibe during the exchange?***

**John:** It's very clinical. It puts you in a semi-mental state of detachment. You're there for a very specific reason. You get a date and federal guidelines for transporting animals. You have to make sure that all of your paperwork is in place, and you have to have a set number of people for a set number of animals. Sometimes it's two people, sometimes it's three people that go [to pick up dogs].

If it's a new lab that I haven't worked with before, then I usually end up ... getting a tour of their facilities. It's almost like they want to prove to me that their animals are being taken care of, and they want me to say positive things when I leave. That's always an interesting thing, and I've seen things that I've wished I hadn't. This one lab that I go to, you can tell ... that the people really do care about their animals. They have enrichment toys for cats and people are walking dogs. It almost looks like a daycare until you think about the work that's being done [there].

But when we pick up animals ... [the process is] like a machine.... Usually while I'm doing the paperwork, the caretakers from the lab are offloading all of our crates, go behind closed doors, [and] ten minutes later ... all of our animals in crates [are] being loaded onto the van. And then it's "thank you very much" and we drive on down the road. There's nothing more to it than that.

You can make small talk all you want, but you always get the feeling that they don't want to dilly-dally. You're there to get the animals and get out. We were very clearly told by the last three places ... to not arrive in a truck or van that states the name of the sanctuary. It's all unmarked.

* * *

***Ellie: What are the demeanors of lab personnel when you meet them?***

**John:** You can tell that the caretakers handing us the animals have been directed not to talk about the animals. We had one caretaker ... that made the mistake of saying that they follow us on Facebook, so they could chart the process of the beagles from their lab going to homes. That caretaker ended up being terminated. They are not supposed to have that knowledge. I'm always personally caught off guard at the level of detachment that the management and officers [at] the facilities have. It's really strange. [At one lab I was asked] what we do for enrichment and exercise [for our animals]:

[Among other things] I told him about an exercise wheel that we have for our cats at the sanctuary, and I showed him a video on my cell phone.... Less than a month later he emailed me a video of his cats ... on the same exercise wheel we have. He wants his animals to be happy and healthy, but when they're not on the exercise wheel, what's happening to them? That dichotomy is just fascinating. A caretaker will say [to me], "...This one loves playing fetch, and if you scratch him by his inner thigh he just kicks and gets so happy." ... They're the ones that will tell us the most amazing stories about the behaviors of the dogs because they've worked with them for three or more years at this facility. It's actually kind of heartbreaking to take a dog away from someone that ... truly loves it. But then again ... the poor dogs are going through hell most of the time.

When I asked [one caretaker] what the dogs were eating and when was the last time they ate [he replied] "I don't know. It's just my job to keep them alive, not fat and happy." That's going back to that level of detachment that many caretakers have. It's depressing.

* * *

***Ellie: How much are you told about what type of testing the dogs were used for?***

**John:** Most of the labs will give us what's called an "Acquisition and Disposition" form. All of the dogs have tattoos. Each dog is listed on this form by tattoo, date of birth, weight, and then they have to have a veterinarian inspection if they are going to cross state lines. All of our dogs come from outside the state of Wyoming.

At the top of these forms is a very generalized statement as to the invasiveness of the research done.... So, some labs give us a little blurb of information about the research. Some labs just don't tell us anything. It depends on the length of time we've been working with the lab, and the type of relationship we have with them.

* * *

***Ellie: What is your process for releasing the dogs from their kennels for the first time?***

**John:** These dogs are coming from such controlled environments that we don't want to immediately overstimulate them. We bring the kennels inside the yurt, and we open them up one at a time and let each dog come out on their own time. If possible, we'll get a check-in weight and do a BAR check (Bright, Alert and Responsive) and a quick physical check to make sure they don't have any scrapes or open wounds. Then the whole process starts from there.

We watch how they interact with the other dogs and start coming up with names and see if they want to eat something. Usually [for] the first two or three days, with the change in diet and everything going on, they have the worst, stinkiest diarrhea. Some of the dogs get so nervous they get sick for a couple of days. It's such a whole new world for them. So many of them have never been outside, have never felt the wind on their face, and they don't know what it's like to walk in grass or on dirt.

This position is one of the most rewarding jobs that I've had in twenty-two years of working in animal sanctuaries. To be there when I pull a dog out of the lab, and see it learn how to be a dog, and then to see it go "home." It's heart-wrenching and rewarding all at once.

* * *

***Ellie: Kindness Ranch is pretty isolated. How do potential adopters of dogs find you?***

**John:** Strangely, it's often not the awareness of animals being used in research that leads people to us. In 2020, about one quarter of the people that have found us are looking specifically for beagles, not necessarily lab animals. They find us by accident. These are my favorite people to interact with and educate. At Kindness Ranch, we don't position ourselves to be anti-lab. We're positioned to be the "alternative" to euthanasia after research is done. That's all we want to be known as.

* * *

***Ellie: What do you see as the biggest barrier to ending research on dogs?***

**John:** It's two-fold. The biggest barrier is we don't have many accepted alternatives yet. Until we find those alternatives, we're not going to be able to eliminate it entirely. That being said, one of the most unique cases that came through Kindness Ranch, was beagles that were used for narcotics testing.... [In one test] they were being injected with this unknown narcotic, and [the researchers] timed how long it took for the drug to pass through their system.

Our argument on that was, if you can't give a dog chocolate because it's hazardous to its health [as a dog], then why would you test something on a dog that is being designed for human use? How does that actually equate? We have questions on how the research actually correlates to humans. More often than not, it's not a direct carryover to improving human quality of life.

* * *

***Ellie: What is your advice to members of the general public who want to help end research on dogs?***

**John:** On a personal side ... get angry and change it. On a professional side ... [having] compassion, understanding, and empathy while you raise public awareness is key. There's one breeder in South Carolina that supplies between 7,000–8,000 dogs per year to various research facilities all over the country. This breeder is generating [income of] anywhere from $2,000 to $4,000 per dog. If we can begin to raise public awareness and deter labs from purchasing dogs at such an exorbitant cost ... eventually the commodity side of [selling dogs for research] and the financial lure isn't going to be there anymore. It has to be a multi-pronged process ... once we eliminate the financial lure of the breeders and educate the facilities on alternative methods of testing, eventually it will change. It may not happen in my lifetime. That's why it's important to talk to junior high and high school kids. They are the future voters. They can help to change it.[1]

# Part 3

# Saved

## *Stories of Rescue, Rehabilitation, and Second Chances*

An entire summer was devoted to interviewing families for this book who have adopted dogs from research laboratories. The families represented in this book come from across the nation and around the world. While other parts of this book have taken on a more serious tone, this part is all about dogs being dogs. It is also about the people who love and care for them. Therefore, taking into account the dog-human dynamic, the following stories are emotionally touching, heartwarming, humorous, and inspirational.

Each story has a happy ending, even though it might have taken a bit to get there. Each story is a shining example of what wonderful family pets dogs from research laboratories make. In fact, many former research dogs don't just become pets—they are actually changing people's lives for the better. Giving back to us after they have given so much already. Then again, that is what dogs do.

# 12

# Ambassadors for Freedom

## Teddy

**Breed:** Beagle

**Research History**: Teddy was one of 36 beagles being used as part of a one-year pesticide test commissioned by Corteva Agriscience for its new fungicide (Adavelt®). The beagles, including Teddy, were force-fed the fungicide every day for nearly a year at a laboratory in Michigan. The laboratory's plan was to then kill all the beagles in July 2019 and assess their organs for damage done by the fungicide.[1]

Fortunately for the dogs, the Humane Society of the United States (HSUS) had been conducting an undercover investigation of this operation and released the laboratory video footage of Teddy and the other beagles to the public on social media in March 2019. Within days, more than 500,000 people signed the HSUS petition demanding the end of the testing and the release of all the dogs. Corteva announced a week later that it had ended the test and in April released the 32 surviving dogs, including Teddy, to the Michigan Humane Society, an HSUS shelter and rescue partner.[2]

**Adoption:** He was adopted in April 2019 by Dave and Greta Rubello who live in St. Claire Shores, Michigan. When Dave and Greta Rubello adopted Teddy, he was just shy of two years old. By then he had already undergone so much abuse and trauma that Teddy's even being alive seemed to be a miracle.

Just an hour after the Michigan Humane Society announced through a post on Facebook on a Friday evening that it was opening the adoption process for the Corteva Agriscience beagles, it received nearly 400 applications. Within days more than 800 people applied to adopt one of the beagles, and Teddy was one of the first to find a new home.

**Dave Rubello, Teddy, and Greta Rubello**

## Greta

I had been following the plight of the Corteva Agriscience beagles closely on social media. I saw a video on social media of the beagles being tortured and force-fed pesticides. I was so sickened that I couldn't even watch the video at first. But I did read the news stories and that was enough for me to feel angry on behalf of these dogs.

Exactly eight minutes after the Humane Society's post on Facebook announcing that it was accepting adoption applications, my husband Dave and I submitted ours. A few days later we got a call. We had all the qualities needed to adopt a beagle from a research lab. We have always had beagles. Teddy would be our fourth. The Michigan Humane Society seemed to like that we had another beagle—a two-year-old female—and a fenced yard. We made an appointment for the next day to meet two of the beagles.

They requested that we bring our beagle Cleo with us to the appointment to meet the two dogs. They brought us into a large room and we waited in one corner until they brought the first dog in. This dog was allowed to get comfortable in the room before we approached. Then we observed how they interacted. The first dog wasn't a good fit. Her nervous energy brought out dominant behaviors in Cleo. Then they brought out a male dog who was quite timid and did not threaten Cleo. They seemed to get along fine, so we were able to adopt Teddy.

I'll never forget my first interaction with Teddy. He came right over to me and put his paws on my leg. I smiled at him and felt like he was reaching out to me. He was so gentle and sweet and obviously afraid that it just melted my heart. In the way he licked my hand, he seemed to understand that we would take care of him and was grateful.

Teddy was quite thin from his ordeal in the laboratory. The Michigan Humane Society also told Dave and me that none of the rescued beagles barked—which is odd for a beagle—and that was certainly true of Teddy. Teddy didn't bark for the longest time. It took him months. Our other dog showed him how. Now Teddy has a funny bark. It's very high-pitched and subtle—very unlike a normal beagle bay. We were so excited when Teddy barked for the first time. I didn't think it was possible because of the chemical testing he endured.

The Corteva Agriscience beagles were raised entirely in cages, so the biggest challenge for Teddy was navigating a house and a yard, when all he had before was a cage. And figuring out how to be with us. He seemed cautious about interacting at first. The potty training was really hard. He seemed confused about where to go if he wasn't outside on the grass. He started using our area rug in the living room and then the throw rugs by the doors. He doesn't want to do the wrong thing. So we've just worked around this and purchased special waterproof mats for the house in case he had an accident inside.

Teddy definitely gets stressed and is frightened by noises he doesn't know. He won't really go in the kitchen because of the noises there that frighten him, like the trash compactor, closing a drawer or opening the ice tray. Even a rustling of a plastic bag can send him running. Teddy was also unsure of how to run at first, and he sort of galloped. Now he's really fast and loves to tear around our yard. Teddy also would not eat his food from a bowl on the ground. Instead we would feed him on a chair in the living room. We even hand-fed him for some time so that Cleo wouldn't take the food from him. Now we place his bowl on the chair and he jumps right up to eat it.

Teddy has become so loving to all of us and just a joy to be with. He's brought us very tender feelings and a chance to make up for what other humans put him through. He will sit calmly on Dave's lap and let him cradle him like a baby. At night he sleeps with us curled up very close like he's leaning on us.

## Dave

Not long after Teddy settled in with us, I received a special invitation. Teddy and I were invited to the Michigan State Capitol in Lansing to meet with Representative Kevin Hertel and Senator Peter Lucido.

Representative Hertel had just introduced Michigan House Bill 4496, which would require research facilities to put cats or dogs no longer being used for testing up for adoption through a Michigan-based animal shelter. The bill would also require laboratories to submit annual reports to the state, providing the number of animals in the lab's possession and the number of animals tested—data that are currently submitted only to the federal government.

We were able to meet the Humane Society activists who had pushed for the beagles' release. Here was a group of people that had fought and fought and fought the good fight to get these dogs freed. This was the first time they had ever seen one of the dogs. They were brought to tears. They were so excited to meet Teddy. They all wanted to take pictures with Teddy, and they threw a reception for us. Teddy also got to tour the inside of the capitol building and took souvenir photos with Senator Lucido and Representative Hertel, who were so happy to meet him.

Besides being a local celebrity in Michigan, these days Teddy is living the good life with us. Teddy loves exploring the beautiful beaches surrounding Lake St. Claire with his sister Cleo or going walking with us on local trails and around the neighborhood. He also enjoys boating on Lake St. Claire, which we often do. There are all kinds of neat smells and sights out there for a dog.

Our experience with Teddy inspired me to start the Facebook page "DOW Beagle Humane Society," a place for all the adopters of the beagles to stay in touch, help each other, disseminate information, and host events to promote adoption of research dogs. I even planned a beagle float featuring all the Corteva Agriscience beagles for a Memorial Day parade in 2020, an event that had to be cancelled due to the coronavirus pandemic.

I am a voice for all research dogs like Teddy. Big companies have been able to hide what they're doing to animals. When it's in the dark, you can't do anything. When it's in the light, we have to speak up, until it changes.[3]

## George

**Breed:** Beagle

**Research History:** In July 2013 seven beagles were rescued from a laboratory near Washington, D.C., by the rescue organization Beagle

**George the beagle assisting Governor John Carney of Delaware in signing the state's Beagle Bill into law in 2018.**

Freedom Project. They included six boys and one girl. No information is available on what type of research they were used for.

**Adoption:** He was adopted in July 2013 at age four by Gail Thomssen who lives in Raleigh, North Carolina. Growing up in a suburban town in Michigan, Gail never realized that she was living near one of the world's largest animal testing laboratories, known as Charles River Laboratories, located just on the outskirts of her neighborhood. As a kid in high school she thought, "Animal testing ... oh, they have mice there." That was the extent of her knowledge of what was going on. She had no idea about the thousands of dogs being used there for research as well.

Little could Gail have guessed then how her past and future would become enmeshed, thanks to a beagle named George. Gail first became aware of dogs' still being used for research experiments around 2011. She saw a story on NBC Nightly News about some beagles rescued from a research lab in Spain that were arriving in the United States. The story went on to explain how this is happening in the U.S. as well.

A few years later, in 2013, Gail was living in Charlotte, North Carolina, when she heard about another rescue of research dogs. This time she jumped in to help. The nonprofit animal rescue group Beagle Freedom Project had just rescued seven beagles from a laboratory near

Washington D.C. These six boys and one girl became known as the "DC7," each named after a Founding Father.

"George" Washington was four years old when he first met Gail and had never been outside a cage before. He had spent his whole life inside a research laboratory. Nothing was disclosed about what testing he had endured.

## Gail

### *New Beginnings*

At this stage of my life, I was working in corporate America. I had spent 15 years working at Bank of America while I was living in Charlotte, and I got really burnt out with the rat race. I knew I wanted to make a change, but I didn't know what that change looked like. I thought, "It will come ... what it is that I want to do." At around that time in 2013 I got George.

George was extremely nervous the first few months. It really took years for him to get over the extreme anxiety. He clung to my side, either next to me on the sofa or next to me at night in bed. I'd carry him outside to go potty. He was terrified of doors. He felt safer outside the house and hid in the bushes when I first got him. I would need to pick him up and carry him inside as he would not step through the doorway. It took him about two weeks of pacing around the backyard before he worked up enough courage to come inside on his own.

I also fed him by hand the first few days and gave him ice chips or droppers full of water since he didn't know (or was afraid) to eat and drink out of a bowl. I pretty much devoted myself to his care for the first few months.

I was still also trying to decide what I wanted to do with my life, and then one day it just came to me. I felt like I was most myself when I was speaking from the heart—and that was when I was talking about George and his story. So, I quit my job at Bank of America and moved to Washington, D.C., to try to get a job at an animal nonprofit organization. I changed careers because of George—that's how much he changed my life.

### *Changing Hearts, Laws and Paws*

Because of my proximity to Washington, D.C., and my newfound passion for research dog rescue, I started working with Beagle Freedom Project, the organization that rescued George. Part of my job was working on the Beagle Bill for both Maryland and Delaware [a state-specific bill which requires research facilities to give cats and dogs a chance at adoption at the end of experiments].

I also testified for both bills. The Beagle Bill in Maryland was a four-year process, and I came in on the second year. George became well known in Annapolis. He would attend lobby day with me. We visited delegates and senators. George went to a convention of counties and met the governor and the attorney general. George was also there the day the Maryland Beagle Bill was signed into law by Governor Larry Hogan on April 24, 2018.

In a Senate meeting in Delaware [where the bill was also passed later in 2018] I was invited to speak, and I brought George up there in the Senate room with me. It's so much more impactful when you have the dog there, and you can tell their story, because people can see them. It softens people. And you have this real story to tell and they can make that link. Just looking the dog in the eye makes a big difference. There's something that resonates with people about what these dogs went through.

George is so calm and sweet—he just draws people in. People love George because he has a heroic story. It's a happy ending for something that may not have been a happy ending. For so many of them [dogs in research] it's not a happy ending.

## *Looking Ahead with Hope*

In July 2018 I accepted a position to be the North Carolina State Director for the Humane Society of the United States. I use George's story to educate others on the fact that animal testing still exists, dogs are used, and that these dogs are most often euthanized at the end of their study. I'll go into meetings with our lobbyist in North Carolina and I'll bring George. They think it's the funniest thing when George jumps up on the table and sits in the middle of the conversation. It just became his thing.

There are a couple of components to ending animals testing on dogs. If you're going to use them for right now, at least give them a life after research and not euthanize the dogs. Why not give them a life? They make great pets. We all look at the end result and try to figure out how we can get there. What are these replacements for dogs in testing? How can we incrementally phase this out? How do you shift a mindset that has been in place for centuries? This also includes exposing the labs. People don't even know where some of these labs are located. That's because big corporations don't want you to know what's going on there.

If we say we're going to end testing on dogs, let's offer solutions against the argument that testing on animals is the only reliable way to gain information pertaining to human health. In this 21st century, how do we not do something with computer models? It is because not enough people are aware and outraged enough to really push it. I hope that we are really getting to that point.[4]

## Bogart

**Breed:** Beagle

**Research History:** On May 10, 2012, there were 20 beagles rescued from a laboratory in San Diego, California. No information is available on the type of testing they underwent. The laboratory's name has never been made public.

**Adoption:** Bogart was adopted in May 2012 at age three by Kelly Selcer and her husband Manos who live in Denver, Colorado.

**Kelly Selcer and Bogart making an appearance at a Beagle Freedom Project red carpet charity event.**

Twenty happy beagles climbed all over one another, romped around in the sunshine and enjoyed their very first tastes of the outdoors. They were at an adoption event at Four Paws Coonhound Rescue & Friends in El Cajon, California. Ranging in ages from three to seven years old, these beagles had never set foot on green grass before and had spent the entirety of their lives inside a research laboratory.

Four Paws had a regular arrangement with the

San Diego laboratory to release dogs to their care when they were no longer needed for research, instead of euthanizing them. This large rescue had been a team effort. While Four Paws kept ten of the beagles, the remaining ten traveled to Los Angeles to be cared for and adopted out by Beagle Freedom Project (BFP)—which named them the "San Diego 10."

## Kelly

## *Following My Path*

I will never forget the day I learned that dogs, mostly beagles, are used in animal testing and research. I had a beagle named Jack for many years before I married my husband Manos. One day a "Facebook friend" shared a post on my page about an organization called the Beagle Freedom Project (BFP) that was rescuing beagles from laboratory testing. As a lifetime animal lover and current beagle mama, I had a roller coaster of emotions as I clicked the links and started down the rabbit hole. I asked myself, "How could I not know?" However, I would quickly find out that I was not the only one who "doesn't know."

From the moment I clicked on that Facebook post, my life changed forever. As a native and then-current resident of Los Angeles, I was particularly interested in BFP because their office was practically in my backyard. Several months after my initial introduction to animal testing and BFP, I learned about an event called Beaglefest. It was a yearly event held in Huntington Beach attended by hundreds of beagles and their humans. My husband and I trekked down to Beaglefest with Jack, and spent the day among beagle-obsessed humans, reveling at the display of happy little beagles everywhere.

At the event there was a table set up representing BFP. I was ecstatic! I spoke with the woman who was there on BFP's behalf. By her side was a beagle named Maynerd who was a laboratory testing survivor. We visited and cuddled with Maynerd, astonished by his incredibly sweet nature. By this time I had read all about BFP and animal testing, but I had never met a survivor in person. It really affected me, to the point that I wanted to adopt a laboratory beagle myself.

I was more determined than ever to submerse myself in BFP and do what I could to help. It didn't make sense at the time, but upon revisiting the timeline of these memories, it was clear to me that I was following a deep magnetic pull that was leading me in a direction I would never have found otherwise. Just a few days after Beaglefest, I began volunteering my time at BFP headquarters.

## The San Diego 10

"He has wires running through his body," I remember the veterinarian saying. Each group of dogs released from a lab comes with its own unique set of issues. This group, the San Diego 10, I was told, was one of the worst to date in terms of the dogs' overall condition. They had rotted teeth, wounds, and stitches all over their bodies. It was discovered from an x-ray that one of the beagles, Pirate, even had a wire implant, its purpose or use unknown. I was angry and heartbroken. Looking at this motley crew I thought of my own beagle, Jack, living in luxury at home. They were no different than Jack; he could have suffered a similar fate.

The San Diego 10 required a lot of care, and some of the dogs were not healthy enough to be entrusted to foster, so they stayed at BFP headquarters, which at this time was located at the home of BFP Director Shannon Keith. I returned every day I could to help Shannon. Besides a lot of cleaning, another important duty was walking the dogs. This was not an easy task. Regardless of age, not a single dog had ever been walked on a leash. Once leashed, they would just stare back up at me. If I was lucky enough to get one dog to walk a few steps, it was almost always followed with an immediate halt and then lying down on the sidewalk, refusing to move.

There was one dog who stole my heart almost instantly. He was one of the only dogs who had no physical sign of surgery or illness. His teeth were in horrendous condition, but other than that, he appeared healthy. He was a little over three years old. He had dark black fur, accented by warm caramel and white. He was really adorable. Whenever I would walk up to him while he was lying on his side enjoying the cool cement in the backyard, he would begin wagging his tail. He wouldn't lift his head or move a muscle. Just wag ... wag ... wag that tail. He was introduced to me as Bogart.

Shannon referred to Bogart as a gentleman. And when I asked to take him home for a few nights as a trial run, she laughed and said, "Yes, sure ... take home the best behaved one!" And so I did.

## Bogart the Ambassador

Though I thought my husband would need some convincing to keep Bogart, there was no need. He was smitten with Bogart's good looks and sweet nature. Bogart adjusted to life in our home easily. He quickly learned the routines from his beagle brother Jack and had minimal accidents in the house. He was a "man of leisure" who quickly learned all the tricks to getting dog cookies.

At this time I was living in Los Angeles, so I was able to attend many BFP events. Bogart was an extremely helpful ambassador, appearing with us at charity events, including one in Beverly Hills, posing for media coverage and marketing photo shoots. I was asked to do a very last-minute interview with the *Huffington Post* for an article they were doing on animal testing. My husband and I dropped what we were doing, grabbed Bogart and rushed to the interview. We arrived to find it was actually a television taping, so Bogart and I took a deep breath and went on live TV. People treated Bogart as a celebrity and he was super tolerant of it.

In 2018 we decided to move to Colorado. We moved because the dogs needed a bigger house, and Los Angeles was getting too expensive to give them the life we wanted them to have. Crazy as that sounds, the decision to move was based on their happiness. My experience with BFP and Bogart has changed my life, my lifestyle, and my values. I have learned how to inspire people to listen. I have a whole new level of compassion and understanding for people and animals. I don't stand in judgment of others, because that's not how you effect change.

Bogart is almost twelve years old now. His hair is mostly white, but he is as spunky and full of life as when we first met. He found his beagle voice spending time around other adopted BFP dogs. He is much more opinionated than ever. He does have an enlarged spleen and heart. I have no idea if that is a result of any testing he endured. I continue to cherish whatever time I have left to enjoy my little gentleman. He is as much a part of me as any other significant influence in my life. I also started a Facebook page for Bogart named *Bogart Saved by the Beagle Freedom Project*. Since then he has collected a worldwide following, and people continue to donate to BFP in Bogart's name even today.[5]

## Laila

**Breed:** Beagle

**Research History:** In August 2017, five female beagles were rescued from an undisclosed laboratory in Pennsylvania by the Beagle Freedom Project (BFP). They were known as the "Rocky V," each dog receiving the name of a famous female boxer. One of the beagles, Laila Ali, has two scars on her head resembling holes for screws. Screws may have been used to attach some sort of mechanical device through her skull to her brain, a research procedure still used in laboratories today.

**Adoption:** She was adopted in August 2017 at age five by Ryan and Sarah Webster who live in Alexandria, Virginia. Living just outside Washington, D.C., Ryan and Sarah were looking for a social group to join with their two beagles, Mason and Ralphie. Both avid beagle enthusiasts, they were hoping to meet other beagle-lovers in the area, since they had recently moved from California. After searching online, they stumbled upon a "beagle happy hour" hosted by the BFP. Ryan and Sarah were excited to get involved, assuming it was a local meet-up event for beagles and their owners.

**Laila being a "spokesdog" for the Beagle Bill in Maryland and getting her photograph taken with Governor Larry Hogan in 2018.**

Unbeknownst to Ryan and Sarah, the event was actually a commemoration of the one-year anniversary of freedom for seven beagles that were rescued from animal testing. There were several "celebrity" beagles from this rescue enjoying the party. While the party was lighthearted, it shined light on an issue that saddened and shocked Ryan and Sarah: the fact that dogs are still being used for research and testing. They both vowed to learn more and help however they could.

## *We're All In...*

### Sarah

I'm a pediatric nurse practitioner, and I didn't realize how much animal testing was still going on, and that beagles were the main breed of dog used. In May 2017, we attended another BFP event called Red, White & Beagle in downtown Washington, D.C. Held in a hotel, this event had a more political theme, because the BFP was trying to promote the "Beagle Bill" in Maryland. This bill would require laboratories to release retired research dogs for adoption as an alternative to euthanasia. The event included a presentation of disturbing videos showing beagles being used for various research procedures in laboratories. Devastated and both in tears, we donated a ton of money that day!

During the event we befriended a lady named Gail and her beagle George, a laboratory survivor, who was also in attendance. We spent a lot of time with George at the event, and helped watch him as Gail went on stage to speak about the Beagle Bill. We must have made a good impression, because two months later I got an urgent call asking us to be foster parents for a laboratory rescue beagle.

## Ryan

We had been involved with several BFP social events by this time and had met some of the beagle rescues. They were so sweet it was hard to imagine people using them for experiments. We had also watched several online videos of "release events," where they let the beagles out of their cages so they can walk on grass for the first time. I got so emotional watching these dogs timidly touch the grass with their paws, expecting pain when they stepped out. It was so touching to watch them slowly come out of their cages and realize that the sun was shining, humans were for petting, and grass was for sprinting. This is why we decided to foster a laboratory beagle. We didn't know anything about the dog we might get. All we knew was that these dogs were special, needed extra love, and we wanted to give it.

## Sarah

On the day of their rescue, the beagles went straight from the laboratory to a BFP volunteer's home, where the dogs were taken to the backyard for release. This was the first time we had ever witnessed a "release event" in person. They filmed us opening the cages and the dogs running around the yard together. We observed them to see which one would be the best fit for our household. One dog was running around and really active. A second one was notably sad and scared. Meanwhile Laila, another one of the dogs, was almost like the forgotten one, and nothing about her really stood out, at first. But, looking back, I believe that she chose us that day.

### Ryan

I got to open one of the beagle's cages and let her out onto the grass for the first time. Then we sat back and let the dogs roam, wander, sniff, and explore. They would come up to us and get pets, and then wander off. It was hard to keep track of them as they ran around. They were all a mix of brown and white coats.

A few of the beagles stole the show with their excitable energy, and that made them more memorable initially. Then our eyes went to Laila. She was just scaling the food table trying to get some treats. I thought to myself in partial amusement, "Laila is locked up for five years, gets five minutes of freedom, and she's like, 'Is that a food table over there?'" She didn't care about anything else.

She was very sociable with us, and often came over for petting, then she would run back to the food table. Our beagle Mason, who ended up being Laila's mentor at our house, was also a total food hound. That's how we knew she would fit perfectly into our pack. As a side note, I found out after the fact that it was Laila's cage I had first opened when the dogs arrived.

## *New Beginnings with Laila*

### Ryan

When we first got Laila home, she appeared so easy and happy that we thought she wasn't going to have any issues. In the living room, we brought her up on the couch with us, covered her with soft blankets, and then turned the television on.

Suddenly we saw another side of Laila. We were watching *Game of Thrones* on a big screen TV. There was a montage of loud scenes, dragon roars, battle clanks, shouting, and flashing lights. Laila ran into the bedroom terrified and sat on the edge of the carpet shaking, head down, and looking fearfully from side to side. From then on, the bedroom became her "safe space." Laila still does not like the TV, even if there's no sound or it's completely off. However, we have made some progress. She is now able to stay in the living room with the TV on for longer periods, as long as one of us is there to encourage her. When guests spend the night at our house, we make sure to let them know that the main guest bedroom is reserved for Laila. I like to joke and say Laila went from a three-foot cage to a master bedroom with a king-size bed.

I understand that dogs in laboratories are fed a very low-quality and inexpensive kibble. Laila ate this food and received no dental care for her five years in the laboratory. Because of this, she has had to have most of her teeth removed. She can still chew, but because she is nearly toothless, her gums get stuck in a "snarl" position which is both funny and sad.

While Laila is tough and a survivor, she is much more of a lover. She is so affectionate that she is pushy about it. If I am lying on the ground, she stands on my chest, head-butts me, and rubs her face on my face. When I pet her, she rolls her head into me to get even more affection. If I stop, she uses her nose to poke my hand and pushes her face into my hand to make sure she gets more pets.

Laila does the same routines every day. For example, in the morning, she runs out of the bedroom to check whether there is food magically waiting in her bowl. As I walk into the kitchen, she runs back to the bedroom and sits on the edge of the carpet with anticipation. As soon as I scoop food into her bowl, she sprints back to get her food.

Laila also has super-powers when it comes to jumping. If we put her outside while we are cooking inside, she will stand outside the door, which is wood at the bottom and glass on top, and go "boing, boing, boing, boing" on her hind legs so she can see the food. Her strong hind legs also allow her to walk like Frankenstein and beg while on the move.

## SARAH

The same year we adopted Laila, the Beagle Bill passed in Maryland. In fact, Laila was a "spokesdog" for the bill and attended the bill's signing in Baltimore, getting her photo taken with Governor Larry Hogan. Laila was also part of a *Show Your Soft Side* media campaign featuring the Baltimore Ravens football team, whose members were helping to promote the Beagle Bill.

We're so proud of Laila. She has become an ambassador for other rescues. We have fostered three laboratory dogs in our home since adopting her. She welcomed them, gently kissed them, and showed them around the yard.

In 2018, we hosted a one-year-of-freedom anniversary party for the "Rocky V" beagles at our home. We invited all the beagles from Laila's rescue, including Lucia, Rhonda, and Gigi. We got them little doggie cakes to eat, and it was so much fun. Only this time, we were not sad or shocked, as we had been at the first BFP anniversary party we attended. We no longer felt helpless about what to do for research beagles. Instead, we were full of joy thinking about how much Laila has enriched our lives.[6]

# 13

# Special Dogs ... Special Love

## *Mini and Maria*

**Breed:** Beagles

**Research History**: In September 2017, the advocacy organization BeagleChina in Beijing rescued more than 25 beagles from experimentation from various laboratories throughout China. Most of the survivors were between the ages of nine and ten and suffered from serious health concerns. Over the course of the fall, BeagleChina was able to find adopters in China for half of the dogs, primarily the younger and healthier beagles. The remaining dogs were moved to rescue centers and cared for while their health was assessed.

***Left to right*: Mini and Maria**

BeagleChina contacted Beagle Freedom Project (BFP) in the United States to help with relocating and adopting the remaining 15 dogs that needed extra medical care. On January 11, 2018, these 15 dogs arrived in the U.S. from Beijing. Three of these beagles had been used for intestinal experiments and required surgery to have metallic wire implants removed from their abdomens. Six others suffered from glaucoma, artificially-induced cataracts due to experimentation, or were already completely blind. Five of the female beagles were ten years of age and had been used for breeding as well.

**Adoption:** Mini and Maria were both adopted by Mary Pryor who lives in Anaheim, California. She adopted Mini in February 2018 at the age of 10, and Maria, who was also 10 years old in September 2018. They are both completely blind.

## Mini

### Mary

We lost our beloved chocolate lab-mix to cancer in December 2017 at age 11. Her name was Rogue Anna Marie and she was the focus of our existence. I had adopted Rogue at just eight weeks of age. Rogue was an only-dog-in-the-house kind of dog. She was around 80 pounds and the love of our lives. She battled cancer for about a year. When Rogue passed away we were beyond devastated.

My sister and I live together, and all of our kids are grown and living on their own. So, when Rogue left us, we had all this love and need to nurture and nowhere to put it. We were absolutely lost without Rogue. I remember at first thinking I'd never adopt another dog; that the grief of losing a dog is too much to bear. But soon after Rogue's passing, we started thinking that maybe sometime in a few years we'd adopt again, or maybe just foster dogs here and there, but not get "tied down."

I don't know why I thought of BFP. I had heard about them several years before and just filed it away in my head. On a whim, I completed an online adoption or foster application for BFP. The form stated that it could take weeks or months to hear back, because BFP doesn't always have dogs available. I indicated on the application that we were interested in fostering an older dog. Because we are older now as well, we didn't want to take on a young dog. We were looking for a dog with a little less energy.

It was just a day or two later when a BFP staffer called me and we chatted. As it happened, they just had a group of dogs rescued from China, and an older female beagle, who was blind, was up for adoption.

We arranged to meet Mini right away. When we first saw Mini, she was in the arms of her foster mom Sara, just limp. Sara asked if I wanted to hold Mini and I said yes. She put Mini in my arms and Mini leaned against me and I fell immediately in love with her. It felt to me that she wasn't scared, just resigned to have to endure whatever was going to happen to her. She never tried to push away. We sat on the sofa and my sister and I held her. We could feel that Mini wanted to be held, talked to, and petted. I turned to my sister and said, "We're adopting her."

Mini continued to crave human contact. She would sleep as close to me as she could and tuck herself up against my neck. She would go potty only on the cement outside, or anywhere in the house, and never in the grass. Mini didn't like grass, and still does not. Being blind, Mini didn't know anything about stairs. It took weeks for her to get confident on our stairs, though she learned the layout of our house very quickly. While Mini doesn't play with toys, she dances, twirls and hops for her food with much abandon.

## Maria

BFP asked us to only foster Maria, knowing we had no plans to adopt another dog. Maria was part of the same rescue as Mini from China, and totally blind just like Mini. Maria was pregnant at the time they flew all of the other dogs over to the U.S., so she had to stay behind and have her puppies. She flew over a few months later with four of her puppies.

Maria was ten years old when she had her last litter. Some of Maria's puppies had already been adopted in China. The four puppies who arrived in the U.S. with Maria also had adoptive homes in place. It was just Maria that needed a place to go. We knew how important fostering is for rescue organizations, so my sister and I were determined not to be "foster failures," to instead remain a reliable foster home for BFP.

Maria was a little more cautious than Mini, and it seemed harder for her to trust her new home situation. She was sound asleep in her bed one day when my sister looked at her and said, "You know, it would be hard for her to go to another home and again learn new things, and again possibly have to learn to get along with another dog." As it was, Mini and Maria got along just beautifully. My sister said, "Maria's going to stay here. This is where she's going to live the rest of her life."

## *Blind and Brave*

We live in a typical California one-story house. There's one big step down to the family room, and another step that goes into the bedroom. Those are the only steps inside the house. There are a couple of steps outside of the house to get into the backyard. Also, our front porch has steps down from it. People advised us to use different scents to help orient Mini and Maria in the house. For example, the smell of peppermint is a signal that stairs are ahead. A rug is then placed right where the stairs begin. But Mini and Maria never needed that. They learned how to get around the house on their own. The front house steps, however, took both Mini and Maria a while to master. Now they go up and down them like it's nothing.

Maria has one eye that is enlarged and we often have our veterinarian check it for glaucoma. She doesn't need any treatment for that eye at this point. It's basically just a useless eye. If it starts causing her any pain, it will have to come out. Maria's other eye is small and also what is called a "dead eye." There is no pressure there. She is completely blind.

As for Mini, you wouldn't even know she was blind if you looked at her eyes. She can look right at you. Her eyes look like regular, beautiful, black eyes. My niece calls her "Daredevil"—laughing that Mini can secretly see, but she's not telling us. But our veterinarian has told us, "Nope, she can't see any light ... nothing," and says it does look like cuts were made to her corneas. Our vet is always looking into Mini and Maria's eyes, trying to figure out what happened to make them blind. So far it's a mystery.

## *Lessons to Live By*

Both Mini and Maria are great little ambassadors. We can take them anywhere and people fall in love with them. Mini and Maria both like people very much and are always happy to meet them. Their tails start wagging right away. People say to me, "Oh my gosh, that must be so hard. I can't believe you have two blind dogs." And it is true, we do have to carry them a lot because they can't get in or out of the car. And, when Maria goes outside, she won't come back in on her own. My sister always has to pick her up and bring her inside. This may be more than some people would want to do.

On the other hand, Mini and Maria don't have the energy of a two-year-old dog that we need to keep up with. So, I always think they are not that hard to take care of. But, I had to learn patience. Mini and

Maria had ten years of doing things a certain way, and now we were asking them to change that. In this way, Mini and Maria have changed me fundamentally, because I'm not a patient person by nature. I learned quickly that being impatient got me nowhere with Mini and Maria. Patience was the number one requirement for helping them navigate their lives outside of a cage.

I often look at Mini and Maria and think, "I can't believe for ten years you suffered like that." The overwhelming feeling of wanting to make it stop for other dogs engulfs me. Then I think about how adopting Mini and Maria gave me a purpose at a time in my life when I was completely lost. I guess you could say we saved each other on this unexpected journey together.[1]

## Leo

**Breed:** Beagle

**Research History**: In August 2015, four beagles were rescued from an undisclosed laboratory. The beagles, all 16-month–old males, were used to test a new human male contraceptive drug. The rescue organization, Kindness Ranch, nicknamed them the "Teenage Mutant Ninja Turtles," each dog receiving the name of one of the characters. Leo suffers from severe cluster seizures. He also has abnormally large nipples, most likely due to hormones he received during the study.

**Nancy House and Leo**

**Adoption:** He was adopted in September 2015 by Nancy House who lives in Denver, Colorado. Nancy's first introduction to dogs being used for scientific research happened during her childhood in the 1960s when a television commercial showed beagles strapped down and being forced to smoke cigarettes. As a dog lover, this was heartbreaking for Nancy watch.

Nancy, a scientist herself, has a bachelor's degree in geology/geophysics and a master's degree in geophysics. Her 40-year professional career has focused on the application of leading-edge geophysical interpretation for multinational corporations as well as for small independent oil companies. While Nancy understands the value of experimentation, she has questioned the benefits of using dogs for testing human conditions.

Nancy's compassion for dogs in research was about to come full circle due to a series of events in her life. Her first beagle, Bubba, passed away from cancer in 2012. In 2015, she got laid off from her job. Living in Pennsylvania at the time, Nancy decided to move to Colorado to start her own home-based consulting business. She knew it was the perfect time to adopt another dog but was unsure if she was emotionally ready to commit. So, she decided to begin by fostering a beagle from a rescue organization.

## Nancy

### *Chosen One*

A friend told me about Kindness Ranch, and I liked the approach they had to rescuing former laboratory animals. I felt I could do some good for beagles by fostering and learn techniques for rehabilitating beagles from them and made arrangements to visit and stay there for a few days as a volunteer.

The Teenage Mutant Ninja Turtle beagles had only been there a couple of days when I arrived. I cleaned their pens, played with them outside in the morning before breakfast, and watched the staff teach them basic things like walking on a leash. Raphael was the most confident and eager to play with toys, Leo was curious, and Donatello and Michelangelo were much more shy and reticent to come and play.

While out in the play yard, Leo kept coming up and jumping on the bench to check me out. At some point, he decided I was his "person" and put his front paws on my chest, staring into my eyes. I had not come to adopt a beagle, but I was particularly drawn to him. I went back home, still not sure if I was ready for such a commitment. However, after some contemplation, I wrote Kindness Ranch asking to be considered for adopting Leo. I was informed that I could adopt Leo, but that he needed a couple more weeks at the ranch to become more socialized. We arranged to go on September 13, my son's birthday, to pick him up.

The staff at the ranch told me that Leo would be scared, and that would be okay. At home, I let him out of the kennel that was in the car and took him out to the backyard. He looked around and smelled everything. We ran around together. He was attracted by laughing, and I would let him catch me by lying down on the ground. He would climb up on my stomach and put his paws on my chest as he did when he first met me, letting the world know that he was the boss of me.

## *A New Normal*

Kindness Ranch suggested that I keep his routine as much like theirs as possible for a while, so the first night I put him to bed in his kennel. He did fine as far as I remember. The second night when I tried to put him into his kennel he refused violently, and I decided that I was not going to force him to sleep there.

I enlisted the help of a trainer early on since I realized I needed help. She gave me some good advice on getting Leo more comfortable with going into the kennel whenever I had to leave. Unfortunately, one day I came back from being gone for about an hour and he had broken out of the kennel and had a bloody nose. I did not fully realize how strong his desire to be with me was until this moment. Leo had to have several teeth extracted and two root canals because of the damage he caused biting on the kennel.

After that incident, I was not able to leave him alone without worry. I stopped confining Leo to his kennel and tried leaving him in different rooms of the house. He tore up curtains, blinds, and wood trim trying to get out. Instead of leaving the house, I started begging friends to come over. It was very isolating. In addition to severe separation anxiety, Leo became afraid to go on walks. This started soon after his kennel-breakout incident. We were walking in the neighborhood just fine, but I think Leo's painkiller for his tooth surgery must have worn off, because he was chasing a leaf when all of a sudden his tail went between his legs, and all he wanted to do was go home. From that point on, it took several months to get Leo to go for a walk from the house. I had to put him in the car to go someplace else for a walk.

At one point Leo had free access to the backyard through a doggie door. Leo had broken the fence in the backyard on several occasions to follow me when I left him alone. When I returned, he insisted on getting into the car since I couldn't leave him if he was in there. I decided I needed a new plan for myself and Leo. I got a part-time job for three days a week and seven-hour shifts away from home. I also took Leo to a behavioral veterinarian. She gave Leo some anti-anxiety medications and I re-enlisted the help of a trainer. I also gave Leo free access to the whole house, but locked the doggie door, and installed a pet camera to keep an eye on him.

## *Seizures*

I had had Leo for a few months when I was asked if I would run for president of the Society of Exploration Geophysicists (SEG), an international society of applied geophysicists. I won the election, but it meant that I would be traveling from time to time. I needed to find a suitable boarding facility for Leo. I did find one that Leo seemed to enjoy. They helped get him accustomed to other people and playing with other dogs.

I had to go out of town around Memorial Day, and I arranged for Leo to be boarded. At the boarding facility, the staff members go home after evening feeding and cleaning, so the dogs are left alone. There was a serious thunderstorm during one of the nights. When they came in the following morning, Leo's room was covered with feces and vomit. They called me to come get him because he had been having seizures. Even while they were trying to give him a bath to clean off the vomit, he got aggressive and started seizing again. My daughter went to pick him up, and he had another seizure on the way home. She checked him into the vet hospital, and it took a few days to get his seizures under control. His doctor at the time believed that these seizures were a result an overdose of anti-anxiety medication.

After three calm weeks, I thought the seizures were over. Though I had been told about them, I had never actually witnessed one. But one day, I was sitting in my home office on a conference call with Leo sleeping near me when he suddenly got up and started shaking his head like he had something caught in his throat. After that he went into a massive seizure. A few hours later he had another one as I sat with him. The seizures went on until three in the morning when I finally called the vet and took him to the hospital for treatment.

Leo underwent an MRI, which yielded no obvious reason for the seizures. A new veterinarian thought the seizures could be part of an auto-immune disease. They put him on an anti-inflammatory drug. This helped but did not stop them completely. No one could really pin down what was causing Leo's seizures. Even neurologists could not identify anything definitive. After treating him for several months and having a cluster of seizures every three weeks that could no longer be controlled easily, the veterinarian told me, "You might as well take him home. I don't have any other arrows in my quiver. There's nothing else I can do." I was seriously considering putting Leo to sleep.

In the meantime, I found a pet sitter for Leo, who could stay with him whenever I was not at home. She was a veterinary technician who was experienced in dealing with seizures and who could give him his medications. She fell in love with Leo, and felt strongly that it was not yet time to put him to sleep. At her urging, I consulted with the local pet store where they promoted a raw, ketogenic diet known to help reduce seizures. I also took Leo to a different neurologist, who was much more aggressive with his treatment.

Leo's daily routine now includes four different anti-seizure medications and he is happily seizure-free for nearly two years, except for one episode after breaking into a bag of regular kibble and gorging on that. We would eventually like to reduce his medications, and hope to do so soon. I have a video of almost every seizure he has ever had. That is the only way I could keep track of when they were happening and for how long. It was so sad to see him like that.

## *Love Beyond Measure*

Leo sleeps more than I think he should. He has gained a bit of weight because of the medications. My veterinarian told me, "If it's a choice between having horrible seizures or controlling them and gaining weight, it's okay to be a little bit overweight." As for me, I have been trying to make sure that when Leo wants to play, I drop everything and play, run around with him, and go on lots of walks.

Why have I stuck it out with Leo through all this? Because I just love him. He is like a baby. There was never any doubt in my mind that I would not do whatever it took to help him. Leo picked me to help him. I know people who decided not to go to medical school because of the animal experiments they would have to do. On the other hand, I have another acquaintance who is a professor at a medical school, and when I was talking to her about the plight of research dogs one day, she said, "Well, they're just dogs." That broke my heart.

Leo is a hit at the dog park. I always tell his story and explain why he is different than other dogs and may not be easy to approach. Many people are shocked at the reality that dogs and many other animals are still used in research. Personally, I would like to see legislation that requires very sound scientific reasoning for using any animal to test drugs to be used for people.

Before bed every night, Leo finds his favorite duck toy and buries it in the pillows on my bed. Then he gets down to sleep on his own bed until morning. If I get up first and take a shower, Leo will come out of the bedroom and be curled up on the couch waiting for his breakfast. This is just another "day in the life" with Leo, and I would do it again in a heartbeat.[2]

## Walker

**Breed:** Beagle

**Research History:** In September 2018, there were 13 beagles rescued from a laboratory in the southern United States. Their ages ranged from five months to two years old. The rescue organization Beagle Freedom Project named this group the "Celebration of Survival." No information is available on the type of testing they underwent.

**Adoption:** Walker was adopted in September 2018 at age two by Lily Blavin who lives in Los Angeles, California.

By age 22, when Lily adopted Walker, she had already lived an extraordinary life. From age three she was a professional equestrian competing in hunter jumpers and had won eight national championships. Lily retired from competition at the age of 20 and set her sights on a profession in filmmaking. Lily graduated from college with a degree in liberal arts, and started producing films, including one based on a *New York Times* best-selling book.

Despite her early accomplishments, it is a Beagle Freedom Project (BFP) event she attended in 2014 as a teenager that Lily credits for changing her outlook on life. In fact, she now sits on the board of the BFP and actively works for the rescue organization between producing films. Her myriad tasks include fostering dogs, handling calls from research laboratories, and picking up newly-rescued dogs from the airport.

### Lily

I attended a BFP gala fundraising event in 2014. I had been invited by a friend but had no idea what they did. When I entered the hotel, I saw a few beagles being carried around or being walked on leashes, and I was confused. I later learned that these dogs had been victims of animal experimentation. This reality impacted me so deeply that from that

**Lily Blavin and Walker on his first day of freedom from laboratory life.**

moment forward I decided I would do whatever I could to help these survivors.

I was 20 years old when I was invited to another BFP gala fund-raising event in September 2018. I was a full-time college student living in a one-bedroom apartment at the time. I had already been sitting on the BFP board for a few years. This is where I first met Walker, who had just arrived in Los Angeles after a long drive following his release from the laboratory. He immediately stood out to me because of how sad and broken-down he looked. I jokingly (with a hint of seriousness) said, "I will take him," but was told he already had a foster home lined up.

A few hours later, as the event was winding down, I was told that Walker's foster family had dropped out and the BFP asked if I would take him. Without hesitation, I agreed, on the condition that it was strictly to foster, not adopt. However, by early the next morning, I emailed the BFP adoptions team asking them to send over adoption papers.

Growing up in a dog-loving family, I had lived with at least twenty dogs throughout my childhood. Now, in my apartment, I had two senior rescue chihuahuas, Frederick and Russell. Adding Walker to the mix did not bother me at all. When I agreed to adopt Walker, I had no idea how deep his trauma was, but was told he was one of the "most traumatized dogs that BFP had ever rescued." Indeed, he suffered from severe post-traumatic stress disorder and anxiety. For eight months, I could not pet Walker without his cowering and urinating on himself. He would also run in circles when he got scared, a stress behavior known as *stereotypies,* which in Walker's case probably resulted from him being confined to a small space for years. Walker's circling happened every day for over a year.

Training Walker to go to potty outside out on my apartment's balcony was the toughest part. Even though I have real grass there, at first Walker did not know what grass was, let alone understand why going outside was important. That required a lot of patience. Walker was quiet and sensitive, so I respected that for those first eight months. He preferred to sit on the corner of my bed on the pillows in silence, just observing.

Over time, Walker began venturing out of the bedroom, and soon he began to wander into the living room. This progressed to his joining his Chihuahua "brothers" on walks. Since then, Walker has become the sweetest dog. When he wants cuddles, treats or a meal, he will let me know. A few of his favorite activities are meeting strangers along our fence line and doing "beagle freedom zoomies" as I call them, when he runs around the yard as fast as he can for the fun of it. Other than that, he is a happy couch potato.

Walker had no reason to trust me, but he did. Whenever people compliment Walker, or ask me about him, I say "thank you" and let them know he is a former research animal. I don't know what my future holds because I am still young, but I do know that this issue of rescuing research animals and the Beagle Freedom Project will always be in my life.[3]

# 14

# Two, Three, Four ... Just One Beagle More

Kris and Bert Wood live in California with four laboratory research rescues.

Kris distinctly remembers the incidents that led her to start rescuing laboratory beagles. The first occurred around Thanksgiving 2011 when her mother informed her of 40 laboratory beagles being extricated from a medical testing laboratory in Spain. The rescue organization, Beagle Freedom Project (BFP), had paid for the dogs' transportation to the U.S., and the rescue director Shannon Keith was now putting out urgent calls through the local media for foster homes. Up until this moment, Kris didn't know dogs were still being used for research. She was shocked. Her first thought was to adopt one right away.

She and her husband Bert already had three dogs—two beagles and a German Wirehair Pointer. She remembers her husband saying "We don't need another dog. The last thing I want to do is cart four dogs around in the truck!" Kris, a fourth-grade teacher, tried to put it out of her mind temporarily.

Their five-acre horse ranch in rural Anza, California, was a perfect home for dogs. There was a pond for swimming, three horses, and plenty of space for dogs to explore and play. Bert built and designed three day–event equestrian courses, a sport in which Kris sometimes competed, so the dogs often tagged along for horse shows. In Kris's mind, it was the perfect place and living situation for a traumatized dog to heal and start over.

The second incident happened when she received a new laptop computer for her birthday. The first email she opened was from her sister, also an avid animal lover. The email included video footage of seven newly-rescued laboratory beagles coming out of their crates for the first time. She was overcome with emotion. Her campaign to convince Bert to rescue a laboratory beagle had begun.

Since then, Kris's one-laboratory beagle campaign has turned into four laboratory beagle adoptions. She has become a major advocate for dogs in research and believes that each dog—Chief, Bronco, Roscoe and Wyatt—has changed her life for the better.

## Chief

**Breed:** Beagle

**Research History:** Chief was one of 72 beagles rescued from a testing lab in Barcelona, Spain, in 2011. He was one of 40 dogs transferred to the U.S. for adoption. This group of dogs became known as the "Spanish 40." Chief was used for human drug studies.

**Adoption:** He was adopted in November 2011 at age five.

**Kris Wood and Chief**

### Kris

I wasn't prepared at all to take on Chief. Our first three dogs were from breeders, so I had no idea what to expect with a laboratory rescue dog. I just figured we've got beagles, and I love beagles, so let's get another beagle!

I had been following the Spanish 40 rescue operation and had registered to adopt one of the dogs. I checked the BFP website many times. I waited and waited. Right when I was about to give up, the rescue director Shannon called and said there was a beagle that had just been returned by his foster family and needed a home right away. We were in the car on the way to LA in a heartbeat.

Only a month into his freedom, Chief had already been returned to BFP by his foster homes twice. He had run away from his first home, bolting out of the apartment and becoming lost in downtown Los Angeles for 24 hours. The family was able to find him by hiring a professional dog tracker. Because of this incident, he was labeled a "bolter." Chief next was sent to another foster family. I didn't ask why he had been returned. I just knew I wanted to take him home.

When we first met Chief I was stunned. He was so scared and unsure of everything. He was skinny and had barely any muscle. He had ID tattoos in both ears which usually means they have been in more than one lab. He had dents on the pads of his feet from standing on the wires of the cage for five years. Chief had no personality when we first brought him home. No expression ... nothing. He didn't bark. He hid in the bushes and came out only sometimes to see us. He was petrified of walking through doors, loud noises and anything over his head like ceiling fans. I don't think Chief had feelings at this point ... he was just like, "What are you going to do to me next?"

The first few days were especially challenging. He had no idea how to be a dog, but our other dogs welcomed him right in, and helped him. Chief had to learn everything from scratch. He didn't know how to eat and drink from a bowl and had no social skills with the other dogs. The five acres were a bit overwhelming at first and he would stick to the fence line and just look out. The horses were terrifying and intriguing at the same time. We had to keep eyes on him all the time.

When something is going on that he doesn't like—such as being at the veterinarian, or a getting a bath—he goes into what we call the "mode," signs of post-traumatic stress. He just checks out and stands there, tail down, head down, eyes almost closed, until whatever it is that's happening is over. Chief also has horrible teeth. He's lost almost every single one.

With the help of our other three dogs, and living in such a loving and free environment, these days Chief is over-flowing with personality, very talkative, and has many fun adventures. Some of these adventures are included in a book I wrote about Chief, *From Cage to Couch,* which summarizes Chief's first two years out of the laboratory. Chief has become an ambassador for BFP and we bring him to outreach events to educate people about the realities of animal testing. I strive to purchase only cruelty-free products, and try to persuade others to do the same.

As a fourth-grade teacher, I start the school year introducing myself to my students. Bert has brought Chief into the classroom as part of that. I use Chief's story and other rescue videos of beagles from BFP to educate my students on dogs used for testing. These kids, anywhere between 8 and 10 years of age, are surprisingly affected by it. Some even cry and ask, "Why do they do that?" They have so many questions.

## Bronco

**Breed:** Beagle
**Research History:** Like Chief, Bronco was one of the "Spanish 40"
**Adoption:** He was adopted in 2012 at the age of six.

### Kris

When we brought Bronco home we had four dogs. Chief had now been with us for a year. I was at the one-year reunion party for the Spanish 40 when one of the adopters approached Shannon in tears. They spoke for a while and when we came together to share triumphs of the first year, Shannon said that Bronco was going to need a new home because his fear of the father in the house was getting progressively worse. Bronco had already been with that family for a year.

I shot Bert a text while I was at the party. "There's another Spanish 40" I wrote, and filled him in briefly, including that I wanted to adopt this dog. Bert replied, "See if anyone else will take him." And I texted back, "No ... no one else will take him." Bert is extremely understanding about my rescue missions. He falls in love with these dogs just like I do. Bert has an energy about him that is very quiet and laid back, which is helpful for these traumatized dogs. I also bring home senior hospice dogs from a local dog rescue from time to time, so he supports me in that, too.

From his first family's description, Bronco's fear of their father was extreme. They would take Bronco for walks and he would not want to go back to the house. They would have to go pick him up in the car. And Bronco would never want to be in the same room with the father. The more I thought about it, the more I started to panic. "Oh my God," I thought. " If he's that scared maybe we won't be able to help him either."

Before the family came to drop him off, I had a bit of a meltdown. Bert was out of town, so I was alone to handle the introduction to my dog pack. As it turned out, I was worried for nothing. When Bronco arrived, he jumped out of that car and never looked back, not even when they were ready to leave. I felt kind of bad, but I couldn't help thinking this was going to be a better situation for him. I was so happy to watch him run off with my other dogs—like he was finally home!

**Bronco enjoying a boat ride.**

Bronco turned out to be, even a year out of the lab, much more skittish than Chief. Like Chief, he had ID tattoos in both ears, meaning he may have been in two different labs, and he too had horrible teeth, about half lost. He had a large scar on his hock where the hair never grew back and his gait was very unorthodox.

Bronco was leery of Bert, but not as badly as I feared. He settled in well, except for being frightened of loud noises and voices, ceiling fans, and the fire alarm chirping. We couldn't even watch a program on television if a fire alarm chirped in the program. Bronco would run outside and fall apart emotionally.

We have a pond and Bronco loved to swim. Over time, he turned out to be one of my happiest dogs and one who was most comforting. With our hospice rescues he would just be quiet and let them sit with him. With me, he always seemed to know when I was sad.

He was very particular, almost obsessive, about some things. For example, he had "his chair." When a guest would come over and sit in Bronco's chair, Bronco would just sit there and look at the person as if to say, "That's my chair ... that's my chair ... that's my chair." The same was true of his special spot in our truck. If he wasn't in his spot he would start to lose it.

Bronco was a very soulful guy. Which is weird, because many dogs out of the lab are so apathetic. We called him the Drama King. Bronco passed away from hemangiosarcoma, a type of cancer in 2019. He had the physical as well as the mental scars to really show what he went through.

# Roscoe

**Breed:** Beagle

**Research History:** Released from unknown research studies on the East Coast.

**Adoption:** He was adopted in 2017 at the age of six months.

## Kris

We were ready for a new addition when the Beagle Freedom Project happened to need a foster home for a six-month-old beagle from Georgia. About Roscoe's background we knew only that he'd been in a laboratory for those six months. The BFP wanted us to foster him for only a short while because a "big-name person in Hollywood" wanted to adopt him. The BFP flew Roscoe from Georgia out here to California. But the Hollywood arrangement fell through, thank God, because I could not have given him up. We hadn't had a puppy in a very long time, and I had completely forgotten what having a puppy was like.

Like our other two rescued beagles, Roscoe was very skittish and scared. He was petrified of his collar. Without it, he was fine. But when I put it on he would roll in the dirt to get it off, then go to his safe place on our bed, and freeze. Once, he went almost two days without eating or

*Left to right:* **Wyatt, Chief, and Roscoe**

drinking because of the collar. We called in a dog trainer to help us with the collar issue. It broke my heart that Roscoe had already been in a lab and had a tattoo in his ear. But I also felt relieved that it was for only six months.

## Wyatt

**Breed:** Beagle
**Research History:** Unknown
**Adoption:** He was adopted in 2020 at the estimated age of four.

### Kris

It was spring and someone had reached out to Shannon at the Beagle Freedom Project about a dog in San Diego that needed to be saved. The experience was very unusual and hush-hush. Was this a dog that had been stolen out of a laboratory? Possibly, because it was about the time when many labs were shutting down due to the coronavirus pandemic. But the man who called Shannon provided no details. Instead, he said "I will talk only to you. I will see only you. This is where we have to meet...."

Wyatt is obviously a lab dog, with the tattoo to prove it, and every emotional characteristic. But we have no idea where he's from, how long he's been out, or anything about him. I was extremely nervous about taking Wyatt on.

During his first vet visit we discovered he had ridges on his teeth, most likely from chewing the bars of his cage. He is by far the most scared rescue we've had to date. He does everything he can to run away from most people. I've had moments of panic, thinking we may not be able to help him. Wyatt's tail stayed tucked tight against his rear for a long time. After three months he finally started to wag and carry it up. He bonded very quickly to Roscoe and they have become very close, playing hard all the time.

Wyatt is a "runner": When he gets scared or unsure his first instinct is to run away. He also becomes obsessed over certain things for long periods of time. For example, he began sniffing the fence line of our yard for days, to the point we've had to physically bring him into the house. The few times I have taken Wyatt out on "field trips" his incredible fear is a conversation starter. Many people ask why he is the way he is. I don't think people truly understand what lab dogs go through until they see the remnants of it in an actual dog. Rescuing lab dogs is probably one of the most rewarding things I've ever done.

* * *

While animal rescue groups fund rescue activities, they often cannot fund follow-up medical care for adopted animals. After paying for three dog knee surgeries and losing Bronco to cancer, I understood acutely how expensive medical care can be. So, in 2019 I started a 501c3 charity called the "Cowboy and Rousseau Animal Assistance Fund," whose mission is to raise and provide funds for the medical care of adopted animals with severe illnesses and injuries. The fund is named after two dogs—Cowboy, my first beagle, and Rousseau, a friend's laboratory rescue beagle, who both died of cancer. The fund is open to any rescued dog, not just laboratory dogs.[1]

* * *

Diane and Bruce Vanderpool live in Colorado with two laboratory research rescues:

## *Boomer and Koln*

## Boomer

**Breed:** Beagle

**Research History:** Boomer came from a laboratory on the East Coast in July 2016, where he was used for food studies. The laboratory put Boomer, three other dogs, and a number of cats on a tractor trailer bound for California with other cargo. All the animals were in small crates barely big enough for turning around. They had nothing to eat or drink for the entire trip, which lasted 36 hours.

By the time they arrived at Kindness Ranch Animal Sanctuary in Wyoming, all the dogs and cats were covered in feces and soaked in urine. Boomer, age seven, and another beagle named April, age ten, needed multiple baths because they smelled so foul. As a Kindness Ranch staff member recalled, "I could see the humiliation in their eyes and demeanor that first day. They could barely walk when they arrived."

**Koln, Bruce Vanderpool, Boomer, and Diane Vanderpool on adoption day at Kindness Ranch.**

## Koln

**Breed:** Beagle

**Research History:** Koln was bred in Fort Collins, Colorado, specifically for laboratory testing. He was released from a laboratory in September 2016 at age two. No information is available on what he was used for.

**Adoption:** Both Boomer and Koln were adopted in October 2016 by Diane and Bruce Vanderpool who live in Woodland Park, Colorado.

Bruce has always had an interest in creating something beautiful out of something ordinary. His woodworking business began as nothing more than a hobby. In his spare time, he learned the art of crafting wood with a scroll saw, creating intricate pieces for the purpose of giving them away as gifts for friends and family. Using only collected pieces of dead or discarded wood, Bruce creates mountain-themed wall hangings, lamps, bowls and tables in the workshop behind their house.

Attending up to 12 art shows together each year, Bruce and his wife

Diane share another common interest: their love for rescuing beagles. They had already adopted three beagles together. Six months after their eldest beagle's passing at age 17, they were ready to adopt another. However, what was supposed to be an ordinary adoption process for Bruce and Diane turned into a fortuitous turn of events.

## Diane

### *A Lucky Surprise*

Our last beagle had died in March 2016, and we were without a dog for the first time in many years. We knew we were going to adopt a research dog, because we had been looking into that for a long time. I stopped buying cosmetics tested on animals years ago, and through my involvement in animal rescue, I had become aware that dogs are still used in research.

We had friends who adopted a beagle from Kindness Ranch, so we filled out the paperwork to do the same. We were just a few days away from going on vacation when Kindness Ranch sent me a picture of a beagle named Koln (originally known as Sarge). I looked at him, and something pulled at my heartstrings. I told Bruce, "I think we're ready."

We came back from vacation, knowing Koln was waiting for us. The next weekend, we eagerly drove the five hours it took to get to Kindness Ranch. When we arrived, several staff members took us into the dog play area to meet Koln. I remember that Koln pretty much ignored us. As we were sitting on a bench watching the dogs, another beagle jumped up between us and looked right at Bruce. The staff introduced him as Boomer. Boomer would not take his eyes off Bruce the entire time we talked. We all thought that was interesting.

They asked if we would like to take Koln for a walk, and added, "Would you like to take Boomer also?" We said, "Well, sure!" As we were walking, we noticed that Koln was very skittish, but walked well on a leash. We also noted that every time Boomer stopped to sniff something or lift his leg, Koln followed and did what Boomer did.

I knew from a lot of reading on rescuing research dogs that it often helps to have another dog in the household who is more confident. We already knew we were going to get a second dog. What we couldn't have known was that this second dog would be right here, right now. As we were walking, Boomer stayed very close to my husband. When we got back from our stroll, my husband said to me adamantly, "We can't leave him here. I think Boomer will teach Koln what we can't: how to be a dog."

Even the ranch staff could see in Boomer's eyes that he had chosen my husband as "his person." The sad thing about Boomer was that other dogs would get adopted before him, because everyone thought he was too old. We had adopted our previous beagle from a shelter at age seven, so to us, his age was no big deal. We went to Kindness Ranch to adopt one beagle and came home with two. The night we came home from the ranch, Boomer immediately found my husband's lap, and hasn't given it up since.

## *Patience, Love and Training*

### Diane

Boomer was quite overweight when we got him. We're lucky because our home borders a national forest, giving us access to many trails. Both dogs get walked two to three miles every day, so we were able to get the weight off Boomer fairly quickly. Boomer likes every person he meets, and thinks every person wants to be his friend. He likes other dogs, too. He is an all-around social boy.

Koln, on the other hand, was extremely scared of people, as we soon found out. When we first got home from Kindness Ranch, I put both dogs on leashes and led them into our small, fenced backyard to let them go to the bathroom after the long drive. It took Bruce and me 45 minutes to catch Koln to go inside the house, because he was so afraid of us. His eyes were bugged out, and he was running around in panic mode. I finally was able to grab his collar and calm him down. Bruce and I looked at each other and thought, "Oh my gosh, what have they done to you that you are this afraid?" After this incident we attached Koln to a long rope in the backyard, so we could get him back inside easily. We did that until he got used to approaching us without fear.

We invested in dog training for both dogs. We also have a friend who does "healing touch" on animals, which is incredible to watch, especially with Koln, because he loves it so much. Koln is wired differently. He hasn't developed mentally in some areas. We call him our special needs boy. He doesn't grasp concepts like a regular dog and seems to still have behavioral traits of a puppy.

Koln also has severe separation anxiety. If I get into my car and drive away to go to work, he's fine. But if I leave the house on foot and I'm still on the property somewhere, pulling weeds for example, he goes into a barking frenzy to the point I worry he'll injure himself. If he knows I'm around, but he's not with me, he can work himself into a stupor. The situation with

Bruce was the opposite. It was about a year before Koln started coming to him. He would run from the room whenever Bruce walked in.

### Bruce

Koln now comes to sit with me on the couch and lets me pet him. However, when I stand up he will not come near me.

To take Koln for a walk, I have to walk out to the porch—to be outside. He loves going for a walk and runs circles around me in excitement. But he will not come to me inside the house for his leash and harness. Koln walks great with me. When we come back to the house, I take his harness off, and give him a treat. Then he won't come near me again until it's time to go to bed.

### Diane

Boomer and Koln accompany us to art shows where we display and sell Bruce's woodworking creations. People often comment on the dogs, and this gives us an opportunity to educate them on the realities of animal testing. It also gives Kohn exposure to being around other people. While Koln still has his quirks, after years of patience, love, and training, we can happily say that Koln now prefers to sleep next to Bruce in bed at night. It has been amazing to witness Koln's journey of growth, and Boomer's instant connection to Bruce. These dogs went from being discarded pieces of laboratory equipment to beautiful and valued members of our family.[2]

* * *

Sasha lives in Colorado with two laboratory research rescues:

## *Elliot and Bodhi*

**Adoption:** Both Elliot and Bodhi were adopted by Sasha who lives in California. Sasha adopted Elliot at 16 weeks old in June 2016. She adopted Bodhi at age two and a half in September 2018.

Sasha's two dogs Cooper and Carley were her constant and beloved companions. She had purchased a home with a large backyard just for the dogs. She used to hike several times a week with Cooper, a Wheaten terrier, until he developed a debilitating cervical spinal stenosis. Carley, a Chihuahua beagle mix, was very connected to Cooper, and together they made a happy trio.

Sasha became aware of the rescue group Beagle Freedom Project (BFP) early in 2016. She knew that the pharmaceutical and medical industries did animal testing, but until she heard about it through the BFP she never understood the extent to which dogs are still being used in research experiments. Struggling to grasp the plight of dogs in research, she resolved to champion the work of the BFP. Using her professional skills in marketing, communications and advertising, Sasha began volunteering for the Project, helping with rescue and special events, and garnering media attention for the cause.

## Elliot

**Breed:** Beagle

**Research History:** Elliot was part of a young group of dogs rescued by the Beagle Freedom Project in June 2016. This group was named the "LA 5," and included five dogs ranging in age from 16 weeks to three years old. It is unclear whether Elliot was used for research "in utero" or if she was a "discard." A "discard" is a dog that is purposefully bred for some type of research, but for some reason can't or doesn't end up getting used. "Discards" are usually killed. Elliot was to be euthanized.

**Elliot on her first day of freedom from laboratory life.**

## Sasha

I was helping the BFP with public relations for a rescue release in Los Angeles. Cooper was very ill and I had been thinking about adopting another dog out of deep concern for Carley, who I knew would be devastated when the time came for Cooper to leave us. It was nothing more than a thought, because I worried about introducing a new dog into our home while Cooper's health was failing. Would it be too upsetting?

While I was at the release event, I asked one of the BFP team members whether they had fosters for all the dogs. I knew that sometimes fosters and adopters are not in the immediate area and may need to travel to get their dog. I thought, "If they need a foster home for a night or two, I could do that." When I offered, their response was, "Thank you. We're covered." So, I went about the day working with media and interacting with guests.

A little while later, the adoption coordinator approached me and said they did in fact need a foster for a few nights. Again, I questioned whether it was the right thing to do, thinking about Cooper who needed a lot of care. I didn't think a puppy was a great fit and hoped for one of the older dogs. Then, they placed one of the puppies in my arms. Oh my gosh … how could I say "no" to that! I kept asking, "It's only for a night or two, right?" They kept assuring me, yes.

The puppy's name was Loretta and she was only 16 weeks old. She was very precocious and confident. I took her home and was quickly becoming attached to her spunky, sweet personality. Knowing adoption was an option, that night, I called to ask how long I had before they needed to know if I would keep her. They told me to take all the time I needed. A few days later, I called to ask if I could keep her. She became Elliot, aka Ellie, and her adoption was finalized on June 30, the anniversary of my father's passing the year before.

Even as a puppy, Elliot was so wise and knowing, and very gentle with Cooper. I have a video of her coaxing him out of bed when he was struggling to walk. Elliot would pull him gently by the face out to the yard. It was amazing to watch. Despite my worries, Elliot caused no stress, no jealousy. Instead, she brought us all so much joy and positive energy, and Cooper loved her.

Cooper passed away on September 15, just a few months after Elliot's arrival. Carley took Cooper's death very hard, as I suspected she would. Elliot saved both of us during that difficult time. Even though she's tiny for a beagle, weighing in at only 20 pounds, she has the gift of being a great healer. She has an uncanny ability to calm other anxious rescue dogs and show them the ropes.

# Bodhi

**Breed:** Beagle

**Research History:** In September 2018, there were 12 beagles rescued from a laboratory in the southern United States. Their ages ranged from five months to two years old. The rescue organization Beagle Freedom Project named this group the "Celebration of Survival." No information is available on the type of testing they underwent.

## Sasha

Bodhi (initially named "Parker") was part of a highly anticipated BFP rescue including a dozen dogs coming from a laboratory across the country. There was a need for foster homes for these dogs, and I volunteered to help under the strict agreement that I would just foster. I already had three dogs at this time, and I was managing some significant professional changes in my life. It was not the right time to add another dog to our pack.

**Bodhi ... could there be paper for me on this desk?**

On the day of the release, I didn't care which dog I was given to foster. I just wanted to give one of them a good start to their new life. A BFP team member asked if I would be willing to take one of the higher-trauma dogs, named Bodhi. They felt my home would be a good environment to begin his recovery.

By the time Bodhi arrived at my house he was in great distress. He arrived with another dog from the lab, who also spent the night with us until his foster family could get him the next day. Bodhi frantically ran and paced the fence line of my house. He was confused and frightened of everything. He peed on anything in sight: the walls, the floors, and the furniture. He slept sitting up in a doorway with his lab mate curled at his feet. But even on that first, most stressful evening, I could see the sweetness in his eyes. He just had to learn to trust.

After two days, I could no longer bear how badly Bodhi smelled. The odor coming from him was a mixture of urine and a musty, hospital smell. It was time to give Bodhi a bath. He was terrified, so we took it very slowly. Even so, my t-shirt was in tatters at the end of the ordeal from his clawing and panicking, but he soon surrendered and allowed me to cleanse him—removing another layer of life in the lab.

Besides smelling bad, Bodhi had a number of physical ills. He was very thin. His ribs protruded so badly that I thought they would cut through his skin. He was 16 pounds when I got him, at least half the weight of an average beagle. Bodhi is now 24 pounds, still thin, but healthy.

At first Bodhi wasn't very stable on his feet. He had never run before, and he stumbled and fell a lot. Bodhi also suffered from gastroenteritis, which took months to get under control. I ended up fostering him for longer than expected because of this, and we became very bonded. And so, from fostering I moved to adopting Bodhi. He was our boy and completed our pack.

## *An Odd Paper Obsession*

Bodhi has an odd obsession with paper. He is fast and sneaky and will do just about anything to get to a paper towel, tissue, desk papers, calendar, or any other paper product. If I get up from my home office desk and leave the room, he will run in, put his paws up on the desk, and search for any paper left there that he can grab. He tears it apart and eats it. The first several weeks his stools contained wads of paper!

I've gotten good at limiting Bodhi's access to paper by closing all doors in the house where there might be paper, like the bathrooms. Sometimes Bodhi gets paper anyway. If the mail arrives while I'm in another room, Bodhi will grab it. He's my personal postal delivery system.

## *Rescue Dogs Award Show*

Steadily, Bodhi has gained confidence. Little by little I showed him the comforts of carpet, a sofa and a bed. A few minutes at a time was all he could handle, but each time his trust grew. Now he is the most affectionate, happy, and loving dog.

On February 16, 2020, the Hallmark Channel aired the first night of their 2020 *American Rescue Dog Show.* Mixed breeds and purebreds vie for top honors over the two-night event in categories that include Best in Special Needs, Best Ears, and Best in Underbite. Taping for the show took place in Los Angeles, and the BFP had a large group of dogs that were part of the "Best Ears" competition. I took both Elliot and Bodhi to be a part of that. They trotted around and showed their ears to the judges. Bodhi was very nervous about the whole thing, but it helped that his social butterfly sister Elliot was with him, showing off in style.

Being a mom to a research dog survivor is very much a lifestyle. My closest friends are women who have rescued dogs from labs, and all of my purchases are driven by a product's cruelty-free status. I help educate and guide others to live a cruelty-free life. Elliot and Bodhi have changed my life profoundly. They remind me every day that life and freedom are so very precious.[3]

# 15

# Beagles Take a Hike … Adventures in the Outdoors

## Winnie

**Breed:** Beagle

**Research History:** Winnie was used in multiple research studies, including a flea and tick study and a human drug study. She has a tattoo on her belly and another in her ear. No other details are known.

**Adoption:** She was adopted in May 2014 at age four by Shannon and Joe Malone who live in Bozeman, Montana.

**Winnie hiking on a mountain trail in Montana.**

Known for world-renowned fly fishing, dramatic mountains for hiking, mountain biking, rock climbing, skiing, hunting, backcountry exploring, and impressive wildlife, Bozeman, Montana, is an outdoor lover's paradise. Picture cowboys herding free-range cattle on horseback, high-mountain meadows full of purple and yellow wildflowers, bison roaming in the distance, and big blue sky as far as the eye can see. That is the backdrop for one fortunate laboratory beagle's new beginning.

It is as stark a contrast to the indoor florescent lights and steel cage bars of a laboratory dog's sterile life as one could imagine. Yet, these two worlds intersected serendipitously one spring day when Shannon and Joe, avid hikers and campers, decided to adopt a beagle named Winnie.

## Shannon

My husband and I already had two beagles. When our older beagle, Mac, passed on, we knew we wanted to adopt another beagle. I was looking on Petfinder one day and discovered Kindness Ranch Animal Sanctuary in Wyoming. We loved their mission of providing sanctuary to former research animals, and that was something we wanted to support.

Since we love hiking and camping, we were searching for a beagle to include in our adventures and be a buddy for our female beagle Kraken. It was strange because when we were looking at dogs on the Kindness Ranch website, Winnie was not listed there. Even when I was emailing Kindness Ranch about adopting one of their dogs, she was not one of the dogs mentioned to us as a possibility.

Initially, we were interested in getting a male beagle. However, upon our arrival at Kindness Ranch and a visit to the cottage where all the male dogs were living, we did not find one that we really connected with. So, we went over to the cottage where the female beagles were being kept. My husband was sitting there watching the dogs that were being shown to us when we noticed a beagle named Winnie who was still in her kennel. She was staring up at Joe with her big, beautiful eyes and wagging her tail. A Kindness Ranch caretaker noticed this too and said "Oh, she's picking you out!" So, they let her out of her kennel, and she went right over to Joe.

Winnie was a little nervous when we first got her, especially on the car ride home. She was panting and wide-eyed the whole way. For the first week she stayed in her crate, but we were lucky because her anxiety was minimal compared to other laboratory beagles I've heard about. It helped that we already had Kraken to show her how to use the doggy door to go outside.

At first Winnie was timid. Over a month or so, she started to open up. I remember how excited she was to discover her toys in the toy basket. I also remember one of the first times she played with Kraken. They were chasing each other around the house. Unfortunately, Winnie was not accustomed to stairs and she slid down them while chasing Kraken. She was uninjured and kept playing. One of her biggest fears was riding in the car. That changed the first time she got brave enough to put her snout out of the window and take a whiff of the passing breeze. From that moment on she became okay with riding in the car. Now she is better at it than Kraken.

Winnie is the sweetest, most docile dog. She is extremely motivated by food and likes to snuggle and play outside. Winnie has brought much happiness and love to our family. She loves walks, toys, food, and love from her people. Winnie especially loves camping. She has the natural instinct to dig little dens when we are at our campsite, and she is very good at it. She also loves to sniff all the gopher holes around the tent, and sleep in my sleeping bag. To date Winnie has hiked roughly 730 miles since we adopted her, and she loves it! She has also camped and traveled all over Montana, Wyoming, and Idaho.

We tell Winnie's story whenever we have the chance. I think it is good to share our research dog's story because it makes it more real. She sadly has the tattoos on her ear and belly that mark her forever. When I show these to people it really hits home. These animals are living beings. They were not created for the purpose of research and cruelty, or to be bred for humans to use as "things," and a means to an end. In the case of Kindness Ranch, they are angels who are giving these dogs a chance to experience life.[1]

## Scarlet

**Breed:** Beagle

**Research History:** In August 2012, four mother beagles and seven puppies were rescued from a Northern California research laboratory by the Beagle Freedom Project (BFP). Scarlet was one of the mothers. All the mother beagles were young, and they had already had their puppies when the BFP rescued them. The laboratory did not know which puppies belonged to which mother. Tests were performed on the puppies "in vitro," meaning while in the womb.

**Brigitte Pascual and Scarlet hiking the Switzer Falls Trail in California.**

**Adoption:** Scarlet was adopted in October 2012 at age one by Brigitte Pascual who lives in Glendale, California.

Within thirty minutes of Los Angeles County and the city of Glendale are hundreds of hiking trails. The Angeles National Forest, San Gabriel Mountains, and Griffith Park are a few of Brigitte's favorite areas to train for mountaineering. She has summited Mount Kilimanjaro, a 19,341-foot dormant volcano in Tanzania, and successfully trekked to Everest Base Camp at 17,650 feet in Khumbu, Nepal. Brigitte has also completed the Tour du Mont Blanc, a famous hike around the Alps through France, Switzerland, and Italy. It was on a local training hike with friends and her beagle Heidi when Brigitte first learned that beagles were being used for research.

## Brigitte

Our hiking group included my friend and my friend's cousin. The hike was around ten miles. When we finished, my friend's cousin said she wasn't going to bring this up because it might upset me, but asked if I was aware that companies did research on beagles. At the time I was not aware of this. She said she used to work at Pfizer, a pharmaceutical corporation headquartered in New York City. She told me they did research on beagles, and that the laboratory where this research was done was so secret that employees of the company couldn't access it.

When I arrived home that evening, I immediately started researching online about testing on beagles. This is when I stumbled upon the Beagle Freedom Project. I felt sadness and disbelief. I have been a beagle-owner for a long time and beagles have a special place in my heart. After finding out about animal testing, I wanted to do whatever I could to help. At this time I had my eight-year-old beagle Heidi and had just purchased a house. I thought it was time to rescue another dog and decided to reach out to the BFP.

I put my name in to adopt a beagle named Savannah that I saw on the BFP website. A week later I received a phone call which was more like an interview. I was asked at the end of the call if I wanted to come and meet Savannah. I was very excited and scheduled a date and time to visit. When I got there, I sat in the courtyard of the BFP director's home, where the newly-rescued beagles were being kept. I held Savannah on my lap. While I was sitting with Savannah, another sweet little dog kept coming over to see me. I felt a connection right away with this other dog whose name was Scarlet. However, there was another couple there looking to adopt Scarlet. As it turned out, Savannah also had others looking to adopt her, and it was decided that another family would be a better fit.

As I drove home, I couldn't get little Scarlet out of my mind. Not long afterwards, I got another call from the BFP. They told me that Savannah had been adopted, but that Scarlet was still available and did I want her. My heart started to pound faster. I immediately said, "Yes!" What struck me most about Scarlet when she first arrived at my house was that she had no leg muscles. Her legs were as thin as sticks. She was underweight. She was uncoordinated. My guess is that she wasn't out of her cage much in the laboratory, if at all.

The first time I took Scarlet for a walk, everything scared her. The sound of stepping on a leaf. The sound of the wind or a car passing by. Luckily, Scarlet bonded with me right away, and she has been my little shadow ever since. Scarlet's gait is also very unusual. When she walks, she doesn't bend her knees, but instead swings her legs out to the side. Her walk resembles more of a "waddle" to the point that people comment on it. Thankfully, she doesn't have any pain associated with this issue.

My beagles have always trained with me for my mountaineering adventures. Heidi helped me train for my hike up Mount Kilimanjaro. We would run canyons together for at least six miles several times per week. When I got Scarlet, we started hiking in the Angeles National Forest together. Hiking helped build muscles in her legs, and she also loved it. We still hike regularly; however, now that she has gotten older, I try to limit our hikes to three or four miles.

What many people don't know about beagles is that they are working dogs. If they are used for hunting, they are out running all day looking for rabbits. Beagles are also very adaptable. They can be the greatest couch potato or, like my beagles, little athletes. When I pull their leashes out, my beagles go wild with excitement. They enjoy going out, although I have learned to be patient because there's a lot of sniffing time associated with hiking beagles.

I spent a lot of time volunteering and fostering for the BFP. I was always impressed by how resilient these dogs were after everything they had experienced.

After adopting Scarlet, I adopted another mother dog, a little pit bull with puppies named Abigail, who was found in a high-kill shelter. Then, in July 2018 I adopted yet another mother beagle, named Maddie, rescued from a laboratory. Because my first beagle, Heidi, had also been a rescued beagle mom, at one point I had four mother dogs living in my home. Needless to say, Mother's Day is a very special occasion in my household.[2]

## Dug

**Breed:** Beagle
**Research History:** Dug was rescued from an undisclosed phar-

maceutical laboratory with 11 other beagles. He and one other dog from the group had seizures from drug withdrawals a short time after they were released from the lab. No information is available on what type of testing they endured.

**Dug (*left*) and his buddy Chunky on a hike in Colorado.**

**Adoption:** Dug was adopted in June 2019 at age five by Lillian and Niels Larson who live in Erie, Colorado. After years of traversing the country between New York, Connecticut, Pennsylvania, and California for school and work, Lillian and Niels finally settled down in Erie, Colorado. Just a short drive from Boulder and the Rocky Mountains, they enjoyed hiking every weekend with their then-only dog Chunky, a puggle they adopted in 2014 at the age of one. Chunky accompanied them everywhere, from hikes and dog parks to outdoor patio dining and road trips.

Chunky was quite particular about what other dogs were allowed in the home, so when Lillian and Niels decided to adopt another dog, Chunky had a say in the matter. After fostering a few dogs Chunky did not form a bond with from a local animal shelter, Lillian and Niels became aware of a rescue organization called Kindness Ranch in Wyoming, only a three-hour drive away. The ranch's unique "guest yurt" accommodations for potential adopters to test a new dog in a home setting appealed to them. Chunky would accompany them and help choose his new buddy.

## Lillian

Once we learned about the mission of Kindness Ranch, we were excited to understand more and play a part in helping these research dogs. When we adopted Chunky, he too had been skittish and timid, so we felt confident that we could help a dog with this background.

On the Kindness Ranch website we saw a beagle named Dug, and we decided we wanted to meet him. However, once we arrived, the ranch director thought that Dug would not be a good fit for our active lifestyle, because Dug refused to walk while on a leash. We live in a townhome, so any dog we adopted would need to adjust to walking on a leash with us to go outside.

## Niels

Since Dug did not seem to be the best option, we were introduced to three other beagles at the ranch. Chunky's opinion on what dog we chose was paramount. We would adjust our lives accordingly. Chunky did not connect with any of these dogs, and even got grumpy with one of them. When Dug was eventually introduced to the group, Dug went right up to Chunky, and the two of them walked off together. Dug had chosen his buddy, and Chunky had accepted him.

As for us, Dug was wary and stayed an arm's-length away. We asked if we could take Dug back with us to the guest yurt for the night for a trial run, which did not go very well. Dug was a basket case. He did not want to hang around us. We tried to take him for a walk, which turned out to be impossible. He just sat there. It took a lot for him to get moving. He was very shut down.

While Dug did sleep with us and Chunky in the bed that night, there was not a lot of change in his behavior the next morning. He did not acknowledge us. We had to make a decision. We asked ourselves, "Is this a too big a challenge for us?" Since Dug would not walk on a leash, would I literally have to carry him every time he had to go out? And how long would that last? We voiced our concerns, but we wanted to give Dug a chance.

## Lillian

When I first met Dug, I was not sure that he was all there mentally. The ranch director let us know that Dug had seizures when they first rescued him. The ranch brought in neurologists from Boulder who determined it was probably drug withdrawal that caused the seizures. They gave him a clean bill of health and said he would mostly likely not have any more.

Along with his completely shut down behavior, we questioned our capabilities for taking on such a dog. Dug, however, gave us reason to hope when he finally let us pet him. When we first arrived home, Dug was afraid of many things. He did not like being cornered, tight spaces, or doorways, and did not trust the food we gave him. He "safe-zoned" on particular pieces of furniture in each room of the house. Anytime he saw us he would run and jump on his safe spot and observe us from there. He also had many accidents in the house.

While he was unsure of his leash and harness, with some encouragement Dug quickly learned to walk with us. We typically walk two to four miles daily around the neighborhood. At first Dug would plop down and not want to walk any more. Often, I would be stuck on the road and have to call Niels to come home from work to pick us up. Luckily Niels and I have flexible work schedules and are able to take Dug and Chunky on longer walks, or drive to a dog park. Dug even comes to work with me occasionally to see different scenery. We place a lot of emphasis on exercising our dogs' bodies and minds.

## Niels

Dug cannot bark. Instead of the typical beagle bay, he makes a rough grumbly noise. When he tries to howl, a little squeak comes out. We are sure that is because the laboratory removed his vocal chords, as they often do to keep the dogs from barking.

Before getting Dug, I was ignorant of the fact that beagles are used in research. I would notice the cruelty-free label on products and it was always a rabbit. No offense to rabbits, as I believe all life should be respected, but I thought research was being done on rats and bunnies. I was oblivious to it. When I found out dogs are also used for research, I immediately downloaded the Cruelty Cutter app on my phone and scanned everything in our house.

Everything Dug does warrants a picture because he finds the cutest ways to display his emotions. For example, he loves eggs. As soon as an egg is being cooked, Dug knows and he will get up from wherever he is and start sniffing. Once the egg is being served he loses all control. He tries to climb on the table for eggs. He will do whatever he possibly can to get the eggs. If I'm walking up the stairs with a plate of eggs, he's tripping over himself like he forgot how to walk up stairs. I have never seen a dog act like that before. He has normal dog behavior for chicken or steak, but he goes completely crazy for eggs.

Lillian and I are relatively logical people and go with the flow. We are never really "down" in life. These days, whenever there is a problem at work or at any point in life I look at Dug. He spent five years in a laboratory cage with some degree of suffering during that time. Now he is a happy dog, always wagging his tail. If Dug can do it, how can I not bounce back from something tough in my life?

When we would first take Dug to the dog park, you could tell something was "off" about him. People would ask us why he was so skittish. It was great segue for us to talk about Dug as a laboratory beagle. But we do not get those questions anymore. He is just like a normal dog.[3]

# 16

# Wild West Beagles

## Texas

### *"Texas McGee Killer Talsma"*

**Breed:** Beagle

**Research History:** Texas was rescued from an undisclosed laboratory by Kindness Ranch Animal Sanctuary. No information is available on what type of research he was used for.

**Adoption:** He was adopted in August 2017 at age four by Nicki S. and Wayne T. who live in Belle Fourche, South Dakota.

On the northern slopes of the world-famous Black Hills in Western South Dakota, Texas McGee Killer Talsma, or "Texas" for short, officially lives in the Wild West. The town of Belle Fourche, where Texas lives with Nicki and Wayne, was officially designated in 1959 as the "Geographic Center of the Nation." Legendary Western figures such as Wild Bill Hickok and Calamity Jane frequented this area at one time, and gold was discovered nearby in the late 1800s. It is a place where the West still rings true and people still say "howdy." It is also the place where Texas "struck it rich" with his new family.

#### Nicki

We had just lost our 17-year-old Labrador retriever, Chloe, in July 2017. She had been Wayne's dog. When I met Wayne, Chloe was eight years old, so she became my dog, too. Chloe was a "once in a lifetime" dog and losing her was devastating for Wayne and me. I knew our next dog had big shoes to fill.

I thought Wayne would wait a few months before looking for another dog, but he started looking soon after Chloe's death. We wanted a second dog to keep our other dog Maxwell, a beagle, company. I just left it up to him. I said to Wayne, "You'll know when you want another dog, and you'll know what kind of dog you want when you see it." It didn't matter to me what type of dog we got.

Wayne started looking around at local shelters and at all different breeds. He happened to see a photo of Texas online one day, standing in a play-bow stance, and he said to me, "I think I want that one." I put in our application to Kindness Ranch to adopt Texas, and we did a phone interview. Once our application was approved, we packed up Maxwell and all three of us traveled down to Kindness Ranch in Wyoming, about a three-hour drive from Belle Fourche, to pick up Texas.

Texas was outside when we met him, and he was very shy. He sniffed us a little bit, but mostly kept his distance. He also met Maxwell, and they seemed to get along fine, which was great. "Shy" and "timid" were words I used to describe Texas when we first got home. But looking back I think he was instead terrified. He was hesitant to do anything in the beginning and would shut down regularly. His shut-downs are a super-submissive mode where he sits, makes no eye contact, drops his head, and doesn't move. There is no alertness about him, he looks sad, and his eyes are dull. Texas remained in shut-down mode for the first few days after we got him. He had his tail tucked all the time, wrapped around him.

**Wayne, beagles Texas and Maxwell, and Nicki**

At the time we got Texas I was working at a dog boarding and daycare facility. I had seen many dog demeanors, attitudes, and behaviors on the job, but I had never seen anxiety and submissiveness as severe as Texas had. It took longer than I thought for Texas to come around to us, and we were at a loss for what to do to help him feel better. We talked about the possibility that we'd bitten off more than we could chew. However, we knew how much we were able to offer Texas. He needed our help, and we buckled down and started getting back into some daily routines.

Maxwell was happy as a clam to have another dog around again. While Texas would follow Maxwell all around, he remained reserved to us. Whenever we would try to pet Texas he would sit, look away, and go into shut-down mode. After a few months Texas became less shy around me, but continued to be wary of Wayne. Eventually, though, Texas came around to him, too.

We noticed other odd behaviors, such as his strange attention to detail. If anything is out of place or moved, such as pictures on the wall, he gets obsessed with that spot. We have to put him in his kennel until his attention shifts. He also has a propensity to look upward a lot. Clouds scared him at first, but that has gotten better. He will still just randomly look up high whenever he's inside or outside. He definitely has quirks, enough that I lovingly call him my "little weirdo."

Texas is the best little sitter in South Dakota! If you walk up to him he automatically sits, whether you tell him to or not. He can also be a goober about sitting and gets forceful about it. If he sits in front of you and he thinks you are not paying attention to him, he'll get up, walk a few steps then sit down forcefully again as if to say, "Did you see me? Did you see me? I did it!" Also, when he gets excited he spins around and around like a top—there's no stopping him.

Texas is a great walker and has been from the first day we got him. In fact, he's the best walking dog I've ever had. He walks at my hip, or a bit behind me, never pulling on the leash. If I drop the leash by accident, he stops right way and stays with me.

I used to call Texas "Muffin" as a nickname. One day Wayne said, "I'm not going to call our dog 'Muffin.' He's not a muffin." As shy as Texas was, Wayne said he needed a tough name, so other dogs knew he wasn't a sissy dog. He needed a name like "Bulldozer" or "Killer." That's how the name "Killer" stuck and is now part of his full given name. I think Texas needed to be in our family. He has gotten Wayne and me to work together more and helped build a new pack with the four of us. Chloe was a once-in-a lifetime dog. I think Texas is, too.[1]

## Marty

**Breed:** Beagle

**Research History:** Marty was rescued from a pharmaceutical research laboratory in Colorado by Kindness Ranch Animal Sanctuary

Ellie and Marty on a walk in the snow on the high plains of Montana.

in April 2014. He was used for human drug studies. No other information is available.

**Adoption:** He was adopted in June 2014 at age six by Ellie (this book's author) and Jeremy Hansen, who live in Billings, Montana.

Ellie's morning began like any other, sipping from a mug of coffee and scrolling through Facebook at the kitchen table. Her two dogs—Max, a beagle, and Tyee, a rat terrier—lounged lazily on the living room couch. Ellie remembers freezing suddenly when on Facebook she came upon an undercover video of a beagle being euthanized after a scientific experiment in a research laboratory. It was a graphic, heart-wrenching and unforgettable experience.

## Ellie

The video and what it represented took hold of me, hard. I sobbed loudly and my husband Jeremy came into the room wondering what was the matter. My right brain wanted me to run into the streets and scream, "Hey everyone, did you know this is happening! They are using dogs for science experiments! We have to do something!" My logical side instructed me to begin educating myself on the issues surrounding animal research and testing.

Over the next few weeks I found an animal sanctuary in Wyoming called Kindness Ranch that specializes in rescuing dogs from research laboratories. Jeremy and I applied to adopt one of these dogs, preferably a beagle since we already had a beagle and understood the breed well. Here was my chance to help.

We had cared for special needs dogs before through our local animal shelter's foster program. Our fosters included a beagle puppy with a broken leg and severe food aggression issues. We helped her heal physically and emotionally, and she was adopted into a loving home. Then came Mr. T, an obese Chihuahua rat terrier mix who suffered from grand-mal seizures. Mr. T, who could barely walk when we first got him, lost five pounds under our care and became a favorite patient at our veterinarian's physical therapy department, where he went swimming three days a week for four months. Despite his seizures, Mr. T was adopted as well.

Our application to Kindness Ranch was followed by a lengthy phone interview to ensure that we were prepared to handle the rehabilitation needs of a former laboratory research dog. The dog would most likely not be house-broken, have never walked on a leash, never walked up or down stairs, and the list went on.

Finally, our application was approved, and we were invited to Kindness Ranch to pick out our new dog. My heart soared, and I quickly made arrangements for our six-hour drive from Billings to Hartville, Wyoming, where the sanctuary was located.

We chose a day in late June to make our trek. The drive from the city of Billings (population 109,000) to Hartville, Wyoming (population 61) is a long stretch of highway crossing several mountain passes interspersed by barren landscapes of sagebrush, prairie grass and rocky plateaus as far as the eye can see. I was too excited to sleep as my husband drove. I remember gazing out the window wondering how much my life would be different tomorrow.

## *Frozen in Fear*

His muscles were frozen solid, rigid and unbending. I had never felt muscles so tense as I picked him up and set him gently on the grass. Many fearful dogs would struggle, try to flee, or even bite. With me touching him, all this dog could do was freeze. Physically, his body was preparing for the worst. Who could blame him? He had spent the first six years of his life living in a cage and being used for pharmaceutical drug testing in a laboratory in Colorado. To him, people meant being stuck with needles, or worse. His upbringing was far from that of a normal dog, and his fear of humans was extreme.

I knelt next to him as he remained in his contorted position—not quite sitting, not quite standing. All I was offering him was a chance to go potty on the cool green grass, since we still had a six-hour drive ahead of us to reach home. Meanwhile, our other two dogs pranced around happily, marking trees, sniffing and exploring. Their carefree mannerisms were a sharp contrast to this beagle's stoicism.

This rigid, fearful dog was the one we were rescuing among the many we had spent hours with at Kindness Ranch. He was a light-colored beagle named Marty. Unlike some of the other rescue dogs being rehabilitated at the ranch, after almost three months Marty had not made much progress.

## *Baby Steps*

Many people say that their rescue dogs "chose" them, but Marty definitely did not choose me. I chose him because he would not come near me. He was terrified of me. He paced. He seemed petrified of staying in one place too long. Any sudden movement or noise would make him flee.

As we lifted Marty gently into the dog kennel in our car, his body went rigid again, like he was bracing himself for something bad. I was nervous, too. What had I just gotten myself into? But I knew Marty needed us, and that we could help him learn how to live in the outside world. Kindness Ranch agreed that our current lifestyle of being able to bring our dogs to work with us would benefit Marty greatly. My heart was pounding as I signed the adoption paperwork.

When we finally reached home, I put the dogs—three now—in our fenced backyard. Marty started exploring right away. Whenever I poked my head over the fence to take a peek, he would glance at me and run away in terror. When I finally got him inside our house, he was so nervous he pooped all over the kitchen and family room floors.

That night, I couldn't sleep. I got up at 5 a.m. to let Marty out. I opened the door to the backyard and he bolted into the yard. The sun was just coming up and it was cool, so I threw a sweater on over my pajamas. I sat on the deck with one of my favorite books and started to read out loud. Marty came to sit beside me on the deck. As long as I stayed seated and didn't look at him, he let me stroke his head and his beagle-soft floppy ears.

Often, Marty could not move for fear, so I carried him. I carried him compassionately, knowing this was temporary and that he would soon find his courage and strength. He did not know how to go up or down stairs, or through doorways. So, we carried him. After a few weeks, Marty started looking to us for help to cross his fear thresholds. He was finally communicating and starting to become curious instead of shutting down and freezing.

One morning, I awoke to let him outside, and when he saw me he wagged his tail for the first time. It was a simple gesture, but coming from Marty it had so much meaning. I folded Marty lovingly into my daily routines, and involved him in everything our family did under the big Montana sky. We walked and jogged. Hiked, camped, boated, and fished. Marty became quite the backcountry hiker. At first he stayed on a leash, but by the end of the summer, he was free to roam, sniff, and chase chipmunks with the other dogs. His confidence had grown tremendously in just three months.

Marty taught me some valuable lessons. One of the most important was that I had to learn to wait for him to see the world in a different light by supporting him in his decisions to do what made him feel safe. I never treated him as a victim, but as a survivor.

I also learned from him the value of not living in the past, as we humans often do. Now that he has learned to trust again, Marty has chosen to live every day to the fullest, as most dogs do. Tail wagging

... jumping for joy when I get home ... sitting at my feet as I prepare his breakfast and dinner ... getting excited about going out for a walk ... snuggling on the couch at night. When an animal's soul awakens, a beautiful light shines out.

## *A Visit to Prison*

Since we adopted Marty in 2015, he has become a sort of poster-dog for rescues from research. Marty was featured in *Animal Wellness Magazine* and *All Animals Magazine*. He has appeared on the local news and has made appearances for the Humane Society of the United States' "End Animal Testing Campaign" across the state of Montana. Marty is also one of the inspirations for this book.

In April 2019, Marty accompanied me to the Montana Women's Prison. I was invited to be a speaker for the inmates who are part of "Prison Paws," a program in which inmates learn how to train dogs through positive reinforcement methods. We were invited by the prison's program director to help educate the inmates on the issues of animal testing on dogs.

As I watched Marty interact with the 30 or more prisoners attending the session, I was overcome with compassion. Marty freely socialized with the ladies, sometimes lying quietly at their feet. I was pleasantly surprised to see how calm and giving Marty was. Marty inspired the prisoners to write letters to their legislators on the issue of animal testing, and to spread the word to friends and family about buying products not tested on animals. Watching Marty that day, I thought of how far he had come in four years. While once he was behind bars himself and scared of the world, he was now a brave delegate.[2]

# 17

# Part of the Family

## Chandler

**Breed:** Hound mix

**Research History:** Chandler was rescued along with five other large hounds in December 2014 from an undisclosed laboratory. They had all been used to test a weight-loss drug. The rescue organization

**Best friends.... Chandler with his new baby human brother.**

Kindness Ranch named them the "Friends" hounds after the television show's famous characters Joey, Monica, Chandler, Ross, Phoebe, and Rachel.

**Adoption:** Chandler was adopted in August 2015 at age two by Erica and Kyle Ridgeway, who live in Sheridan, Wyoming. Erica did not start looking specifically for a laboratory research dog. In fact, at the time she was not even aware that research on dogs was an ongoing practice. An emergency room nurse in the trauma unit of the local hospital, Erica had just lost her beloved dog Ruger, a large hound mix. Ruger had been her emotional support dog through her college and early adult years. His passing in 2015 after a long battle with megaesophagus was devastating.

Erica knew she had to find another hound to help fill the hole in her heart. She began searching for hound dogs in Wyoming online, and that is when Chandler's photo appeared. She remembers the photo vividly. He was wearing a green bowtie for St. Patrick's Day, and he was clearly not impressed. Noticing how handsome he looked, Erica resolved to get him.

## Erica

I had no idea what the Kindness Ranch was. I did not know we had a facility that rescues research animals in Wyoming. Trying to rescue a dog from research was not something I sought out. A visit to Kindness Ranch is eye opening in a sad way. You see all the animals at the ranch, and it makes you think about the animal testing that is going on. In day-to-day life, this is not something that is visible to the general public.

I knew I was going to take Chandler home with me. Whatever problems he had I knew we would work out. Luckily, Chandler was housetrained by the time we got him. My husband Kyle and I were both very involved with Chandler's training. We had a kennel set up for his own "safe space" for quite a while. The first few weeks he preferred being in his kennel to being with us. When we first got home, we also discovered that Chandler did not know how to walk up or down stairs. I remember Kyle going down on his hands and knees trying to show Chandler how to use the stairs.

Chandler has a few quirky behaviors, one of which is his fear of flies. He hides in the basement stairwell when there is a fly in the house. I don't know if the sound of a fly buzzing bothers him, or what else it could be. At first, we weren't sure why he would start to panic and run for the basement. Then one day we saw a big fly in the house and made the connection. It was just flying, not chasing or landing on him.

Chandler is a big dog and I often think to myself, "Chandler, you could eat that fly if you wanted to!"

Another odd behavior is Chandler's reaction to food. Initially, we would try to keep his food bowl full, mostly because we felt so bad about his background in weight-loss studies. We wanted to give him whatever made him happy. However, a few months later, his weight had ballooned from 70 pounds to over 90. Chandler is now on a food schedule, and much to his dismay, he gets an allotted amount of food per day.

I have never seen a more food-motivated dog. When it gets close to mealtime, Chandler will start barking and whining. Then he starts play-bowing and slapping the floor with his two front paws, frantically. He starts jumping around in circles, like a bucking bronc at a rodeo. He does not eat anything fancy. It's just dog kibble. However, given his obsessive affinity for food, I wonder what connection this behavior has to the weight-loss drug he was subjected to at such a young age.

In 2019 I had a baby, our first child. When we brought our daughter home from the hospital, Chandler was terribly confused as to what the baby was. He was a bit aggressive. I was worried we would have to do intensive therapy with him for the baby's safety and his own comfort. At the advice of our veterinarian, we got Chandler a vibrating training collar. Any time he would get too excited around the baby, we would vibrate his collar and he would walk away. We only had to vibrate his collar twice. Since then he has been great with his baby "sister." In fact, they are best friends.[1]

## Roofus

**Breed:** Beagle

**Research History:** Roofus was part of a group of ten dogs that came from a Midwest laboratory where they were tested, most recently, with flea and tick vaccines. He has two tattoos, which usually means he was used for another unknown study. The rescue organization Kindness Ranch named each dog after Golden Globe and Grammy winners. Roofus was a Grammy-winning "Electronic Music" artist for 2020.

**Adoption:** He was adopted in May 2020 at age two by Lisa F. and her family, who live in Centennial, Colorado.

With schools closed to protect against Covid-19 infections, Lisa and her husband felt it was the perfect time to get another beagle. Their first beagle had died in 2017, and their eldest dog had just passed away in early 2020. Quarantined together at home without a dog, the family began looking at beagle rescues in the area, including Kindness Ranch. Lisa and her husband had only one stipulation: that the dog be good around children. Their two boys, ages six and eight, were used to being around older dogs. Their youngest son was concerned about getting a dog that would scare him.

**Roofus**

Nevertheless, a sociable, rambunctious two-year-old beagle named Roofus was recommended to them by Kindness Ranch as a great family dog. In May, once Kindness Ranch—closed for a time against COVID-19, too—opened its doors back up to the public, they decided to go meet Roofus.

## Lisa

I never knew dogs would be subjected to procedures that I now know happens in laboratories. I had pictured something fairly innocent, like a rat trying to find its way through a maze. Nothing about being force-fed poisons, or other things I've since read about. We wanted to provide a beagle from a laboratory, who had had a difficult start to life, with a family who would love him.

We have a house in the suburbs with a fenced yard. There is a park across the street. Our kids play many sports, and we enjoy taking our dogs with us to sit on the sidelines. We spend all our time together as a family, and we wanted our new dog to be included in that.

The first time we met Roofus at Kindness Ranch, he wanted nothing to do with us. I understood, as there were four of us trying to meet him all at once. But we could see how much he loved the ranch staff members. He kept running back to them, asking to be picked up. They assured us that he would open up to us as well. It was hard to know whether we were making the right decision by taking him home with us. We didn't want him to be uncomfortable or scared. At the same time, we knew we could give him a wonderful life.

It seems so silly to me now, but as we were driving to pick up Roofus, my mother-in-law mentioned that he wouldn't be house trained. "Of course he wouldn't," I thought to myself, but didn't realize the depth of trauma these dogs go through until I met Roofus.

Our first days with Roofus were challenging. The first night home, we turned on the ceiling fan in our room and he was terrified. He was very cautious about anything new. He had to learn how to walk on a leash. While he picked that up quickly, he rarely made it through a walk without something scaring him to the point he would tuck his tail between his legs. He would not take treats from us and was wary about any food we gave him. He also barely made a sound. We weren't sure whether he still had the ability to bark until one day we finally got a howl.

It's really hard to know what will scare Roofus. Once we took him to a brewery, a common place where we live for dogs to accompany their owners. We figured he'd be with us and happy to sit outside. Instead, he took one look at the fifteen or so people sitting at the different tables and tried to run back to the car. He was visibly shaking for a few minutes before he settled down.

## *Advice for Families*

Roofus loves chasing tennis balls. One thing that has been difficult for our family is a common puppy trait—nipping. One day, Roofus seemed to realize that the kids were fun to play with. They were throwing the ball for him, and he was chasing it. Everything was going really well until Roofus jumped up and nipped one of the children, breaking the skin. It was very clear he was playing, and not being aggressive. Of course, the kids were afraid after that. We solved the problem by monitoring playtime more closely, and now when everyone starts getting too excited, we de-escalate and move on to another activity.

Not every laboratory dog will do well with young children. There's an unknown quantity about the whole situation. My kids are now old enough to play on their own, so I can give Roofus my undivided attention as needed. Also, I question whether a laboratory dog should be a family's first dog, because it is a lot to take. Not only would you be adjusting to having a dog in the house for the first time, but you'd also have to deal with the dog's other unique characteristics. That would be really be difficult.

We love Roofus, and as a family, we're all in. Even though he has been more difficult than any dog I've had before, we're so glad that he's with us.

## *A Child's Perspective*

We told our kids that Roofus's job had been to work in a laboratory, and that they tested things on him, but we don't know what that means. They don't fully understand how awful that is. They just know he wasn't in a place where he was loved. They understand that his life before this was sad, and he doesn't know how to act as normal dogs do. I tell them he has to learn all the things that happen in a house or with a family, because he doesn't have any experience with that. Here's what my eight-year-old son wrote about Roofus:

> It's nice to have a dog back in the house again. A puppy is very playful and if you get too playful, he can accidently bite you. Roofus is very good with kids most of the time. When he is having some Roofus alone time he is not good with kids. He's learning things super fast. He's scared when you approach him.
>
> Roofus got rescued from Kindness Ranch and before that he was basically just a lab dog. He was tested by scientists. That makes me sad because they don't let the dogs play. Now he can play and just not be scared of all the things around him.[2]

# Maycie

**Breed:** Beagle

**Research History:** In October 2019, nine beagles were rescued from a research laboratory by Kindness Ranch Animal Sanctuary. Maycie (then known as "X-Ray") was one of the female beagles in this group. No information is available on where she came from or what she was used for.

**Adoption:** Maycie was adopted in November 2019 at age four by Paula and Jeff Bowie who live in Sheridan, Wyoming.

Paula, her husband Jeff, and their four children are an approved foster family for the National Brittany Rescue and Adoption Network. Prior to adopting Maycie, they already had two dogs of their own, a four-year-old Brittany and a one-year-old beagle. They have a large backyard where dogs can play and relax in, and they enjoy taking their dogs for walks, and as part of the family for fly fishing, kayaking, and camping.

Paula remembers that one of the first online posts she saw by Kindness Ranch was in 2018 around Christmas time. The video showed all the dogs in their kennels about to get their Christmas presents. The staff opened the kennels and she could see how happy the dogs were. Not just for the treats and toys, but also the loving human interaction. Having recently learned that dogs are still regularly subjected to research experiments, Paula knew the mission of Kindness Ranch was a cause her whole family would stand behind.

**Jeff Bowie and Maycie**

## Paula

There was such a cute picture of a dog named Gracie on the Kindness Ranch Facebook page. We thought for sure this would be the perfect fit for our family and other dogs. We happened to be in Casper, Wyoming, for a volleyball tournament, just two hours from Kindness Ranch. We decided that while we were down on that end of the state, we would visit. So Jeff and I, along with our youngest teenage daughter Brooklyn, her boyfriend Seth, and Rebecca—our exchange student from Italy—all went to meet Gracie.

As it turned out, Gracie wanted nothing to do with us. However, there was another very sweet, shy dog that seemed to connect with Jeff. This dog's name was X-Ray, a temporary name given by Kindness Ranch because the tattoo in her ear began with the letter "X." Once Jeff picked her up to snuggle, we knew that she was the one. Even when he put her down to play with the other dogs, she wanted to stand close to Jeff.

We changed her name to Maycie. At the time of her adoption, we still had two teenage children living at home. She was easy going from the start, and not hyper at all. Interestingly, the behavior of our other two dogs toward Maycie was different from the start than anything I'd seen before, even with the foster dogs we often had. I think they sensed Maycie was different, and they were both so gentle around her, as if they didn't want to scare her.

The first night with Maycie was a reality check. At bedtime, we put her in bed with us so we could give her reassurance and love. She did not know what to do. She stood still, almost paralyzed for forty minutes before she finally relaxed enough to lie down. We knew then that that getting to "normal" with her would take time.

We also noticed that Maycie was missing all her front teeth, both top and bottom. We guessed it was from chewing on cage bars in the laboratory.

Maycie did not want to go down any stairs in the house, so at first we would carry her down. It took her about a week to go down the three steps from our deck to the ground outside. I video recorded the event like a proud mother, feeling that excitement when a child reaches a milestone.

### Jeff

My three daughters and Seth's two sisters began doing research on animal testing after we adopted Maycie. Once they learned how animals are killed to test cosmetics, and other chemicals, they all made an instant switch to cruelty-free make-up and threw their other make-up, creams, and soaps in the trash. As their dad, I thought that was pretty cool. Now when they need something new, they research the product to make sure it's cruelty-free.

One reality check I had with Maycie was her nightmares. Once or twice a week during her first six weeks with us Maycie would wake up suddenly, growling and snarling at my face. She never tried to bite or attack me, but I could tell she was very scared. Each time this happened, Paula and I would turn the lights on. I think that helped Maycie visualize where she was. A few times her nightmare episodes were so bad that I had to leave the room to get her to calm down.

Maycie's nightmares were the only time she's ever shown any aggression toward me or anyone else. Whatever was going on in her head during these episodes might have been defensive, or something like Post-Traumatic Stress Disorder. While I was growing up my family raised springer spaniels, so I've been around dogs my whole life. Yet, I'd never seen anything akin to Maycie's nightmares. It was scary, but we worked through it, and her nightmares have disappeared.

## PAULA

We have shared our experience with our family and friends, encouraging them to buy products that are cruelty-free. Most people are shocked that animal testing still continues. We also encourage people to adopt rescued dogs.

Maycie's impact has grown beyond us.

While Seth, our daughter Brooklyn's boyfriend, was with us at Kindness Ranch, he became attached to a sweet beagle named Tessa. Only a few weeks later, Seth's family decided to adopt Tessa.

In June 2020, Brooklyn graduated from high school. For her final exam in public speaking, she decided to do a presentation on laboratory testing on animals. Because through Maycie she had personal experience with this topic, Brooklyn could speak from her heart and received an excellent grade, while at the same time teaching others.[3]

18

# Sharing the Gift of Healing

## Connor

**Breed:** Beagle

**Research History:** Connor was rescued by the Beagle Freedom Project from a biomedical research facility at a university in the Washington, D.C., area. He and one other dog were the only two dogs released from this laboratory at this time. Nothing is known about what type of research they were used for.

**Adoption:** He was adopted in November 2016 at age ten months by Mary Beth Stoddard and Ken Nelson, who live in Palm Beach Gardens, Florida.

Far from the atmosphere of a biomedical laboratory cage, Connor now lives in paradise. Palm trees and tropical breezes are part of his daily routine, as is the important job of patrolling the pristine beaches along Florida's

**Mary Beth Stoddard and Connor in a Christmas photograph at the beach in Florida.**

southern Atlantic Coast. Living only eight minutes from Jupiter Beach, one of the most popular dog beaches in the state, Connor is a frequent visitor there, routinely inspecting mangrove trees, finding shells to sniff, and uncovering treasures that wash onto shore.

Mary Beth knows what university Connor came from but has promised to keep this information confidential, so as not to jeopardize the possible release of additional dogs. Connor was hookworm positive while kept in the lab, which delayed his release for about ten days.

## Mary Beth

### *Early Memories*

I was between five and seven years old when I became aware of animal testing. My first exposure was a People for the Ethical Treatment of Animals (PETA) pamphlet. It showed pictures of chemical hair dyes being dripped into the eyes of live rabbits. At that young age, I started having anxiety attacks and a sense of helplessness. The knowledge that humans were intentionally torturing animals was making me physically ill, which resulted in my first visit to a professional therapist as I was having difficulty sleeping at night. As a result, I have been shopping for cruelty-free products as long as I can remember.

My first introduction to dogs being used for research was a social media post by the Beagle Freedom Project (BFP), which showed beagles taking their first steps of freedom from a laboratory. I had owned two rescue beagles previously and did not realize there were organizations that could pull dogs out of laboratories. I reached out to the BFP to inquire how I could help.

At this time Ken and I lived in northern Virginia and had one senior-age beagle named Darwin. We were avid hikers and our home backed up to a state park. I would often take Darwin for long hikes through the woods there. I had offered to foster or adopt a beagle from BFP, and it wasn't long after when I got a call that BFP had been able to negotiate the release of a dog from a university laboratory nearby.

My rendezvous point for getting Connor was at a veterinarian's office, where I met a woman who had picked him up from the laboratory. I first saw him through the exam room window. His body was very long for a beagle and his tail was seriously shaped like a hook or a question mark, but he was absolutely adorable. He slept on my lap contently for the entire drive home.

## *Bouncing Off the Walls*

Once I got home with Connor it was a different story. I brought him into the living room to meet Darwin and he went nuts. Connor zoomed around so fast that he ran into the wall multiple times. He was literally bouncing off the walls! At first, I was excited to see him running around and enjoying himself, however moments later I realized it was a manic episode—not happiness. Connor had no idea what to do with all his new space. He wasn't afraid. He just had no idea how to function. Even his sense of balance was off.

I learned early on that Connor had extreme resource guarding issues over food and toys and would often lunge at and try to attack Darwin. Connor had no sense of pack mentality, or socialization skills with other dogs. I worked with a local dog trainer to help us correct his aggressive behavior.

I could not imagine how Connor survived the first ten months of his life living in a small laboratory cage. His high energy, problem-solving skills, and intelligence are beyond any other dog I've known, and I had an incredible border collie which is arguably one of the smartest dog breeds. It takes him only a few minutes to learn new tricks and commands. Also, when we first got Connor, he never had an accident in the house and automatically followed Darwin's lead on where to go outside.

When Darwin passed away, Connor developed severe separation anxiety. Since I had to bring Darwin to the vet's office for his final moment, I believe Darwin's "disappearance" affected Connor emotionally. He no longer tolerated me leaving the house. I would often come home to find door frames and windowsills completely chewed up. Once I came home to see the custom drapes shredded on the floor. Ultimately Connor caused about $4,000 in damage to our house and as a result I did most of the house repairs myself to afford them.

We had to find a solution to his new destructive behavior. I worked with a veterinary dog behavioral specialist, who put him on anti-anxiety medication, and set up some dog cameras to monitor him. It was stressful to think that our departure was causing him so much anxiety.

We decided to adopt another dog, a black Labrador retriever named Corvus. While I was advised that getting a second dog would not solve Connor's separation anxiety issues, Connor and Corvus became instant best friends. Connor and Corvus played a lot, and Connor quickly became interested in his toys again. However, just as I was told, Connor's separation anxiety did not improve.

We continued to work with the behaviorist. One of the commands we taught Connor was "bed," where the desired action was for Connor to go lie on his bed and stay there until we used a release command. We started in baby steps, at first with taking only a few steps away from him, to being able to leave the room. He has now learned his bed is a comforting place, and that if he stays there, we will always come back. He can now self-soothe, and no longer needs to take so many different types of medication.

Connor loves being around people. Because he doesn't seem afraid, people often ask me incredulously, "He was used in a lab?" However he does not like veterinarians in white coats. During Connor's first visit to our veterinarian's office, he literally screamed and screamed then pooped all over himself! I had to cancel several veterinarian appointments because Connor would get so upset once he was in the exam room. Fast forward: now Ken and I live in Florida, Connor loves to visit his new veterinarian because he wears normal clothes—no white coat.

## *The Empath*

Beginning in February 2017, tragedy began striking like lightning all around me. I had Connor for only about three months when my eldest brother died at age 49. We had been very close. After my brother died, my family and I, who were deeply grieving his loss, began focusing our energies on his girlfriend who was pregnant with his child. Turning my attention to the baby helped me cope and gave me hope that a part of my brother would survive. However, in July 2017, the baby—his daughter—was stillborn.

That October, Darwin passed away. Then in January 2018 my nine-year-old niece unexpectedly passed away. Needless to say, with all the deaths happening around me within a ten-month period, I was hanging onto my emotional well-being by a thread.

One of the things that got me out of bed each day during this difficult time was Connor. I absolutely believe Connor is an empath. Whenever I was feeling sad, even if Connor was in a different room than me, he would come running to give me "hugs" to cheer me up and offer comfort. Even now, if I'm upset and sitting in my chair, Connor will come find me, and put his paw on my leg to get my attention. I've learned to then sit on the floor and let him put his paws up on both sides of my neck and push his head into my forehead. The more I cry, the harder he hugs me.

I also joined a BFP support group. With the assistance of other devoted owners of former laboratory dogs, I was able to overcome the initial challenges I encountered with Connor. Additionally, some of these women have become my absolute best friends and helped save me from my grief. Spending time with Connor and my BFP family reminds me not to focus on past hurts, but to live in the present moment.[1]

## Pearl Grace

**Jodie Lee and Pearl Grace modeling her K9 Sport Sack.**

**Breed:** Beagle

**Research History:** Pearl Grace was part of a group of beagles that was used for flea and tick treatment research. She was purposely impregnated in order to research side effects the treatment had on her and her puppies. No information is available about what happened to her puppies. No information is available on the laboratory she came from. While she was used for several studies in her life, this is the only one for which any details were provided. She was rescued by the Kindness Ranch Animal Sanctuary.

**Adoption:** She was adopted in January 2020 at age four by Jodie and Bob Lee who live in Broomfield, Colorado.

### *Definition of Grace*

> Unmerited divine assistance given to humans for their regeneration or sanctification.
>
> —Merriam-Webster

As a massage therapist helping clients recover from severe auto and workplace injuries, Jodie recognizes the value of acceptance and letting go of the past. She herself is no stranger to traumatic events. One such event occurred while she was dog-sitting for her good friend Ashlee's dog, a beagle named Bark Ranger. Often for weeks at a time, Bark Ranger would stay at Jodie's home, and they became quite attached. One day, as they were traveling together in her car, Bark Ranger jumped out of the window. Screeching to a halt, Jodie jumped out of the car and ran into traffic, frantically trying to save his life. Unsuccessful in retrieving him, she watched in horror as a truck ran over and killed him.

## Jodie

That moment when Ashlee's beagle died in my arms, my legs physically stopped working. I could not even move. My mouth could barely get words out as I called Ashlee to tell her that her dog was dead and gave her directions to where to come pick us up.

Overcome with guilt, I was afraid to face Ashlee when we got back to my house. As it turned out, I had no reason to be afraid. As I was on the floor, collapsed in shock and grief, she gently picked me up. I said, "Ashlee, I don't know why you're being kind to me at this point. If you don't ever want to speak to me again, I would understand." She looked at me with what I understood to be pure "grace," and replied, "Jodie, I'm not mad at you. And even if I were mad at you, it wouldn't do any good, because you're already madder at yourself than anyone is ever going to be." Ashlee had given me this "grace," but I didn't know what to do with it. I didn't feel I deserved it. As the years passed by, the word "grace" kept coming to mind, but I didn't understand—then—why.

My husband Bob and I had a beagle of our own named Tator Bean at this time. He was so full of life, and everything he did made us laugh. He really helped me heal after the tragic loss of Bark Ranger. Tator was also my best friend. He left no moment unlived. The intensity and presence of mind he possessed was the biggest blessing of my life.

Then, on New Year's Day 2020, Tator suddenly died. He just fell over after dinner, shook for a minute, and was gone. Tator was only six years old. Our hearts were so broken after Tator's death I have no words to describe the sadness we felt. But I decided that Tator's "energy" would live on in my heart. I resolved to pass on to my next beagle the energy—that special friendship—Tator had given me.

## *Finding Grace*

Two of the four beagles I have owned over the past thirty years were from abusive backgrounds, and I know how forgiving and sweet beagles can be under the worst circumstances. When I first heard about animal testing on dogs, I wrongly assumed that the dogs lived otherwise normal lives, and I was distraught as I uncovered the truth.

When it was finally time to open our home to a new beagle, I searched online for a beagle retired from research. This is how I found out about Kindness Ranch. At this time, we also had a thirteen-year-old border collie. Tator had been her best friend, and we wanted to fill the void in our home after Tator's passing.

Kindness Ranch informed me about a dog named Heather. They said she was very friendly, so I was expecting to connect with her immediately, using biscuits and cuddles. Instead, Heather was hesitant to approach. She finally accepted a biscuit, but as soon as the biscuit was in her mouth, she ran away from me to eat it. I realized that connecting with Heather was going to take time.

It didn't matter to me how traumatized Heather was or how much work it would take to gain her trust, I was going to give her the "grace" my friend Ashlee had bestowed upon me years ago. Like Heather, my life had been marked with trauma. I understood the importance of moving forward instead of dwelling in the past. We would use "grace" to heal together. Fittingly, on adoption day I changed Heather's name to Pearl "Grace."

## *Adventures with Grace*

The first few weeks with Pearl Grace were a challenge. She startled at the smallest noises and paced and peed in the house and on our furniture. She spent most of her days on the sofa in the kitchen, so we covered it with fuzzy blankets, pillows, and dog toys. We also quickly figured out how to quietly and slowly open doors and cabinets. She was so nervous she wouldn't eat. I tried to feed her cuts of ham, chicken, and beef, but no, not a bite. It took her two weeks to feel comfortable enough to eat while we were in the room.

We usually walk three miles a day with our border collie, and since Pearl Grace had no experience with a leash, that was a learning process, too. The first day I put a leash on her for a walk, it took us one hour to meander a half mile! Even afterwards, she would often stop and refuse to keep walking. We called it "the stall." Sometimes, after a mile of walking, I would have to carry her home.

I realized this issue would not go away soon, and solved the problem with a *K9 Sport Sack,* a backpack designed to carry dogs. Pearl Grace feels so safe in her backpack that we have used it regularly to introduce her to new things. She now comes biking and paddle boarding with me in her backpack and loves it.

One of Pearl Grace's first adventures with us was a road trip to the California Coast. Pearl Grace and I were walking along the boardwalk at Ventura Beach, when we met a retired couple who were walking their dog. When I told the woman that we had just adopted Pearl Grace as a rescue from animal testing, she replied, "Well, they must have been testing makeup on her, because she is just so beautiful!" She missed the point entirely and didn't understand what testing Pearl Grace had really endured, but I found her remark funny and it made me laugh—something I really needed.[2]

# 19

# International Rescues—United Kingdom

## *Going Undercover: Three Beagles Rescued*

In 2013, an undercover investigation by Cruelty Free International, an organization campaigning to end animal experiments, revealed lethal experiments being conducted on puppies at a United Kingdom–based veterinary subsidiary of a United States pharmaceutical company in Cambridgeshire. The eight-month long investigation uncovered shocking video footage of puppies as young as four to five weeks old being used to test animal vaccines. After the experiments, the puppies were routinely killed and dissected.

During the course of the investigation, 92 beagle puppies and 10 adult nursing female beagles were killed by the laboratory. Video footage showed some of the puppies panicking and struggling as they were injected with the needles used to euthanize them. Healthy mothers were also killed, almost always without any apparent attempt to find them adoptive homes, according to the undercover investigator. However, the undercover investigator was able to secure the release of two nursing female beagles and one beagle puppy before the story was released to the press.[1]

Following the Cruelty Free International investigation and its subsequent campaign for animals to be released from laboratories wherever possible, the U.K. government released new guidance on how laboratories could find homes for animals considered suitable for a new life. The stories of one of the freed female beagles, Missy, and the puppy, Oliver, are told below.

## Missy

**Research Background:** Missy came from a beagle breeding supplier in the Netherlands and was imported into the United Kingdom while pregnant, along with other pregnant females. Missy was a breeding female used to produce puppies for animal vaccine research.

**Missy in a United Kingdom laboratory with puppies in 2013. This photograph was taken as part of an undercover investigation conducted by Cruelty Free International. © Cruelty Free International. Reprinted with permission from Cruelty Free International.**

**Adoption:** Missy was adopted in December 2013 at six years old by Sarah Kite who lives in the United Kingdom.

## Sarah

I have a university degree in psychology and am trained as a mental health social worker. However, most of my working life has been spent employed in the animal protection field. I have been campaigning on behalf of animals for over forty years, for most of that time working with Cruelty Free International. While there, I managed the investigations unit, media efforts, and campaigns against the use of animals in research.

In 1988, I worked undercover in a contract testing laboratory in the United Kingdom to expose the plight of beagles used in toxicity testing. I have also spent a few years living in the United States, co-managing a sanctuary for non-human primates in Texas. Some of the monkeys there had been released by laboratories. I am currently an advisor to Cruelty Free International and also co-founder of a new project—Action for Primates.

When Missy joined us, I had three other rescued dogs in my home. My husband and I live in a rural location, and we have a large garden and field that is ideal for dogs. I had many years of experience taking care of rescued dogs, including beagles. I adopted Missy because she was the more institutionalized and nervous of the two dogs.

Missy is a small tri-colored beagle. At first, she was nervous about almost everything and very skittish. She would hide in the garden and it was very difficult to persuade her to come back into the house. Two things caused Missy the most anxiety at the beginning: going through doorways and walking on a lead. She would not go to the bathroom while a lead was on.

Although she has improved considerably since then, she still has what we call her little "ghosts" from the past. For example, she still has issues with walking through the back door, and it sometimes takes many attempts before she will re-enter the house. Indoors, her safe spot became the top of an old wooden sea chest, so we put a dog bed there for her. She continues to use it.

Missy is a very sweet dog. She is not especially active, but every now and then she becomes very excitable and will dash around in circles, wagging her tail, and soliciting attention. It is lovely to watch her hurtle about. She is obsessed with food. Mealtime and treats cause her great excitement. She also enjoys lying in the sun.

While adopting Missy has been challenging, she is a dear dog and it has been wonderful to watch her grow in confidence and enjoy her new life. We have been fortunate to be able to provide her with a quiet, peaceful environment that has enabled her to thrive.[2]

## Oliver

**Research Background:** Oliver was born on September 24, 2013. He was removed from his mother, Latifa, along with his siblings at just five weeks old to be used in tests along with 29 other puppies. Latifa, who was only four years old, was killed after her puppies were taken away because she had served the company and was of no further use. When the Cruelty Free International undercover investigator picked Oliver up to bring him to a rescue organization, he had green permanent marker all over his head. It was a mark to tell Oliver apart from his brother Bailey, as they were both lemon- and white-colored. Bailey was killed the morning Oliver was rescued.

**Adoption:** Oliver was adopted in July 2015 at 22 months old by Sheila who lives in West Midlands, United Kingdom.

**Oliver all grown up.**

## Sheila

I have lived with former laboratory dogs since 1991. That's when I adopted my first two, Hazel and Bramble, who came from Perrycroft Farm Kennels, one of Britain's biggest breeders of laboratory animals at that time. Perrycroft became national news in 1990 when over 70 of the 100 beagles they shipped to a pharmaceutical company in Sweden suffocated to death in the pick-up van used to transport them, due to the van's faulty ventilation system. Perrycroft was charged with animal cruelty and eventually the facility closed down. This event got me on the campaign trail to save laboratory dogs.

In 1997 I was actively involved in rescuing 176 beagles from Consort Bioservices in Herefordshire after persistent protests and campaigns caused them to shut down. I had helped to re-home many dogs then and kept one for myself, a beagle named Sam. When I found out about Oliver, he was with a foster family and needed a permanent home.

I was then living in rural Gloucestershire. My dogs are my life. We have always gone on long countryside walks, and I have done the sport of agility with two of them. Everything I do is based around my dogs. When I got Oliver, I had three other dogs—two Beagles and a Trailhound. While I do not have any formal qualifications in animal behavior, I am experienced with special-needs dogs and have spent many years helping dogs with a troubled background.

Oliver was very scared of men and wasn't at ease if there was a man around or even if he knew there was one nearby, such as when out walking etc. He would want to hide and get away if he could. He is now much more confident around men and will even wag his tail if he meets a male now.

If there was a difference in the room, like a coat hanging up or a different pair of shoes on the floor that weren't there before, he would be terrified and wouldn't eat. He wouldn't eat if he heard a noise coming from inside or outside the house, like a car driving by or voices. If I moved from one spot in the room to another spot, he would stop eating and would not eat for the rest of day.

Oliver still has a little anxiety and noise-sensitivity, but when I look at him now I realize how far we have progressed. His confidence has grown so much. Despite his background, Oliver is extremely loyal, loving, and kind. He is also very sensitive by nature. His favorite activities of the day are taking a walk, eating some food, and then chilling out on his favorite spot on the sofa.[3]

# 20

# International Rescues—Italy

## *Thousands of Beagles Find Freedom*

In July 2012, approximately 3,000 beagles intended for animal testing were confiscated from the breeding facility Green Hill, an Italian branch of the United States company Marshall Bioresources located in Brescia, Italy. This factory farm had provided dogs for research laboratories all over Europe, with beagles specifically bred for testing purposes.

Due to Green Hill's high mortality rates (6,023 deaths of beagles between 2009 and 2012) the Court of Brescia found Green Hill guilty of animal cruelty and ordered the permanent closure of the facility in January 2015. All rescued dogs were successfully adopted through the activist groups LAV-Antivivisection League and Legambiente.[1]

## Artù

**Research Background:** Artù was rescued from Green Hill.

**Adoption:** Artù was adopted in August 2012 at five months old by Samanta Stefano who lives in Faloppio, Italy.

### Samanta

This is the story of my Artù, who as I write is now eight years old. I remember the heat as it was yesterday and the endless journey to pick up Artù. The target seemed to be a distant goal thousands of kilometers from my home even though it was only a little over an hour. But when you look forward to "that moment," time never seems to pass. I think I drove at an insane speed, but "he" couldn't wait any longer. "He" was waiting for me.

Finally, I arrived in front of the gate of the kennel. The excitement caused my legs to tremble. The beating of my heart increased. And then ... there they were. Two boxes full of yelping puppies who, despite their very young age, have already known hell. Someone tells me, "Choose which one you want." And I remember I thought, "Choose? And how can I choose?" They all had the same right to have a free and happy life, and someone who would love them and take care of them.

**Samanta Stefano and Artù**

Shortly afterward, I found myself with a puppy in my arms. He had chosen me. He had taken the step towards me. The look we exchanged in that moment is indelibly imprinted on my mind. And that's when I made him a promise: whatever happened, he would never go back to Green Hill. He was never going to be a lab "rat." And I kept that promise.

It was so hot that day, but I didn't feel the heat anymore. What I had in my arms was a bewildered puppy, with big ears and lost eyes. I remember the depth, the sweetness, and the melancholy of his gaze. I remember the stiffness of that little body when I held it tightly to me, filling it with kisses. I remember the acrid, pungent smell that has nothing to do with today's clean scent. I was terrified of hurting him, and of not keeping him in the right way. Yet I have had dogs since I was born. But Artù did nothing, not even a movement, not even a moan. He stood there trying to figure out who I was.

The first night at home I spent watching him, enchanted and incredulous while he, exhausted, slept peacefully clutching his first soft toy. The days to come were the beginning of the exciting discovery of a whole new world that had nothing to do with the cages of Green Hill warehouses: sunlight, grass in the meadows, rain, snow, and the company of the good part of humans.

He did no barking nor emitted any sounds for several months. From what the veterinarian told me, this was due to the trauma he endured in captivity. He had giardia, otitis and a bit of dermatitis around his mouth and, of course, the tattoo in his ear (which fortunately is hardly readable today) that carried a number followed by the infamous BSGH (Brescia Green Hill) symbol. For at Green Hill he was not a sentient being, but just a number.

It took months, a lot of effort, and love to get him over his fears. Artù had to "learn" to be a dog because, up until then, he had been denied all rights. He watched everything with the curiosity typical of puppies but suffered from uncontrolled fear of doors slamming, the television volume being too high, the noise of home appliances, motorcycles, car horns, black garbage bags, and men in glasses and hats. I took him everywhere with me: on vacation, to restaurants, and to see my friends.

Since the beginning Artù has shared his space with three cats, a mixed-breed rescue dog from Puglia named Nerone, and a Maltese named Sofia. I live in an area surrounded by greenery, so in the morning before going to work, we all take an hour's walk in the woods together. In the evening we watch TV on the sofa and at night we sleep in bed next to each other. Artù loves to sleep long under the covers and is the last one to get up.

Fortunately, the months spent in Green Hill left no significant psychological trauma and Artù's initial fears vanished. When I watch him sleep peacefully on his stomach, I can't help but think what would have happened to him if he hadn't been released, and this thought hurts my heart, because I am aware that too many dogs have not been so lucky and they experience the horror of vivisection every day.

Artù choosing me that day of August 4 gave me the opportunity to make myself useful and active in fighting against vivisection, against the mistreatment of animals, and to fight for their rights to be recognized and finally be considered sentient beings. I changed my habits and my lifestyle. I became a vegetarian. I no longer buy products tested on animals. I also created an animal rights group on Facebook—"The Beagle Families in Foster Care," which has more than 1,000 members. Through this page I try to sensitize people towards our animal brothers regardless of the species they belong to.

Before the magistrate transformed the provisional custody of the

Green Hill beagles into definitive custody, I spent months in anguish. I participated in all the hearings of the trials against Green Hill, in events, and demonstrations. Then, finally, the long-awaited decree from the Brescia Public Prosecutor's Office arrived, which ruled that Artù was mine legally—even if he was mine from the first embrace.[2]

## Giulia and Giò

**Research Background:** Giulia and Giò were rescued from Green Hill.

**Adoption:** Giulia and Giò were adopted in July 2012 at five months old by Vania who lives near Milan, Italy.

### Vania

I was an executive for a large company in the food sector. I have always had animals, but mostly cats, because with my job they were

**Giulia (*left*) and Gió as puppies on rescue day from the Italian Green Hill breeding facility in July 2012.**

easier to manage, as I was very often traveling around the world on business. Eventually, I discovered my love of dogs, above all the Newfoundland breed. I came to have 14 Newfoundlands and I had to make a life decision about leaving Milan to make space for my growing animal family.

I purchased a large farmhouse in the countryside about eighty kilometers from Milan, close to hills, and with a lot of land for my dogs. I changed my job and became a freelance sales associate in the food world. Now I rarely leave my home so that I can care for my animals. I have always rescued my dogs from difficult situations such as fights, abandonments, and situations of neglect. I even have a goat rescued from a slaughterhouse.

At the end of July, when the adoption order had arrived for the 3,000 beagles, the problem was that in Italy, July and August are months dedicated to holidays. There was a general fear that there would not be enough adopters at that time. So, I found myself outside the Green Hill property helping out, sorting dogs going to various associations and shelters. It was on July 31 that I was assigned my own two five-month old babies.

I had initially asked to adopt a mother with puppies because I knew that they would be the most difficult to care for. But I learned that these mothers were entrusted to the rescue centers for their protection, as they were in really bad condition. So, Giulia and Giò were given to me instead.

It is very difficult to describe my feelings for Giulia and Giò as we left Green Hill behind. I could only cry as I started to drive them home, because I realized I was the first person who had ever given them affection. When I loaded Giulia and Giò into my car, I was told to keep them in their carriers for their safety. However, as I turned around the corner driving away from Green Hill, I stopped and freed them in the car. I could not bear the thought of them in a cage any longer.

The thing that really moved me was seeing Giulia and Giò make contact with the world for the first time. They had never seen the sky and they had never seen a meadow. At five months old, these two little creatures discovered what was outside that one cage they had inhabited. I looked at their eyes and all their amazement and this was enough for me. I knew that they were finally free and that they would have plenty of time to really start living.

Both Giulia and Giò came out of Green Hill with bad cases of giardia, a parasitic infection of the intestines. And, even though Green Hill was only a place used to *breed* experimental dogs, I can argue the opposite as both Giulia and Giò had already been used for testing.

Giulia had two cuts at the height of the ovaries, badly stitched. After many checks by my veterinarians, we never understood what type of experimentation she was subjected to, as her ovaries were intact. More than anything else, the vets ventured the hypothesis that some device had been implanted under her skin. As for Giò, she had no scar, but a furrow around the muzzle as if some mask-like device had been applied to her. For over four years I was not able to caress or touch her face.

I assigned the two beagles to a room which adjoins the kitchen of the house. At night they slept inside, and during the day I had them meet, very slowly, with the four large dogs I had at home. During the day Giulia and Giò could play outside using both a large garden and a covered area outside the home so that they could get in and out whenever they wanted.

Giulia (the one who arrived with the scars) was very scared, and every time she heard my voice rise (never with them but with my other dogs), she would sit and put her head inside her hind legs exactly where she had the scars. So, even in the moments of play with my other dogs, I avoided raising my voice so as not to make her uncomfortable. Giulia has always been considered the weaker of the two, physically as well, because she was very thin when they handed her to me, and much more delicate. Giò, on the other hand, has always been more brazen, with a more toned physique. She had an enormous need to be in my arms to be caressed and kissed. She needed more contact with humans.

I started to teach Giulia and Giò how to play ball, but above all I concentrated on their nutrition because, in my opinion, they were quite undernourished and did not eat the right food. So, I settled the food issue immediately (obviously with the advice of my veterinarians) and immediately started the therapy against giardia.

During these first days, Giulia and Giò went out with me and I showed them the garden. The first time they saw the garden it was exciting because they didn't know what the grass was and they were afraid to put their feet in it. When they realized that it wouldn't hurt, they started running for hours, chasing each other and jumping in the grass.

Now that eight years have passed since I got Giulia and Giò, I look back at how they taught themselves, a little bit at a time, to bring out their feelings and to trust me. Their "look" is unique. It is a "look" of good feelings. It is a "look" that always thanks me, fills me with joy every time I see it, and makes me understand that saving Giulia and Giò was one of the few true successes of my life.[3]

# Chapter Notes


## *Foreword*

1. Jamie Chambers et al., "Dog-Human Coevolution: Cross-Cultural Analysis of Multiple Hypotheses," *Journal of Ethnobiology* 40, no. 4 (2020): 414–433, https://doi.org/10.2993/0278-0771-40.4.414.
2. "Love Animals? Support Animal Research," Foundation for Biomedical Research, September 2018, https://fbresearch.org/wp-content/uploads/2018/09/Love-Animals-SUPPORT-Animal-Research-4th-Printing.pdf.

## *Preface*

1. Pema Chödron, *Welcoming the Unwelcome: Wholehearted Living in a Brokenhearted World* (Shambhala Publications, 2019), 2–6.
2. "Dogs Used in Testing and Research," compiled by The Humane Society of the United States, 2020.

## *Chapter 1*

1. Andreas-Holger Maehle, "Literary Responses to Animal Experimentation in Seventeenth and Eighteenth-Century Britain," *Medical History* 34 (1990): 40. English novelist Francis Coventry (1725–1759) became best known for *The History of Pompey the Little*, a story following the lap-dog Pompey on his journey from master to master, eventually falling into the hands of vivisection to be dissected alive, although Pompey finally escaped this terrible fate, reflecting Coventry's critical attitude towards animal experimentation as being supplemental and superfluous.
2. James Gordon, "Ancient Dog DNA Shows Early Spread Around the Globe," *New York Times*, October 29, 2020, https://www.nytimes.com/2020/10/29/science/ancient-dog-dna.html.
3. Brandon Keim, "The Genius of Dogs: Understanding Our Best Friends," *National Geographic*, 2020, 66.
4. Nuno Henrique Franco, "Animal Experiments in Biomedical Research: A Historical Perspective," *Animals: an open access journal from MDPI* 3, no. 1 (March 2013): 238–39, doi:10.3390/ani3010238. https://www.ncbi.nlm.nih.gov/pmc/articles/PMC4495509/pdf/animals-03-00238.pdf
5. Bruce Jennings, "Animal Research," in *Bioethics*, 4th ed. (Michigan: Macmillan, Reference USA, 2014), 218–220.
6. Keim, "The Genius of Dogs," 66.
7. Franco, "Animal Experiments," 238–39.
8. Aysha Akhtar, *Our Symphony with Animals: On Health, Empathy, and Our Shared Destinies* (Pegasus Books, 2019), 112.
9. Akhtar, *Our Symphony with Animals*, 113.
10. Jennings, "Animal Research," 220.
11. "Research Animals: Dog," AnimalResearch.info, accessed August 27, 2020, http://www.animalresearch.info/en/designing-research/research-animals/dog/.
12. James A. Serpell, "The Unique Role of Dogs in Society," March 27, 2019, Public Workshop on the Uses of Dogs in Biomedical Research, National Academies Keck Center Building in Washington, DC, video 14-Panel 2, https://vimeo.com/showcase/5891666/video/328466953.

13. Franco, "Animal Experiments," 256.

14. A.W.H. Bates, "Vivisection, Virtue, and the Law in the Nineteenth Century," in *Anti-Vivisection and the Profession of Medicine in Britain*, Palgrave Macmillan Animal Ethics Series (2017): 16–17, https://www.researchgate.net/publication/318655168_Vivisection_Virtue_and_the_Law_in_the_Nineteenth_Century.

15. Franco, "Animal Experiments," 241.

16. Jennings, "Animal Research," 221.

17. Jennings, "Animal Research," 219.

18. Charles G. Gross, "Claude Bernard and the Constancy of the Internal Environment," *The Neuroscientist* 4 (September 1998): 380, doi:10.1177/107385849800400520. https://www.researchgate.net/publication/247752430_Claude_Bernard_and_the_Constancy_of_the_Internal_Environment.

19. Inès Barthélémy, Christophe Hitte, and Laurent Tiret, "The Dog Model in the Spotlight: Legacy of a Trustful Cooperation," *Journal of Neuromuscular Diseases* 6, no. 4 (2019): 422–423, doi:10.3233/JND-190394, https://www.ncbi.nlm.nih.gov/pmc/articles/PMC6918919/.

20. Bates, "Vivisection, Virtue, and the Law," 16–17.

21. Greg Murrie, "Death-in-Life: Curare, Restrictionism and Abolitionism in Victorian and Edwardian Anti-Vivisectionist Thought," chap. 15 in *Animal Death*, edited by Jay Johnston and Fiona Probyn-Rapsey (Sydney University Press, Australia, 2013), 258, www.jstor.org/stable/j.ctt1gxxpvf.21.

22. Gross, "Claude Bernard," 380.

23. Murrie, "Death-in-Life," 261.

24. Murrie, "Death-in-Life," 262–64.

25. Murrie, "Death-in-Life," 262–64.

26. Gross, "Claude Bernard," 381.

27. Franco, "Animal Experiments," 249–50.

28. Gross, "Claude Bernard," 383.

29. Franco, "Animal Experiments," 250.

30. P. Berche, "Louis Pasteur, From Crystals of Life to Vaccination," *Clinical Microbiology and Infection* 18, no. 5 (October 2012): 4, https://doi.org/10.1111/j.1469-0691.2012.03945.x.

31. Berche, "Louis Pasteur," 5.

32. Franco, "Animal Experiments," 253.

33. Daniel Engber, "Where's Pepper?" *Slate*, June 1, 2009, http://www.slate.com/articles/health_and_science/pepper/2009/06/wheres_pepper.html.

34. Michael Specter, "Drool: Ivan Pavlov's Real Quest," *New Yorker*, November 17, 2014, https://www.newyorker.com/magazine/2014/11/24/drool.

35. Engber, "Where's Pepper?"

36. Specter, "Drool."

37. Engber, "Where's Pepper?"

38. "Research Animals: Dog," AnimalResearch.info, accessed August 27, 2020, http://www.animalresearch.info/en/designing-research/research-animals/dog/.

## *Chapter 2*

1. A.W.H. Bates, "Vivisection, Virtue, and the Law in the Nineteenth Century," in *Anti-Vivisection and the Profession of Medicine in Britain*, Palgrave Macmillan Animal Ethics Series (2017): 29, https://www.researchgate.net/publication/318655168_Vivisection_Virtue_and_the_Law_in_the_Nineteenth_Century.

2. Bates, "Vivisection, Virtue, and the Law," 21.

3. Bates, "Vivisection, Virtue, and the Law," 29.

4. Elizabeth Jane Timms, "Queen Victoria's Dogs," *Royal Central*, August 1, 2018, https://royalcentral.co.uk/features/queen-victorias-dogs-106695/.

5. E.M. Tansey, "The Queen Has Been Dreadfully Shocked: Aspects of Teaching Experimental Physiology Using Animals in Britain, 1876–1986," *AJP Centennial* 19, no. 1 (June 1998): S20, https://journals.physiology.org/doi/pdf/10.1152/advances.1998.274.6.S18.

6. Emma Hopley, *Campaigning Against Cruelty: The Hundred Year History of the British Union for the Abolition of Vivisection* (British Union of Abolition of Vivisection, 1998), 2.

7. Hopley, *Campaigning Against Cruelty*, 2.

8. National Anti-Vivisection Society (website), "The History of the NAVS," https://www.navs.org.uk/about_us/24/0/299/.

9. Hopley, *Campaigning Against Cruelty*, 3–4.

10. "Prosecution at Norwich. Experiments on Animals," *The British Medical*

*Journal* 2, no. 728 (December 1874): 751–52, http://www.jstor.com/stable/25240021.

11. Greg Murrie, "Death-in-Life: Curare, Restrictionism and Abolitionism in Victorian and Edwardian Anti-Vivisectionist Thought," chap. 15 in *Animal Death*, edited by Jay Johnston and Fiona Probyn-Rapsey (Sydney University Press, Australia, 2013), 261, www.jstor.org/stable/j.ctt1gxxpvf.21.

12. Bates, "Vivisection, Virtue, and the Law," 26.

13. Hopley, *Campaigning Against Cruelty*, 1.

14. Bates, "Vivisection, Virtue, and the Law," 26–28.

15. Bruce Jennings, "Animal Research," in *Bioethics*, 4th ed. (Michigan: Macmillan, Reference USA, 2014), 221.

16. American Anti-Vivisection Society (website), "Our History," https://aavs.org/about/history.

17. "The Zoophil-Psychosis," *New York Times*, July 11, 1909, https://archive.nytimes.com.

18. Craig Buettinger, "Antivivisection and the Charge of Zoophilia–psychosis in the Early Twentieth Century," *The Historian* 55, no. 2 (December 1993): 277, https://doi.org/10.1111/j.1540-6563.1993.tb00896.x.

19. Buettinger, "Antivivisection," 280.

20. Buettinger, "Antivivisection," 281.

21. Buettinger, "Antivivisection," 284.

22. Buettinger, "Antivivisection," 287.

23. Coral Lansbury, "The Brown Dog Riots of 1907," in *The Animals Reader*, eds. Linda Kalof and Amy Fitzgerald (Bloomsbury Academic, 2007), 311–314.

24. Hopley, *Campaigning Against Cruelty*, 20.

25. Coral Lansbury, "The Brown Dog Riots," 315.

26. Lansbury, "The Brown Dog Riots," 318.

27. Hopley, *Campaigning Against Cruelty*, 20.

28. Lansbury, "The Brown Dog Riots," 319.

29. Hopley, *Campaigning Against Cruelty*, 20.

30. A.W.H. Bates, "The Research Defence Society: Mobilizing the Medical Profession for Materialist Science in the Early-Twentieth Century," in *Anti-Vivisection and the Profession of Medicine in Britain*, Palgrave Macmillan Animal Ethics Series (2017):153–154, https://www.researchgate.net/publication/318656592_The_Research_Defence_SocietyResearch_Defence_Society_Mobilizing_the_Medical_Profession_for_Materialist_Science Science_Nature_of_in_the_Early-Twentieth_Century.

31. Hopley, *Campaigning Against Cruelty*, 34–35.

32. Bates, "The Research Defence Society," 155–57.

33. Daniel Engber, "Where's Pepper?" *Slate*, June 1, 2009, http://www.slate.com/articles/health_and_science/pepper/2009/06/wheres_pepper.html.

34. Bernard Unti, "Frank McMahon: The Investigator Who Took a Bite Out of Animal Lab Suppliers." White paper included in The Humane Society Institute for Science and Policy Animal Studies Repository, 2013, http://animalstudiesrepository.org/acwp_awap/22.

35. Unti, "Frank McMahon."

36. Unti, "Frank McMahon."

37. "The Photography of Stan Wayman," *LIFE* (website), accessed October 20, 2020, https://www.life.com/photographer/stan-wayman/.

## Chapter 3

1. National Academies of Sciences, Engineering, and Medicine, "Necessity, Use, and Care of Laboratory Dogs at the U.S. Department of Veterans Affairs" (National Academy of Sciences, 2020). https://doi.org/10.17226/25772.

2. Nina Hasiwa et al., "Critical Evaluation of the Use of Dogs in Biomedical Research and Testing in Europe," *ALTEX* 28, no. 4 (April 2011): 329, https://www.altex.org/index.php/altex/article/view/492/503.

3. Peter Singer, *Animal Liberation*, rev. ed. (HarperCollins Publishers, 2009), 63.

4. Singer, *Animal Liberation*, 63.

5. "A Brief History of Animals in Space," National Aeronautics and Space Administration, accessed May 31, 2020, https://history.nasa.gov/printFriendly/animals.html.

6. Alice George, "The Sad, Sad Story of Laika, the Space Dog, and Her One-Way Trip into Orbit," *Smithsonian Magazine*, April 2018, https://www.smithsonianmag.com/smithsonian-institution/sad-story-laika-space-dog-and-her-one-way-trip-orbit-1-180968728/.

7. A.W.H. Bates, "State Control, Bureaucracy, and the National Interest from the Second World War to the 1960s," in *Anti-Vivisection and the Profession of Medicine in Britain*, Palgrave Macmillan Animal Ethics Series (2017): 184, https://www.researchgate.net/publication/318655521_State_Control_Bureaucracy_and_the_National_Interest_from_the_Second_World_War_to_the_1960s.

8. George, "The Sad, Sad Story of Laika."

9. George, "The Sad, Sad Story of Laika."

10. Bates, "State Control, Bureaucracy, and the National Interest," 184.

11. "A Brief History of Animals in Space," National Aeronautics and Space Administration.

12. George, "The Sad, Sad Story of Laika."

13. Benjamin Haley et al., "Past and Future Work on Radiobiology Mega Studies: A Case Study at Argonne National Laboratory," *Health Physics* 100, no. 6 (June 2011): 3, https://www.ncbi.nlm.nih.gov/pmc/articles/PMC3784403/.

14. Haley et al., "Past and Future Work," 3.

15. Haley et al., "Past and Future Work," 12.

16. Haley et al., "Past and Future Work," 3.

17. Haley et al., "Past and Future Work," 3.

18. Haley et al., "Past and Future Work," 9.

19. Lawrence K. Altman, "12 Dogs Develop Lung Cancer In Group of 86 Taught to Smoke," *New York Times*, February 6, 1970, https://archive.nytimes.com.

20. National Academies of Sciences, Engineering, and Medicine, "Necessity, Use, and Care of Laboratory Dogs at the U.S. Department of Veterans Affairs."

21. National Academies of Sciences, Engineering, and Medicine, "Necessity, Use, and Care."

22. Katy Taylor and Laura Rego Alvarez, "An Estimate of the Number of Animals Used for Scientific Purposes Worldwide in 2015," *Alternatives to Laboratory Animals* 47, no. 5–6 (2019): 205, https://journals.sagepub.com/doi/pdf/10.1177/0261192919899853.

23. "Dogs Used in Testing and Research," compiled by The Humane Society of the United States, 2020; for further discussion see United States Department of Agriculture (website), "Research Facility Annual Summary and Archive Reports," last modified September 23, 2020, https://www.aphis.usda.gov/aphis/ourfocus/animalwelfare/sa_obtain_research_facility_annual_report/ct_research_facility_annual_summary_reports.

24. "Dogs Used in Testing and Research," The Humane Society.

25. "Class B Dealers," American Anti-Vivisection Society (website), accessed October 28, 2020, https://aavs.org/our-work/campaigns/class-b-dealers/.

26. "Tests on Dogs," compiled by Cruelty Free International, August 2020.

## *Chapter 4*

1. Jim Keen, "Wasted Money in United States Biomedical and Agricultural Animal Research," in *Animal Experimentation: Working Toward a Paradigm Change*," eds. Kathrin Herrmann and Kimberley Jayne (Leiden; Boston: Brill, 2019), 245, https://doi.org/10.1163/9789004391192.

2. Lindsay J. Marshall et al., "Recommendations Toward a Human Pathway-based Approach to Disease Research," *Drug Discovery Today* 23, no. 11 (November 2018): 1824–25, https://doi.org/10.1016/j.drudis.2018.05.038.

3. Marshall et al., "Recommendations," 1824–25.

4. Gail A. Van Norman, "Limitations of Animal Studies for Predicting Toxicity in Clinical Trials: Is it Time to Rethink Our Current Approach," *JACC: Basic to Translational Science* 4, no. 7 (October 2019): 848, https://doi.org/10.1016/j.jacbts.2019.10.008.

5. Jarrod Bailey and Michael Balls,

"Recent Efforts to Elucidate the Scientific Validity of Animal-based Drug Tests by the Pharmaceutical Industry, Pro-testing Lobby Groups, and Animal Welfare Organizations," *BMC Medical Ethics* 20, no. 16 (2019): 5, https://doi.org/10.1186/s12910-019-0352-3.

6. Bailey and Balls, "Recent Efforts," 5.

7. Jarrod Bailey, Michelle Thew, and Michael Balls, "An Analysis of the Use of Animal Models in Predicting Human Toxicology and Drug Safety. *Altern Lab Anim* 42, no. 3 (June 2014): 181–199, https://www.wellbeingintlstudiesrepository.org/cgi/viewcontent.cgi?article=1123&context=acwp_arte.

8. *Good Medicine*. "Averting Drug Disasters: How to Stop the Next Pharmaceutical Catastrophe," Spring 2016, https://pcrm.widencollective.com/portals/vfv1ozlu/GoodMedicine.

9. Aysha Akhtar, "The Flaws and Human Harms of Animal Experimentation," *Cambridge Quarterly of Healthcare Ethics* 24 (2015): 410–16, https://www.researchgate.net/publication/281780611_The_Flaws_and_Human_Harms_of_Animal_Experimentation.

10. National Academies of Sciences, Engineering, and Medicine, "Necessity, Use, and Care."

11. National Academies of Sciences, Engineering, and Medicine, "Necessity, Use, and Care."

12. Humane Society of the United States, comments submitted to the *Institute for Laboratory Animal Research (ILAR)* for the National Academies of Sciences, Engineering, and Medicine study "Necessity, Use, and Care of Laboratory Dogs at the U.S. Department of Veterans Affairs, 2020," submitted June 11, 2019.

13. Elisa Passini et al., "Humans in Silico Drug Trials Demonstrate Higher Accuracy Than Animal Models in Predicting Clinical Pro-Arrhythmic Cardiotoxicity," *Frontiers in Physiology* 8, no. 668 (September 2017): 1–2, https://www.ncbi.nlm.nih.gov/pmc/articles/PMC5601077/pdf/fphys-08-00668.pdf.

14. University of Oxford, Department of Computer Science (website), Blanca Rodriguez, accessed November 24, 2020, https://www.cs.ox.ac.uk/people/blanca.rodriguez.

15. Physicians Committee for Responsible Medicine, "Dog Experiments at Wayne State: Decades of Pain and Futility," October 7, 2019, https://www.pcrm.org/sites/default/files/2019-10/REPORT%20-%20Dog%20Experiments%20at%20Wayne%20State%20-%2010.07.19_0.pdf.

16. Rita A. Halpin et al., "The Absorption, Distribution, Metabolism and Excretion of Rofecoxib, a Potent and Selective Cyclooxygenase-2 Inhibitor, in Rats and Dogs," *Drug Metabolism and Disposition* 28, no. 10 (2000): 1245.

17. Van Norman, "Limitations of Animal Studies," 847.

18. Duff Wilson, "Merck to Pay $950 Million Over Vioxx," *New York Times*, November 22, 2011, https://www.nytimes.com/2011/11/23/business/merck-agrees-to-pay-950-million-in-vioxx-case.html.

19. Van Norman, "Limitations of Animal Studies," 846–47.

20. Rimplejeet Kaur, Preeti Sidhu, and Surjit Singh, "What Failed BIA 10–2472 Phase I Clinical Trial? Global Speculations and Recommendations for Future Phase I Trials," *Journal of Pharmacology & Pharmacotherapeutics* 7, no. 3 (July-September 2016): 1–2, https://www.ncbi.nlm.nih.gov/pmc/articles/PMC5020770/?report=reader.

21. *Good Medicine*. "Averting Drug Disasters."

22. Kaur, Sidhu, and Singh, "What failed BIA 10–2472," 1–2.

23. Van Norman, "Limitations of Animal Studies," 845.

24. Lindsay Marshall. Recorded Zoom Interview with Ellie Hansen. September 25, 2020.

25. Jarrod Bailey. Recorded Zoom Interview with Ellie Hansen. June 22, 2020; for further discussion see Jarrod Bailey, "Lessons from Chimpanzee-based Research on Human Disease: The Implications of Genetic Differences," *Alternatives to Laboratory Animals-ATLA* 39, no. 6 (December 2011): 527–540, https://www.wellbeingintlstudiesrepository.org/cgi/viewcontent.cgi?article=1027&context=acwp_lab; Jarrod Bailey, "Monkey-based Research on Human Disease: The Implications of Genetic Differences," *Alternatives to Laboratory Animals-ATLA* 42 (November

2014): 287–317, https://www.wellbeingintlstudiesrepository.org/cgi/viewcontent.cgi?article=1024&context=acwp_lab.

26. Lindsay Marshall. Recorded Zoom Interview, September 25, 2020.

27. Jarrod Bailey. Recorded Zoom Interview, June 22, 2020; for further discussion see Jarrod Bailey, "Does the Stress of Laboratory Life and Experimentation on Animals Adversely Affect Research Data? A Critical Review," *Alternatives to Laboratory Animals-ATLA* 46 (December 2018): 291–305, https://www.researchgate.net/publication/329416611_Does_the_Stress_of_Laboratory_Life_and_Experimentation_on_Animals_Adversely_Affect_Research_Data_A_Critical_Review.

28. Jarrod Bailey. Recorded Zoom Interview, June 22, 2020; for further discussion see Jarrod Bailey, "Recent Advances in the Development and Application of Human-Specific Biomedical Research and Testing Methods," *Center for Contemporary Sciences* (October 2020), https://contemporarysciences.org/resources/13.

## *Chapter 5*

1. "Ridglan Farms Inc," Laboratory Animal Science Buyers Guide (website), accessed April 23, 2020, http://laboratoryanimalsciencebuyersguide.com/Listing/Company/1185399.

2. "Beagle," American Kennel Club (website), accessed April 23, 2020, https://www.akc.org/dog-breeds/beagle/.

3. "Dogs Used in Testing and Research," compiled by the Humane Society of the United States, 2020.

4. "Marshall Beagle"" Marshall Bioresources (website), accessed November 24, 2020, https://www.marshallbio.com/marshall-beaglesr; "Mongrels/Hounds," Marshall Bioresources (website), accessed November 24, 2020, https://www.marshallbio.com/mongrelshounds.

5. "Ridglan Farms Inc," Laboratory Animal," http://laboratoryanimalsciencebuyersguide.com/Listing/Company/1185399.

6. "Dogs Used in Testing and Research," compiled by the Humane Society of the United States, 2020.

7. "Toxicity Testing on Dogs Exposed," compiled by the Humane Society of the United States, 2019.

8. Kitty Block, "HSUS Undercover Investigation Shows Beagles Being Poisoned with Pesticides and Drugs, Killed at Animal Testing Lab," A Humane World (blog), *The Humane Society of the United States*, March 12, 2019, https://blog.humanesociety.org/2019/03/hsus-undercover-investigation-shows-beagles-being-poisoned-with-pesticides-and-drugs-killed-at-animal-testing-lab.html.

9. "Toxicity Testing on Dogs Exposed."

10. Block, "HSUS Undercover Investigation."

11. Emily Smith, "Life Beyond the Laboratory: Michigan Dogs Blossom Following Release from Testing Facility," *Animal Sheltering Magazine*, Fall 2019, https://www.animalsheltering.org/magazine/articles/life-beyond-laboratory.

12. Jarrod Bailey. Recorded Zoom Interview with Ellie Hansen. June 22, 2020.

13. Stanley Coren and Edwin Rutsch, "How to Build a Culture of Empathy with Dogs," *Center for Building a Culture of Empathy*, filmed August 28, 2012, YouTube video, http://cultureofempathy.com/References/Experts/others/Stanley-Coren.htm.

14. Claudia Fugazza, Ákos Pogány, and Ádám Miklósi, "Recall of Others' Actions after Incidental Encoding Reveals Episodic-like Memory in Dogs," *Current Biology* 26 (December 2016): 3209–3213, https://doi.org/10.1016/j.cub.2016.09.057.

15. Simon Worrall, "Yes, Animals Think and Feel. Here's How We Know," *National Geographic*, July 15, 2015, https://www.nationalgeographic.com/news/2015/07/150714-animal-dog-thinking-feelings-brain-science/.

16. Gregory Berns, *What It's Like to Be a Dog: And Other Adventures in Animal Neuroscience* (New York: Basic Books, 2017).

17. National Research Council, "Regulation of Animal Research," *Science, Medicine, and Animals* (Washington, DC: The National Academies Press, 2004), 29–30, https://doi.org/10.17226/10733.

18. Sarah Kenehan, "The Moral Status of Animal Research Subjects in

Industry: A Stakeholder Analysis," in *Animal Experimentation: Working Toward a Paradigm Change*," eds. Kathrin Herrmann and Kimberley Jayne (Leiden; Boston: Brill, 2019), 217, https://doi.org/10.1163/9789004391192.

19. Lindsay Marshall. Recorded Zoom Interview with Ellie Hansen. September 25, 2020.

20. Kathleen Conlee. Recorded Conference Call with Ellie Hansen. June 22, 2020.

21. Bruce Jennings, "Animal Research," in *Bioethics*, 4th ed. (Michigan: Macmillan, Reference USA, 2014), 222.

22. National Research Council, "Regulation of Animal Research," 31–32.

23. Conlee. Recorded Conference Call.

24. Jim Keen, "Wasted Money in United States Biomedical and Agricultural Animal Research," in *Animal Experimentation: Working Toward a Paradigm Change*, eds. Kathrin Herrmann and Kimberley Jayne (Leiden: Brill, 2019), 247, https://doi.org/10.1163/9789004391192.

25. Lawrence A. Hansen and Kori Ann Kosberg, "Ethics, Efficacy, and Decision-making in Animal Research," in *Animal Experimentation: Working Towards a Paradigm Change*, eds. Kathrin Herrmann and Kimberley Jayne (Leiden: Brill, 2019), p. 283, https://doi.org/10.1163/9789004391192.

26. National Research Council (U.S.) Committee on Scientific and Humane Issues in the Use of Random Source Dogs and Cats in Research, *Scientific and Humane Issues in the Use of Random Source Dogs and Cats in Research* (Washington DC: National Academies Press (U.S.), 2009), 17–19, https://www.ncbi.nlm.nih.gov/books/NBK32671/, doi:10.17226/12641.

27. National Research Council (U.S.) Committee on Scientific and Humane Issues in the Use of Random Source Dogs and Cats.

28. National Research Council, "Regulation of Animal Research," 32.

29. Discussion, March 27, 2019, Public Workshop on the Uses of Dogs in Biomedical Research, *National Academies Keck Center Building* in Washington, DC, video 15-Panel 2, https://vimeo.com/showcase/5891666/video/328467114.

30. Jerrold Tannenbaum and B. Taylor Bennett, "Russell and Burch's 3Rs Then and Now: The Need for Clarity in Definition and Purpose," *Journal of the American Association for Laboratory Animal Science* 54, no. 2 (March 2015): 131, https://www.ncbi.nlm.nih.gov/pmc/articles/PMC4382615/.

31. W.M.S. Russell and R.L. Burch, "Chapter 2: The Concept of Inhumanity," in *The Principles of Humane Experimental Technique*, Johns Hopkins Bloomberg School of Public Health (website), https://caat.jhsph.edu/principles/chap2a.

32. Stacy Lopresti-Goodman and Justin Goodman. Recorded Zoom Interview with Ellie Hansen. August 17, 2020.

33. Lopresti-Goodman and Goodman. Recorded Zoom Interview.

## Chapter 6

1. James A. Serpell, "The Unique Role of Dogs in Society," March 27, 2019, Public Workshop on the Uses of Dogs in Biomedical Research, National Academies Keck Center Building in Washington, DC, video 14-Panel 2, https://vimeo.com/showcase/5891666/video/328466953.

2. Gregory Berns, *What It's Like to Be a Dog: And Other Adventures in Animal Neuroscience* (New York: Basic Books, 2017), 237–239.

3. Lynda Birke, "Into the Laboratory," in *The Animals Reader*, eds. Linda Kalof and Amy Fitzgerald (Bloomsbury Academic, 2007), 325.

4. Birke, "Into the Laboratory," 328.

5. Kathleen Conlee. Recorded Conference Call with Ellie Hansen. June 22, 2020.

6. "Meet Teddy: Rescued from Cruel Research," The Humane Society of the United States, December 26, 2019, YouTube video, https://www.youtube.com/watch?v=NQ0GzWFrM54.

7. Aysha Akhtar, *Our Symphony with Animals: On Health, Empathy, and Our Shared Destinies* (Pegasus Books, 2019), 196.

8. Lesley A. Sharp, *Animal Ethos: The Morality of Human-Animal Encounters in Experimental Lab Science* (Oakland: University of California Press, 2019), 157–158.

9. Sharp, *Animal Ethos*, 174.

10. Sharp, *Animal Ethos*, 231–32.

11. Lopresti-Goodman and Goodman. Recorded Zoom Interview.

12. Sharp, *Animal Ethos*, 236.

13. Serpell, "The Unique Role of Dogs in Society," video 14-Panel 2.

14. David Grimm, "Opening the Lab Door" *Science*, June 29, 2018, https://science.sciencemag.org/content/360/6396/1392.long.

15. Lawrence A. Hansen and Kori Ann Kosberg, "Ethics, Efficacy, and Decision-making in Animal Research," in *Animal Experimentation: Working Towards a Paradigm Change*, eds. Kathrin Herrmann and Kimberley Jayne (Leiden: Brill, 2019), 281, https://doi.org/10.1163/9789004391192.

16. Grimm, "Opening the Lab Door."

17. Cristina Corbin, "University Under Fire for Breeding Golden Retrievers with Muscular Dystrophy," *New York Post*, November 1, 2017, https://nypost.com/2017/11/01/university-under-fire-for-breeding-golden-retrievers-with-muscular-dystrophy/.

18. Scottie Andrew and Saeed Ahmed, "Paul McCartney Asked a Texas University to Stop Testing on Dogs," *CNN*, June 27, 2019, https://www.cnn.com/2019/06/27/us/paul-mccartney-stop-animal-testing-texas-trnd/index.html.

19. Alexia Fernandez, "James Cromwell Arrested at Texas A&M University While Protesting Dog Lab Testing at the School," *People*, October 31, 2019, https://people.com/movies/james-cromwell-arrested-peta-protest/.

20. Tom L. Beauchamp and David DeGrazia, *Principals of Animal Research Ethics* (New York: Oxford University Press, 2020), 2–3.

21. David DeGrazia. Recorded Conference Call with Ellie Hansen. June 19, 2020.

22. Discussion, March 27, 2019, Public Workshop on the Uses of Dogs in Biomedical Research, National Academies Keck Center Building in Washington, DC, video 15-Panel 2, https://vimeo.com/showcase/5891666/video/328467114.

23. DeGrazia. Recorded Conference Call.

24. Akhtar, *Our Symphony with Animals*, 181.

## *Chapter 7*

1. Harvard University, "Lung-on-a-Chip Wins Prize for Potentially Reducing Need for Animal Testing," *Wyss Institute*, February 26, 2013, https://wyss.harvard.edu/news/wyss-institutes-lung-on-a-chip-wins-prize-for-potentially-reducing-need-for-animal-testing/.

2. Barry Teater, "Feds Award $24 M for Wake Forest Lung-on-a-Chip Studies," *North Carolina Biotechnology Center*, October 9, 2019, https://www.ncbiotech.org/news/feds-award-24m-wake-forest-lung-chip-studies.

3. National Academies of Sciences, Engineering, and Medicine, "Necessity, Use, and Care of Laboratory Dogs at the U.S. Department of Veterans Affairs," (prepublication copy, National Academy of Sciences, 2020). https://doi.org/10.17226/25772.

4. Physicians Committee for Responsible Medicine, "Dog Experiments at Wayne State: Decades of Pain and Futility," October 7, 2019, https://www.pcrm.org/sites/default/files/2019-10/REPORT%20-%20Dog%20Experiments%20at%20Wayne%20State%20-%2010.07.19_0.pdf.

5. Karl D'Souza, "Technology to Transform Lives: The SIMULIA Living Heart Model," *NAFEMS Benchmark* (July 2015), https://www.3ds.com/fileadmin/Industries/life-sciences/pdf/NAFEMS-Benchmark-Technology-to-Save-Lives-LHP-07-01-15.PDF.

6. Dassault Systemes (website), *The Living Heart Project*, accessed October 7, 2020, https://www.3ds.com/products-services/simulia/solutions/life-sciences/the-living-heart-project/.

7. D'Souza, "Technology to Transform Lives."

8. D'Souza, "Technology to Transform Lives."

9. Javier Barbuzano, "Organoids: A New Window Into Disease, Development and Discovery," *Harvard Stem Cell Institute*, November 7, 2017, https://hsci.harvard.edu/organoids.

10. Jihoon Kim, Bon-Kyoung Koo, and Juergen A. Knoblich, "Human Organoids: Model Systems for Human Biology and Medicine," *Nature Reviews Molecular Cell Biology* 21 (2020): 571–584, https://doi.org/10.1038/s41580-020-0259-3.

11. Barbuzano, "Organoids: A New Window Into Disease."

12. Kim, Koo, and Knoblich, "Human Organoids," 571–584.

13. Nick Cooney, *Change of Heart: What Psychology Can Teach Us About Spreading Social Change* (New York: Lantern Books, 2011), 43.

14. Cooney, *Change of Heart*, 162.

15. "European Directive 2010/63," Understanding Animal Research, last edited February 21 2018, https://www.understandinganimalresearch.org.uk/openness/european-directive/; for further discussion see Kathrin Herrmann, "Refinement on the Way Towards Replacement: Are We Doing What We Can?" in *Animal Experimentation: Working Towards a Paradigm Change*, eds. Kathrin Herrmann and Kimberley Jayne (Leiden: Brill, 2019), 3–38, https://doi.org/10.1163/9789004391192.

16. "EU Regulations on Animal Research," European Animal Research Association, accessed November 26, 2020, https://www.eara.eu/animal-research-law.

17. "Adverse Outcome Pathways (AOPs)," Biomed21 Collaboration, accessed November 26, 2020, https://biomed21.org/; for further discussion see Kathrin Herrmann, "Refinement on the Way Towards Replacement: Are We Doing What We Can?" in *Animal Experimentation: Working Towards a Paradigm Change*, eds. Kathrin Herrmann and Kimberley Jayne (Leiden: Brill, 2019), 30, https://doi.org/10.1163/9789004391192.

18. Rebecca Ram, "Extrapolation of Animal Research Data to Humans: An Analysis of the Evidence," in *Animal Experimentation: Working Towards a Paradigm Change*, eds. Kathrin Herrmann and Kimberley Jayne (Leiden: Brill, 2019), 367, https://doi.org/10.1163/9789004391192.

19. *Directive to Prioritize Efforts to Reduce Animal Testing* (September 10, 2019) (memorandum of Andrew R. Wheeler, Administrator of the United States Environmental Protection Agency).

20. "About Us: Center for Alternatives to Animal Testing," Johns Hopkins Center for Alternatives to Animal Testing (CAAT), https://caat.jhsph.edu/; For further discussion see Christiane Baumgartl-Simons and Christiane Hohensee, "How Can the Final Goal of Completely Replacing Animal Procedures Successfully Be Achieved?" in *Animal Experimentation: Working Towards a Paradigm Change*, eds. Kathrin Herrmann and Kimberley Jayne (Leiden: Brill, 2019), 103–04, https://doi.org/10.1163/9789004391192.

## Chapter 8

1. Jarrod Bailey. Recorded Zoom Interview with Ellie Hansen. June 22, 2020.

2. Lindsay Marshall. Recorded Zoom Interview with Ellie Hansen. September 25, 2020.

3. Bailey. Recorded Zoom Interview.

4. Marshall. Recorded Zoom Interview.

5. Stacy Lopresti-Goodman. Recorded Zoom Interview with Ellie Hansen. August 17, 2020.

6. Bailey. Recorded Zoom Interview.

7. Marshall. Recorded Zoom Interview.

8. Bailey. Recorded Zoom Interview with Ellie Hansen. June 22, 2020.

9. David DeGrazia. Recorded Conference Call with Ellie Hansen. June 19, 2020.

10. Bailey. Recorded Zoom Interview.

11. Marshall. Recorded Zoom Interview.

12. Lopresti-Goodman. Recorded Zoom Interview.

13. DeGrazia. Recorded Conference Call.

## Chapter 9

1. Beagle Freedom Project, "Help Pass the Beagle Freedom Bill," accessed on December 7, 2020, https://bfp.org/state/.

2. Stacy M. Lopresti-Goodman, "A Comparison of Former Laboratory Dogs' With Non-laboratory Dogs' Psychological and Behavioral Characteristics" (Poster presented at the Tenth World Congress: Alternatives and Animal Use in the Life Sciences, Seattle, WA, August 2017); Stacy M. Lopresti-Goodman, "Psychological and Behavioral Characteristics of Beagles Released from Laboratories"

(Poster for the Annual Meeting of the Eastern Psychological Association, New York, NY, March 2019).

3. Dorothea Doring et al., "How Do Rehomed Laboratory Beagles Behave in Everyday Situations? Results from an Observational Test and Survey of New Owners," *PLoS One* 12, no. 7 (July 25, 2017): 1–22, https://doi.org/10.1371/journal.pone.0181303.

4. Laura Hänninen and Marianna Norring, "The First Rehoming of Laboratory Beagles in Finland: The Complete Process from Socialization Training to Follow-up," *Alternatives to Laboratory Animals* 48, no. 3 (2020): 116–126, https://doi.org/10.1177%2F0261192920942135.

## Chapter 10

1. Shannon Keith. Recorded Zoom Interview with Ellie Hansen. June 24, 2020.

## Chapter 11

1. John Ramer. Recorded Conference call with Ellie Hansen. June 13, 2020.

## Chapter 12

1. "Toxicity Testing on Dogs Exposed," compiled by The Humane Society of the United States, 2019.

2. Emily Smith, "Life Beyond the Laboratory: Michigan Dogs Blossom Following Release from Testing Facility," *Animal Sheltering Magazine*, Fall 2019, https://www.animalsheltering.org/magazine/articles/life-beyond-laboratory.

3. Rubello, Dave (Research dog adopter). Phone interview by Ellie Hansen. April 27, 2020; email messages to author, April 2020.

4. Thomssen, Gail (Research dog adopter). Phone interview by Ellie Hansen. May 4, 2020; email messages to author, May 2020.

5. Selcer, Kelly (Research dog adopter). Phone interview by Ellie Hansen. June 12, 2020; email messages to author, June 2020.

6. Webster, Ryan and Sarah (Research dog adopters). Phone interview by Ellie Hansen. June 20, 2020; email messages to author, June 2020.

## Chapter 13

1. Prior, Mary (Research dog adopter). Phone interview by Ellie Hansen. August 20, 2020; email messages to author, August 2020.

2. House, Nancy (Research dog adopter). Phone interview by Ellie Hansen. June 15, 2020; email messages to author, June 2020.

3. Blavin, Lily (Research dog adopter). Phone interview by Ellie Hansen. June 17, 2020; email messages to author, June 2020.

## Chapter 14

1. Wood, Kris (Research dog adopter). Phone interview by Ellie Hansen. June 5, 2020; email messages to author, May-June 2020.

2. Vanderpool, Diane and Bruce (Research dog adopters). Phone interview by Ellie Hansen. June 22, 2020; email messages to author, June 2020.

3. (Research dog adopter). Phone interview by Ellie Hansen. July 14, 2020; email messages to author, July 2020.

## Chapter 15

1. Malone, Shannon (Research dog adopter). Phone interview by Ellie Hansen. June 8, 2020; email messages to author, May-June 2020.

2. Pascual, Brigitte (Research dog adopter). Phone interview by Ellie Hansen. July 7, 2020; email messages to author, June-July 2020.

3. Larson, Lillian and Niels (Research dog adopters). Phone interview by Ellie Hansen. June 12, 2020; email messages to author, June 2020.

## Chapter 16

1. (Research dog adopter). Phone interview by Ellie Hansen. June 26, 2020; email messages to author, June 2020.

2. Hansen, Ellie (Research dog

adopter). The author of this book contributed her own personal story.

## Chapter 17

1. Ridgeway, Erica (Research dog adopter). Phone interview by Ellie Hansen. June 15, 2020; email messages to author, June 2020.

2. (Research dog adopter). Phone interview by Ellie Hansen. June 19, 2020; email messages to author, June 2020.

3. Bowie, Paula and Jeff Bowie (Research dog adopters). Phone interview by Ellie Hansen. July 7, 2020; email messages to author, June-July 2020.

## Chapter 18

1. Stoddard, Marybeth (Research dog adopter). Phone interview by Ellie Hansen. June 24, 2020; email messages to author, June 2020.

2. Lee, Jodie (Research dog adopter). Phone interview by Ellie Hansen. June 23, 2020; email messages to author, June 2020.

## Chapter 19

1. "Dog and Cat Experiments at MSD Animal Health," Cruelty Free International, https://www.crueltyfreeinternational.org/what-we-do/investigations/dog-and-cat-experiments-msd-animal-health-0; Ted Jeory, "Graphic Content: Horrifying Video Shows Puppies and Kittens Tested at UK Laboratory," *Express*, March 2, 2014, https://www.express.co.uk/news/uk/462546/Horrifying-BUAV-video-investigation-shows-puppies-kittens-ripped-apart-in-UK-animal-lab.

2. Kite, Sarah (Research dog adopter). Email interview by Ellie Hansen. November 8, 2020.

3. (Research dog adopter). Email interview by Ellie Hansen. November 7, 2020.

## Chapter 20

1. LAV, "Green Hill Found Guilty: Court of Brescia Convicts Rondot (Executive Manager), Bravi (Director) and Graziosi (Veterinarian) for Animal Abuse and Illegal Killing of Animals, Occurred in the Italian Beagle Breeding Facility Intended for Animal Testing; All the 3,000 Beagles Are Definitively Confiscated and Will Remain with Their Families!" News release, January 23, 2015; LAV, "Green Hill: Supreme Court Rejects Appeal; This Is the Final Conviction! The Line of Defence Based on the Concept of a Disposable Dog Product for Laboratory Use Has Been Demolished," News release, April 10, 2017

2. Stefano, Samanta (Research dog adopter). Email interview by Ellie Hansen. August 16, 2020.

3. (Research dog adopter). Email interview by Ellie Hansen. August 18, 2020.

# Bibliography

Listed here are writings, conference recordings, and videos that have guided the academic portions of this book. The sources represent one of the most comprehensive collections on the use of dogs in research including historical, scientific, and ethical viewpoints.

For many readers, the study of why and how dogs are used in scientific research may be of interest. Further, the resources listed below have been chosen as tools to help build awareness in all the aspects of research on dogs; encourage educated discussion; and facilitate compassion and cooperation as we work—in our own unique ways—to make the world a better place for both humans and animals.


Akhtar, Aysha. "The Flaws and Human Harms of Animal Experimentation." *Cambridge Quarterly of Healthcare Ethics* 24 (2015): 410–16. https://www.researchgate.net/publication/281780611_The_Flaws_and_Human_Harms_of_Animal_Experimentation.

Akhtar, Aysha. *Our Symphony with Animals: On Health, Empathy, and Our Shared Destinies.* Pegasus Books, 2019.

Altman, Lawrence K. "12 Dogs Develop Lung Cancer In Group of 86 Taught to Smoke." *New York Times,* February 6, 1970. https://archive.nytimes.com.

American Anti-Vivisection Society. "Our History." https://aavs.org/about/history.

Andrew, Scottie, and Saeed Ahmed. "Paul McCartney Asked a Texas University to Stop Testing on Dogs." *CNN,* June 27, 2019. https://www.cnn.com/2019/06/27/us/paul-mccartney-stop-animal-testing-texas-trnd/index.html.

Bailey, Jarrod. "Does the Stress of Laboratory Life and Experimentation on Animals Adversely Affect Research Data? A Critical Review." *Alternatives to Laboratory Animals-ATLA* 46 (December 2018): 291–305. https://www.researchgate.net/publication/329416611_Does_the_Stress_of_Laboratory_Life_and_Experimentation_on_Animals_Adversely_Affect_Research_Data_A_Critical_Review.

Bailey, Jarrod. "Lessons from Chimpanzee-based Research on Human Disease: The Implications of Genetic Differences." *Alternatives to Laboratory Animals-ATLA* 39, no. 6 (December 2011): 527–540. https://www.wellbeingintlstudiesrepository.org/cgi/viewcontent.cgi?article=1027&context=acwp_lab.

Bailey, Jarrod. "Monkey-based Research on Human Disease: The Implications of Genetic Differences." *Alternatives to Laboratory Animals-ATLA* 42 (November 2014): 287–317. https://www.wellbeingintlstudiesrepository.org/cgi/viewcontent.cgi?article=1024&context=acwp_lab.

Bailey, Jarrod. "Recent Advances in the Development and Application of Human-Specific Biomedical Research and Testing Methods." *Center for Contemporary Sciences,* October 2020. https://contemporarysciences.org/resources/13.

Bailey, Jarrod, and Michael Balls. "Recent Efforts to Elucidate the Scientific Validity of Animal-based Drug Tests by the

Pharmaceutical Industry, Pro-testing Lobby Groups, and Animal Welfare Organizations." *BMC Medical Ethics* 20, no. 16 (2019): 5. https://doi.org/10.1186/s12910-019-0352-3.

Bailey, Jarrod, Michelle Thew, and Michael Balls. "An Analysis of the Use of Animal Models in Predicting Human Toxicology and Drug Safety." *Alternatives to Laboratory Animals* 42, no. 3 (June 2014): 181–199. https://www.wellbeingintlstudiesrepository.org/cgi/viewcontent.cgi?article=1123&context=acwp_arte.

Barbuzano, Javier. "Organoids: A New Window Into Disease, Development and Discovery." *Harvard Stem Cell Institute,* November 7, 2017. https://hsci.harvard.edu/organoids.

Barthélémy, Inès, Christophe Hitte, and Laurent Tiret. "The Dog Model in the Spotlight: Legacy of a Trustful Cooperation." *Journal of Neuromuscular Diseases* 6, no. 4 (2019): 422–423. doi:10.3233/JND-190394, https://www.ncbi.nlm.nih.gov/pmc/articles/PMC6918919/.

Bates, A.W.H. "The Research Defence Society: Mobilizing the Medical Profession for Materialist Science in the Early-Twentieth Century." In *Anti-Vivisection and the Profession of Medicine in Britain.* The Palgrave Macmillan Animal Ethics Series, 2017. https://www.researchgate.net/publication/318656592_The_Research_Defence_SocietyResearch_Defence_Society_Mobilizing_the_Medical_Profession_for_Materialist_ScienceScience_Nature_of_in_the_Early-Twentieth_Century.

Bates, A.W.H. "State Control, Bureaucracy, and the National Interest from the Second World War to the 1960s." In *Anti-Vivisection and the Profession of Medicine in Britain.* The Palgrave Macmillan Animal Ethics Series, 2017. https://www.researchgate.net/publication/318655521_State_Control_Bureaucracy_and_the_National_Interest_from_the_Second_World_War_to_the_1960s.

Bates, A.W.H. "Vivisection, Virtue, and the Law in the Nineteenth Century." In *Anti-Vivisection and the Profession of Medicine in Britain.* The Palgrave Macmillan Animal Ethics Series, 2017. https://www.researchgate.net/publication/318655168_Vivisection_Virtue_and_the_Law_in_the_Nineteenth_Century.

Baumgartl-Simons, Christiane, and Christiane Hohensee. "How Can the Final Goal of Completely Replacing Animal Procedures Successfully Be Achieved?" In *Animal Experimentation: Working Towards a Paradigm Change.* Eds. Kathrin Herrmann and Kimberley Jayne. Leiden; Boston: Brill, 2019. https://doi.org/10.1163/9789004391192.

Beagle Freedom Project. "Help Pass the Beagle Freedom Bill." Accessed on December 7, 2020, https://bfp.org/state/.

Beauchamp, Tom L., and David DeGrazia. *Principals of Animal Research Ethics.* New York: Oxford University Press, 2020.

Berche, P. "Louis Pasteur, From Crystals of Life to Vaccination." *Clinical Microbiology and Infection* 18, no. 5 (October 2012), 4. https://doi.org/10.1111/j.1469-0691.2012.03945.x.

Berns, Gregory. *What It's Like to Be a Dog: And Other Adventures in Animal Neuroscience.* New York: Basic Books, 2017.

Birke, Lynda. "Into the Laboratory." In *The Animals Reader.* Eds. Linda Kalof and Amy Fitzgerald. Bloomsbury Academic, 2007.

Block, Kitty. "HSUS Undercover Investigation Shows Beagles Being Poisoned with Pesticides and Drugs, Killed at Animal Testing Lab." *A Humane World* (blog). *Humane Society of the United States,* March 12, 2019. https://blog.humanesociety.org/2019/03/hsus-undercover-investigation-shows-beagles-being-poisoned-with-pesticides-and-drugs-killed-at-animal-testing-lab.html.

"A Brief History of Animals in Space." National Aeronautics and Space Administration. Accessed May 31, 2020. https://history.nasa.gov/printFriendly/animals.html.

Buettinger, Craig. "Antivivisection and the Charge of Zoophilia—psychosis in the Early Twentieth Century." *The Historian* 55, no. 2 (December 1993): 277. https://doi.org/10.1111/j.1540-6563.1993.tb00896.x.

Chambers, Jamie, Marsha B. Quinlan, Alexis Evans, and Robert J. Quinlan."Dog-HumanCoevolution:Cross-Cultural Analysis of Multiple Hypotheses." *Journal of Ethnobiology* 40, no. 4 (2020): 414–433. https://doi.org/10.2993/0278-0771-40.4.414.

Chödron, Pema. *Welcoming the Unwelcome: Wholehearted Living in a Brokenhearted World.* Shambhala Publications, 2019.

Cooney, Nick. *Change of Heart: What Psychology Can Teach Us About Spreading Social Change.* New York: Lantern Books, 2011.

Corbin, Cristina. "University Under Fire for Breeding Golden Retrievers with Muscular Dystrophy." *New York Post,* November 1, 2017. https://nypost.com/2017/11/01/university-under-fire-for-breeding-golden-retrievers-with-muscular-dystrophy/.

Coren, Stanley, and Edwin Rutsch. "How to Build a Culture of Empathy with Dogs." *Center for Building a Culture of Empathy.* Filmed August 28, 2012. YouTube video, http://cultureofempathy.com/References/Experts/others/Stanley-Coren.htm.

Dassault Systemes (website). *The Living Heart Project,* accessed October 7, 2020. https://www.3ds.com/products-services/simulia/solutions/life-sciences/the-living-heart-project/.

Discussion. March 27, 2019. Public Workshop on the Uses of Dogs in Biomedical Research. *National Academies Keck Center Building* in Washington, D.C. Video 15-Panel 2, https://vimeo.com/showcase/5891666/video/328467114.

Doring, Dorothea, Ophelia Nick, Alexander Bauer, Helmut Kuchenhoff, and Michael Erhard. "How Do Rehomed Laboratory Beagles Behave in Everyday Situations? Results from an Observational Test and Survey of New Owners." *PLoS One* 12, no. 7 (July 25, 2017): 1–22. https://doi.org/10.1371/journal.pone.0181303.

D'Souza, Karl. "Technology to Transform Lives: The SIMULIA Living Heart Model." *NAFEMS Benchmark,* July 2015. https://www.3ds.com/fileadmin/Industries/life-sciences/pdf/NAFEMS-Benchmark-Technology-to-Save-Lives-LHP-07-01-15.PDF.

Engber, Daniel. "Where's Pepper?" *Slate,* June 1, 2009. http://www.slate.com/articles/health_and_science/pepper/2009/06/wheres_pepper.html.

Fernandez, Alexia. "James Cromwell Arrested at Texas A&M University While Protesting Dog Lab Testing at the School." *People,* October 31, 2019. https://people.com/movies/james-cromwell-arrested-peta-protest/.

Franco, Nuno Henrique. "Animal Experiments in Biomedical Research: A Historical Perspective." *Animals: an open access journal from MDPI* 3, no. 1 (March 2013): 238–39, doi:10.3390/ani3010238. https://www.ncbi.nlm.nih.gov/pmc/articles/PMC4495509/pdf/animals-03-00238.pdf.

Fugazza, Claudia, Ákos Pogány, and Ádám Miklósi. "Recall of Others' Actions after Incidental Encoding Reveals Episodic-like Memory in Dogs." *Current Biology* 26 (December 2016): 3209–3213. https://doi.org/10.1016/j.cub.2016.09.057.

George, Alice. "The Sad, Sad Story of Laika, the Space Dog, and Her One-Way Trip into Orbit." *Smithsonian Magazine,* April 2018. https://www.smithsonianmag.com/smithsonian-institution/sad-story-laika-space-dog-and-her-one-way-trip-orbit-1-180968728/.

*Good Medicine.* "Averting Drug Disasters: How to Stop the Next Pharmaceutical Catastrophe." Spring 2016. https://pcrm.widencollective.com/portals/vfvlozlu/GoodMedicine.

Gordon, James. "Ancient Dog DNA Shows Early Spread Around the Globe." *New York Times,* October 29, 2020, https://www.nytimes.com/2020/10/29/science/ancient-dog-dna.html.

Grimm, David. "Opening the Lab Door." *Science,* June 29, 2018. https://science.sciencemag.org/content/360/6396/1392.long.

Gross, Charles G. "Claude Bernard and the Constancy of the Internal Environment." *The Neuroscientist* 4 (September 1998): 380. https://www.researchgate.net/publication/247752430_Claude_Bernard_and_the_Constancy_of_the_Internal_Environment.

Haley, Benjamin, Qiong Wang, Beau Wanzer, Stefan Vogt, Lydia Finney, Ping Liu Yang, Tatjana Paunesku, and

Gayle Woloscha. "Past and Future Work on Radiobiology Mega Studies: A Case Study at Argonne National Laboratory." *Health Physics* 100, no. 6 (June 2011): 3. https://www.ncbi.nlm.nih.gov/pmc/articles/PMC3784403/.

Hänninen, Laura, and Marianna Norring. "The First Rehoming of Laboratory Beagles in Finland: The Complete Process from Socialization Training to Follow-up." *Alternatives to Laboratory Animals* 48, no. 3 (2020): 116–126. https://doi.org/10.1177%2F0261192920942135.

Hansen, Lawrence A., and Kori Ann Kosberg. "Ethics, Efficacy, and Decision-making in Animal Research." In *Animal Experimentation: Working Towards a Paradigm Change*. Eds. Kathrin Herrmann and Kimberley Jayne. Leiden; Boston: Brill, 2019. https://doi.org/10.1163/9789004391192.

Harvard University. "Lung-on-a-Chip Wins Prize for Potentially Reducing Need for Animal Testing." *Wyss Institute*, February 26, 2013. https://wyss.harvard.edu/news/wyss-institutes-lung-on-a-chip-wins-prize-for-potentially-reducing-need-for-animal-testing/.

Hasiwa, Nina, Jarrod Bailey, Peter Clausing, Mardas Daneshian, Marianne Eileraas, Sándor Farkas, István Gyertyán, Robert Hubrecht, Werner Kobel, Goran Krummenacher, Marcel Leist, Hannes Lohi, Adám Miklósi, Frauke Ohl, Klaus Olejniczak, Georg Schmitt, Patrick Sinnett-Smith, David Smith, Kristina Wagner, James D. Yager, Joanne Zurlo, and Thomas Hartung. "Critical Evaluation of the Use of Dogs in Biomedical Research and Testing in Europe." *ALTEX* 28, no. 4 (April 2011): 329. https://www.altex.org/index.php/altex/article/view/492/503.

Herrmann, Kathrin. "Refinement on the Way Towards Replacement: Are We Doing What We Can?" In *Animal Experimentation: Working Towards a Paradigm Change*. Eds. Kathrin Herrmann and Kimberley Jayne. Leiden: Brill, 2019. https://doi.org/10.1163/9789004391192.

Hopley, Emma. *Campaigning Against Cruelty: The Hundred Year History of the British Union for the Abolition of Vivisection*. The British Union of Abolition of Vivisection, 1998.

Jennings, Bruce. "Animal Research," In *Bioethics*, 4th ed. Michigan: Macmillan Reference USA, a part of Gale, Cengage Learning, 2014.

Kaur, Rimplejeet, Preeti Sidhu, and Surjit Singh. "What Failed BIA 10–2472 Phase I Clinical Trial? Global Speculations and Recommendations for Future Phase I Trials." *Journal of Pharmacology & Pharmacotherapeutics* 7, no. 3 (July-September 2016): 1–2. https://www.ncbi.nlm.nih.gov/pmc/articles/PMC5020770/?report=reader.

Keen, Jim. "Wasted Money in United States Biomedical and Agricultural Animal Research." In *Animal Experimentation: Working Toward a Paradigm Change*." Eds. Kathrin Herrmann and Kimberley Jayne. Leiden; Boston: Brill, 2019. https://doi.org/10.1163/9789004391192.

Keim, Brandon. "The Genius of Dogs: Understanding Our Best Friends." *National Geographic*, 2020, 66.

Kenehan, Sarah. "The Moral Status of Animal Research Subjects in Industry: A Stakeholder Analysis." In *Animal Experimentation: Working Toward a Paradigm Change*. Eds. Kathrin Herrmann and Kimberley Jayne. Leiden; Boston: Brill, 2019. https://doi.org/10.1163/9789004391192.

Kim, Jihoon, Bon-Kyoung Koo, and Juergen A. Knoblich. "Human Organoids: Model Systems for Human Biology and Medicine." *Nature Reviews Molecular Cell Biology* 21 (2020): 571–584. https://doi.org/10.1038/s41580-020-0259-3.

Lansbury, Coral. "The Brown Dog Riots of 1907." In *The Animals Reader*. Eds. Linda Kalof and Amy Fitzgerald. Bloomsbury Academic, 2007.

Lopresti-Goodman, Stacy M. "A Comparison of Former Laboratory Dogs' With Non-laboratory Dogs' Psychological and Behavioral Characteristics." Poster presented at the Tenth World Congress: Alternatives and Animal Use in the Life Sciences, Seattle, WA, August 2017.

Maehle, Andreas-Holger. "Literary Responses to Animal Experimentation in Seventeenth and Eighteenth-Century

Britain." *Medical History* 34 (1990): 40.

Marshall, Lindsay J., Christopher P. Austin, Warren Casey, Suzanne C. Fitzpatrick, and Catherine Willett. "Recommendations toward a Human Pathway-based Approach to Disease Research." *Drug Discovery Today* 23, no. 11 (November 2018): 1824–25. https://doi.org/10.1016/j.drudis.2018.05.038.

"Meet Teddy: Rescued from Cruel Research." *The Humane Society of the United States,* December 26, 2019. YouTube video, https://www.youtube.com/watch?v=NQ0GzWFrM54.

Murrie, Greg. "Death-in-Life: Curare, Restrictionism and Abolitionism in Victorian and Edwardian Anti-Vivisectionist Thought." Chap. 15 in *Animal Death.* Edited by Jay Johnston and Fiona Probyn-Rapsey. Sydney University Press, Australia, 2013). www.jstor.org/stable/j.ctt1gxxpvf.21.

National Academies of Sciences, Engineering, and Medicine. "Necessity, Use, and Care of Laboratory Dogs at the U.S. Department of Veterans Affairs." Prepublication copy. National Academy of Sciences, 2020. https://doi.org/10.17226/25772.

National Anti-Vivisection Society. "The History of the NAVS." https://www.navs.org.uk/about_us/24/0/299/

National Research Council. "Regulation of Animal Research." *Science, Medicine, and Animals.* Washington, D.C.: The National Academies Press, 2004. https://doi.org/10.17226/10733.

Passini, Elisa, Oliver J. Britton, Hua Rong Lu, Jutta Rohrbacher, An N. Hermans, David J. Gallacher, Robert J. H. Greig, Alfonso Bueno-Orovio, and Blanca Rodriguez. "Human In Silico Drug Trials Demonstrate Higher Accuracy than Animal Models in Predicting Clinical Pro-Arrhythmic Cardiotoxicity." *Frontiers in Physiology* 8, no. 668 (September 2017): 1–2. https://www.ncbi.nlm.nih.gov/pmc/articles/PMC5601077/pdf/fphys-08-00668.pdf.

Physicians Committee for Responsible Medicine. "Dog Experiments at Wayne State: Decades of Pain and Futility." October 7, 2019. https://www.pcrm.org/sites/default/files/2019-10/REPORT%20-%20Dog%20Experiments%20at%20Wayne%20State%20-%2010.07.19_0.pdf.

"Prosecution at Norwich. Experiments on Animals." *The British Medical Journal* 2, no. 728 (December 1874), 751–52. http://www.jstor.com/stable/25240021.

Ram, Rebecca. "Extrapolation of Animal Research Data to Humans: An Analysis of the Evidence." In *Animal Experimentation: Working Towards a Paradigm Change.* Eds. Kathrin Herrmann and Kimberley Jayne. Leiden; Boston: Brill, 2019. https://doi.org/10.1163/9789004391192.

Russell, W.M.S., and R.L. Burch. "Chapter 2: The Concept of Inhumanity." In *The Principles of Humane Experimental Technique.* Johns Hopkins Bloomberg School of Public Health (website). https://caat.jhsph.edu/principles/chap2a.

Serpell, James A. "The Unique Role of Dogs in Society." March 27, 2019. Public Workshop on the Uses of Dogs in Biomedical Research, National Academies Keck Center Building in Washington, D.C. Video 14-Panel 2, https://vimeo.com/showcase/5891666/video/328466953.

Sharp, Lesley A. *Animal Ethos: The Morality of Human-Animal Encounters in Experimental Lab Science.* Oakland: University of California Press, 2019.

Singer, Peter. *Animal Liberation.* Rev. ed. New York: HarperCollins Publishers, 2009.

Smith, Emily. "Life Beyond the Laboratory: Michigan Dogs Blossom Following Release from Testing Facility." *Animal Sheltering Magazine,* Fall 2019. https://www.animalsheltering.org/magazine/articles/life-beyond-laboratory.

Specter, Michael. "Drool: Ivan Pavlov's Real Quest." *New Yorker,* November 17, 2014. https://www.newyorker.com/magazine/2014/11/24/drool.

Tannenbaum, Jerrold, and B. Taylor Bennett. "Russell and Burch's 3Rs Then and Now: The Need for Clarity in Definition and Purpose." *Journal of the American Association for Laboratory Animal Science* 54, no. 2 (March 2015): 131. https://www.ncbi.nlm.nih.gov/pmc/articles/PMC4382615/.

Tansey, E.M. "The Queen Has Been Dreadfully Shocked: Aspects of Teaching Experimental Physiology Using Animals in Britain, 1876–1986." *AJP Centennial* 19, no. 1 (June 1998): S20. https://journals.physiology.org/doi/pdf/10.1152/advances.1998.274.6.S18.

Taylor, Katy, and Laura Rego Alvarez. "An Estimate of the Number of Animals Used for Scientific Purposes Worldwide in 2015." *Alternatives to Laboratory Animals* 47, no. 5–6 (2019): 205. https://journals.sagepub.com/doi/pdf/10.1177/0261192919899853.

Teater, Barry. "Feds Award $24 M for Wake Forest Lund-on-a-Chip Studies." *North Carolina Biotechnology Center,* October 9, 2019. https://www.ncbiotech.org/news/feds-award-24m-wake-forest-lung-chip-studies.

United States Department of Agriculture. "Research Facility Annual Summary and Archive Reports." Last modified September 23, 2020. https://www.aphis.usda.gov/aphis/ourfocus/animalwelfare/sa_obtain_research_facility_annual_report/ct_research_facility_annual_summary_reports.

University of Oxford. Department of Computer Science. Blanca Rodriguez. Accessed November 24, 2020. https://www.cs.ox.ac.uk/people/blanca.rodriguez.

Unti, Bernard. "Frank McMahon: The Investigator Who Took a Bite Out of Animal Lab Suppliers." White paper included in the Humane Society Institute for Science and Policy Animal Studies Repository, 2013. http://animalstudiesrepository.org/acwp_awap/22.

Van Norman, Gail A. "Limitations of Animal Studies for Predicting Toxicity in Clinical Trials: Is It Time to Rethink Our Current Approach." *JACC: Basic to Translational Science* 4, no. 7 (October 2019): 848. https://doi.org/10.1016/j.jacbts.2019.10.008.

Worrall, Simon. "Yes, Animals Think and Feel. Here's How We Know." *National Geographic,* July 15, 2015. https://www.nationalgeographic.com/news/2015/07/150714-animal-dog-thinking-feelings-brain-science/.

"The Zoophil-Psychosis." *New York Times,* July 11, 1909. https://archive.nytimes.com.

# Index